Feature and Magazine Writing

Action, Angle and Anecdotes

Feature and Magazine Writing

Action, Angle and Anecdotes

David E. Sumner and Holly G. Miller

Blackwell
Publishing

David E. Sumner, Ph.D., is professor of journalism and head of the magazine program at Ball State University, Muncie, Indiana. He teaches courses on introductory magazine writing, advanced magazine writing and magazine editing, and advises the student magazine *Expo.* Within the Association for Education in Journalism and Mass Communication (AEJMC), Dr. Sumner has held numerous offices in its 150-member Magazine Division including chair, research chair and webmaster. He has been a freelance writer for magazines for 30 years and has written three books.

Holly G. Miller holds degrees in journalism from Indiana University and Ball State University. She is a Professional in Residence at Anderson University, Anderson, Indiana, and has taught at Ball State University, Indiana University and Purdue University at Indianapolis and at numerous writers' workshops from Mount Hermon, California, to Cape Cod, Massachusetts. Ms. Miller is senior editor of *The Saturday Evening Post* and author of 13 books and more than 2,000 published magazine articles. Her byline has appeared in such diverse publications as *TV Guide, Country Gentleman, Today's Christian Woman, Indianapolis Monthly, Clarity, Reader's Digest, Writer's Digest* and *The Writer.* She has won awards from the Society of Professional Journalists, Associated Press, Midwest Travel Writers, Society of American Travel Writers, Evangelical Press Association, Multiple Sclerosis Society of America and General Motors Corp. She has served as managing editor of a daily newspaper, contributing editor to *Today's Christian Woman* and consulting editor to *Clarity.*

© 2005 David E. Sumner and Holly G. Miller
All rights reserved

Blackwell Publishing Professional
2121 State Avenue, Ames, Iowa 50014, USA

Orders: 1-800-862-6657
Office: 1-515-292-0140
Fax: 1-515-292-3348
Web site: www.blackwellprofessional.com

Blackwell Publishing Ltd
9600 Garsington Road, Oxford OX4 2DQ, UK
Tel.: +44 (0)1865 776868

Blackwell Publishing Asia
550 Swanston Street, Carlton, Victoria 3053, Australia
Tel.: +61 (0)3 8359 1011

First edition, 2005

Library of Congress Cataloging-in-Publication Data

Sumner, David E., 1946-
   Feature and magazine writing : action, angle and anecdotes /
David E. Sumner and Holly G. Miller.— 1st ed.
      p. cm.
   Includes bibliographical references and index.
   ISBN-13: 978-0-8138-0519-1
   ISBN-10: 0-8138-0519-8 (alk. paper)
   1. Feature writing. 2. Journalism—Authorship. I. Miller, Holly G. II. Title.
   PN4784.F37S86 2005
   808'.06607—dc22

                                                 2004029264

The last digit is the print number: 9 8 7 6 5 4

Contents

Introduction
Reading, Writing and Relevance

Feature articles have taken on new importance in this information age. Because of the immediacy of radio, television and the Internet, people have the ability to receive news as quickly as it unfolds. Listeners, viewers and users can track developing stories and keep up to date on the headline aspects—the who, what, when and where—of an event by tuning in or logging on day or night. By the time the print version of a story arrives on their doorsteps or in their mailboxes, readers already know the facts and are ready for more. They need someone to put the facts into context. That's when the feature writer steps in and goes to work.

A skilled feature writer provides background and explanation, digs into the "why" and "how" of a story, explores the offshoots and ramifications of events and trends and shines the spotlight on the people who populate the news and initiate the trends. If news reporters tell readers "here's what's happening," feature writers add "and here's what it means to you." In a lot of cases, newspaper and magazine feature writers make sense of the news by getting inside, rummaging around and sorting through it.

Journalists used to call feature stories "soft news" because the perception was that they lacked the impact and significance of "hard news." Editors believed that if a feature were nudged off a page by a late-breaking story, no harm was done. The feature article could wait its turn. At some point the editor might slot the story for the lifestyle section of the Sunday newspaper or tuck it in the back of a magazine to fill a place left vacant by a canceled advertisement.

Not so today. Features are all about reading, writing and relevance. Writers who specialize in feature journalism know their readers well.

They know the issues that weigh on their readers' minds or catch their readers' fancy. They understand how to deliver stories in an entertaining and compelling way. They have the skills of a news reporter and the gifts of a storyteller. They know how to gather information and how to assemble it in a riveting package. Their stories often are longer and take more time to research and organize than breaking news stories. Their articles require in-depth and follow-up interviews, contain anecdotes, are accompanied by sidebars and sometimes assume the form of multi-part series.

This book looks at feature writing as an art and a science. The first two sections look at the preparations that feature writers make as they scout for ideas, select slants and conduct research. The third section examines nine types of feature articles and offers samples of several. The fourth section delves into the process that freelance writers follow to market their stories. An appendix offers a "Back to Basics" section for writers who are rusty on the mechanics of grammar and punctuation. Each chapter highlights key terms, which are defined in the "Shoptalk" section at the end of the chapter.

As professional writers and editors ourselves, we've worked both sides of the desk. Our experience outside the classroom includes overseeing the lifestyle section of a daily newspaper, writing newspaper features, editing Web sites, consulting with several national magazines and fulfilling hundreds of freelance feature assignments. This book contains the lessons we've learned along the way.

David E. Sumner
Holly G. Miller

Part I
Preparing to Write Feature Articles

Chapter 1
Capturing Reader Attention

Characteristics of interesting stories include strong action, specific angles and plenty of anecdotes. Magazine and newspaper features share common characteristics, but have differences that make magazine features more complex and challenging to write. Understanding these differences, as well as your readers, will help you create more interesting articles that capture their attention. Here's where we begin:

- Five mistakes of beginning writers
- Prescription for interesting stories
- Differences between magazine and newspaper features
- Characteristics of your readers

So much to read and so little time! Great writers make it easy for their readers by packing the most punch into the fewest words. When most people pick up a magazine or the feature section of a newspaper, they're looking for entertainment, they want to relax or they want specific information. If a guy snoozes with an unfinished **feature article** on his lap, then the publication hasn't done its job. You can't argue that he's too lazy to understand the challenging content. Our sympathies are with him. If he got bored, it's because the writers didn't do their job. Great writing is all about getting through to the reader.

The writer's first goal isn't getting published in a magazine or newspaper. A writer's goal is getting read, which goes a step further. The difference between amateur and professional writers is that amateurs write to please themselves and professionals write to please their readers.

Five Mistakes of Beginning Writers

More than 25 years ago, *Writer's Digest* published an article called "Take Five: The Most Common Mistakes Among Beginning Writers." After reading thousands of articles by novice writers over 20 years, we believe these observations are still true. We will explain these five common mistakes and tell you how to avoid them.

Staying in Your Own Backyard

Too many new writers rely on home-grown situations for articles and personal connections for interviews. You can't be a successful writer by staying in your own backyard. You can't rely on personal experience for article ideas or limit your interviews to family, friends and a few professors. Our hardest job in writing classes is persuading students that they can't depend on personal experiences and interests for their ideas. Some cringe at the thought of calling a stranger to ask for an interview.

Meg Grant, the West Coast editor for *Reader's Digest*, says: "You really have to be fearless about approaching people and getting them to give you what you need. I think they will often give it to you if you ask them." She says that years ago when she worked for *People* magazine, an editor assigned her to interview the families of three children killed by a drunk driver, who was also a celebrity athlete. "The editor told me, 'You have to knock on their door and talk to some of these victims' families. I know you think they don't want to talk to you, but the truth is they do. They want to talk to someone and they want to tell you about their kids.' So I had to go bang on those people's doors and say, 'Would you talk to me?' And he was right. They did want to talk," she says.[1]

The fear of leaving their own backyards still tops the list of mistakes among today's new writers. Some don't read magazines or newspapers enough to know what types of articles editors publish and readers read. That's one reason we're spending two chapters of this book explaining how to do research—one on library and Internet research and another on interviewing.

Too often **stories** depend on parents or siblings as primary sources. The main problem with writing about relatives is not having the necessary objectivity to write about what is of universal interest in their lives. The Model Code of Ethics published by the Associated Collegiate Press says that collegiate journalists, "Should not cover . . . or make news judgments about family members or persons with whom they have a financial, adversarial or close sexual or platonic relationship." Another reason to avoid these convenient sources is that they don't challenge you to venture outside your backyard and learn to locate the kind of experts you will need to discover week after week if you are to become a successful feature writer.

Vague Ideas With Unfocused Angles

Second, some beginning writers want to write about a vague topic with an unfocused **angle**. When we request proposals for story ideas, many come up with a vague notion of some topic that interests them—but not a story idea. For example, some suggest writing about "vegetarianism," on which hundreds of books have been written. "What can you tell us about this subject that hasn't been written before?" and "What is your specific angle?" are always the first questions we ask when someone comes up with an unfocused idea like this.

The prevalence of this second mistake is why we're spending two chapters on developing and focusing ideas. Chapter 2 contains a dozen specific ways to come up with an idea and Chapter 3 suggests how to whittle it down into a publishable angle.

Lack of Strong Evidence and Factual Reporting

Strong, creative writers do a lot of digging. They've learned to be aggressive in finding and asking people for interviews. If any article has half a dozen people quoted, the writer may have interviewed 15 or 20 people and used only the most compelling quotes. One academic study found that the typical Pulitzer Prize winning feature story contained interviews with 53 people.

Jack Kelley, a former senior editor for *People,* says, "Many of the best magazine writers liken their work to mining. They chip and chip until they extract a nugget. Then they chip some more. They are not embarrassed to keep asking questions until they hear what they need. God is in the details, and compelling color, quote and detail do not simply materialize."[2]

Some beginners write articles full of generalizations but lacking detailed evidence that backs them up. Writing skill, while essential, can never carry the article without strong content. Editors want facts, and they love to break stories with information never published by their competitors. Few writers have opinions that are in great demand.

Successful article writing depends on getting facts through interviews and in-depth library research. If you don't do good background research, then you risk asking stupid or irrelevant questions in your interviews.

Lack of Anecdotes in Stories

The fourth mistake is lack of **anecdotes**. Anecdotes are true stories containing one or two people and some quotes, and occur in a specific time and place. They reveal an individual's frailty, courage, character and humor and make the story come alive for the reader. Anecdotes add credibility because they provide real-life examples to the claims and generalizations made by the writer.

Anecdotes are so important to use in stories and so difficult to find that they deserve their own chapter in this book. Anecdotes come from the people you interview. Chapters 5 and 8 explain how to find sources and phrase questions that will bring out the most humorous, insightful and compelling anecdotes.

Boring Articles That Lack Action

Boring, windy articles lacking action constitute the fifth mistake. Many beginning writers use stiff, long-winded content that doesn't fit the tone of today's magazines. We have read hundreds of student articles that sound like condensations of research papers from other courses. Other symptoms of this disease occur with too frequent use of passive-voice verbs, long and convoluted sentences, runaway adjectives and adverbs and a formal academic tone.

Editors eagerly look for stories that move, outrage, alarm, delight or inspire readers. They want to make their readers laugh, cry or get angry. They would rather receive angry letters to the editor than none at all because that means people are reading their publication. A plodding, formal style is a turnoff to every editor.

Chapter 6 tells you how to avoid boring stories by building action into characters and content. It shows how to create action by using people to illustrate abstract ideas and increasing the use of narrative, dialogue, action verbs and active voice.

Prescription for Interesting Stories

Avoiding these mistakes will make your stories interesting. "There is a principle of writing so important, so fundamental that it can be appropriately called the First Law of Journalism and it is simply this: be interesting," says Benton Patterson, a former *Guideposts* editor.[3] People will read only what they find interesting.

Part of this book's title is *Action, Angle and Anecdotes* because we believe that lively action, a fresh, creative angle and lots of anecdotes characterize interesting writing that keeps readers interested and involved. Strong magazine and news features connect emotionally with the reader in a way that is different from a news story. They tug at the heart at the same time they inform and inspire the mind.

Feature stories are sometimes called "human interest stories." Good writers understand people as well as they know the language. Contrary to the stereotype, good writers aren't hermits. They are sensitive, socially connected individuals who have an innate sense for finding and writing stories that interest humans. The more you talk to people, the more you understand what people are interested in hearing and discussing.

Action is one characteristic of interesting stories. "Readers love action, any kind of action, and the story that does not move, that just sits there stalled while people declaim, explain, elaborate and suck their thumbs is justly labeled by some editors as MEGO—My Eyes Glaze Over," says William Blundell.[4]

An angle makes a story interesting because it provides enough detail about a subject to give the reader some fresh, original information. Broad subjects are vague, fuzzy and boring. Fresh angles give insight into old topics. You have to find a tiny slice that no one has cut before from a broad topic (such as "time management" or "weight loss") to make a publishable article out of it.

Anecdotes make articles interesting by telling true stories about people doing things. People like to read stories about people. Many articles begin with an anecdote for a good reason: anecdotes tell a story—a tiny tale that draws us into the larger one. They illustrate the meaning of the information that follows. Nothing is more involving or revealing than human drama, and anecdotes capture drama with impact.

For example, *The Cincinnati Enquirer* published a feature story titled, "Junk Man Salvages a Family," which illustrates "action, angle and anecdotes." The story profiles a 29-year-old junk dealer and single parent who is raising two sons. The man and one of his sons stand on a pile of junk in a salvage yard in the feature photo.[5]

This story conveys action because it tells about the man, who lost his wife a few years earlier, making a career out of buying and selling junk while raising two sons. It has a sharp angle because it's not about just any junk dealer. This dealer is a young, single father whose two sons help him with the business.

Differences Between Newspaper and Magazine Features

Is there a difference between newspaper and magazine features? Magazine features are not simply newspaper features published on glossy paper. Having taught magazine and feature writing for more than 20 years, we've frequently discussed differences between newspaper and magazine journalism. Here's our consensus:

- Newspaper feature writing is shorter and more closely related to current events than magazine feature writing. Consequently, magazine articles have a longer **shelf life** than newspaper articles. For example, magazines in public libraries remain on display shelves for at least a month, whereas most newspapers are changed daily. Newspapers rely on current events for their content while magazines rely on trends and issues among the hundreds of **niche** topics that they cover.
- Newspaper writing aims to please a local audience with a broad range of ages, interests and educational and socioeconomic backgrounds. It's "shotgun writing." Magazine writing is directed toward a geographically diverse but narrow target audience with specific interests and demographic characteristics. It's "rifle writing."
- Newspaper feature writing is generally detached and objective. The personality of the writer remains hidden. Magazine writers have more freedom to display viewpoint, voice, tone and style.
- Newspapers employ large staffs of reporters and a few editors. Magazines employ large staffs of editors and few full-time writers. Most magazines rely on freelance writers for most of their stories. They don't just do this to save money. Because most magazines have a regional or national readership, they want content from a wide range of contributors who resemble their readers. Although large consumer magazines are typically published in New York City, their editors really want their content to reflect the interests of all types of people in all types of places. That's why freelance writers are important to them.
- Newspaper writing requires daily deadlines; magazine writing has monthly deadlines except for a few weeklies and quarterlies. That means readers expect more from their magazines: more complexity,

analysis, originality, depth, sources and accuracy. Magazine writing is more intellectually challenging for the reader and the writer.

Characteristics of Your Readers

Develop a friendship with the reader and keep her in mind while you write. Successful salespeople spend a lot of time nurturing relationships with their customers. Successful writers similarly nurture relationships with their readers. When you write, you always need to ask yourself: "How will the reader react to this? Will this sentence cause the reader to laugh or roll his eyes? Will this paragraph fascinate the reader or send her quickly to another article?"

Good writers need to develop two personalities as they write. The first is the sensitive creator of words and eloquent ideas. But the second is the critical editor, acting on behalf of the reader, who savagely scours the page looking for mistakes and unnecessary material. The editor part of you must be cruel and demand perfection.

Readers roam the aisles of supermarkets and department stores and browse through their magazines. Wal-Mart, for example, now accounts for 15 percent of all single-copy magazine sales. Readers sit at computer terminals surfing through Web sites. They browse through an Atlanta airport newsstand while waiting for their connection. If a title or headline attracts their attention, they pick it up and read. If it holds their attention, they read to the end. Think about this happening millions of times every week, and you get the picture. Editors are paid, writers are paid, magazines are published, Web sites stay in business, and everyone is happy.

You will succeed if you remember these common characteristics of readers:

- They're busy. Unless assigned for study or a job requirement, they are not forced to read magazines, newspapers or the Internet.
- They're intelligent and discerning with higher incomes and educational backgrounds than heavy television viewers.
- They won't finish any articles that bore them.
- They read to fill a specific information need related to their personal or professional interests. For example, many subscribe to trade magazines that help them succeed in their jobs.
- Since national news is available 24 hours a day on electronic media, most people turn to local newspapers for news and features about their local communities.

These characteristics may not describe each reader. If you assume that they do, however, you will work harder and get published more quickly than your peers. An interesting article that attracts and holds the reader begins with an interesting idea. So to find an interesting idea, just turn to Chapter 2, and we'll get started.

Suggested Activities

1. Interview five people from outside your immediate environment. Ask these two questions: "If you start reading a feature article and get bored and stop, what are the most likely reasons?" and "When you find a fascinating article, what are its qualities or characteristics?" Record your answers and discuss them in class.

2. Find an interesting newspaper feature story. Discuss how it would differ in content or focus if it appeared in *Rolling Stone, Maxim, Cosmopolitan* or other popular magazines.

3. Circle the leads from any 10 newspaper articles and 10 magazine features. How many of the magazine features begin with an anecdote compared with the newspaper stories?

Shoptalk

Anecdote: A true story used to illustrate the larger theme of a story. Anecdotes contain one or two central characters, some dialogue or quotations and occur in a specific time and place.

Angle: The specific approach that you take toward covering a broad topic. Think of an angle like a small slice of a large topical "pie." Strong angles reveal fresh, original information.

Feature article: A term used mostly by newspaper journalists to describe stories that aren't "hard news." Magazine journalists use more specific categories such as profiles, how-to, travel, true life narratives and inspirational, all of which may be called "features."

Niche: The narrowly defined content and readership that characterizes most magazines. While most magazines serve a narrow niche within a national audience, most newspapers serve a broad range of interests within a narrow geographic area.

Shelf life: The typical amount of time that a publication may remain in a home or "on the shelf" of a library. Daily newspapers have a shelf life of a few days, whereas monthly magazines may have a shelf life of a few months.

Story: The word "story" is generally interchangeable with "article." Feature and magazine writers like to use "story" because it suggests that the article has some drama or action, as opposed to pure factual information.

Endnotes

1. Telephone interview, Nov. 29, 2003.
2. Telephone interview, Jan. 19, 2004.
3. Benton Rain Patterson, *Write to Be Read* (Ames: Iowa State Press, 1986), 6.
4. William Blundell, *The Art and Craft of Feature Writing* (New York: Penguin Books, 1986), 54.
5. John Johnston, "Junk man salvages a family," *Cincinnati Enquirer*, Oct. 2, 2003, E1.

Chapter 2
The Hunt for Fresh Ideas

The best way to find article ideas is to read. Extensive reading helps you separate original ideas from non-original ideas. Another way is to locate primary and unpublished sources.

This chapter includes a dozen places to look for feature story ideas following these main points:

- Reading precedes originality
- Primary sources create original articles
- The feature values
- Types of articles
- Twelve places to find ideas

An editor once told a writer, "Your manuscript is both good and original, but the part that is good is not original and the part that is original is not good." To make it into print, an article must ooze quality, style and freshness. In short, the most successful magazine and newspaper features inform, provoke thought and introduce the reader to something new.

Reading Precedes Originality

The best way to find an original idea is by reading, reading and reading some more. If you don't know what's been published in magazines, newspapers, books and elsewhere, then you have no way of recognizing an original idea when you find one. Successful feature writers have an insatiable appetite for reading. If you don't, you should question whether this is the right field for you. You cannot be a great writer if you do not read widely, often and passionately.

"The real importance of reading is that it creates an ease and intimacy with the process of writing," writes Stephen King. "It also offers you a constantly growing knowledge of what has been done and what hasn't, what is trite and what is fresh, what works and what just lies there dying (or dead) on the page."[1]

A few years ago, David Sumner, one of the authors of this book, interviewed more than a dozen syndicated magazine and newspaper columnists about their craft. One of the first questions was: "Where do you get ideas for your columns?" Their unanimous answer was "reading."

For example, Dave Barry says, "I read *The New York Times* and *The Miami Herald* every day. When I can, I read *The Wall Street Journal*, which I love. It's different from every other paper. I read *Newsweek, Esquire, Sports Illustrated, Harpers* and *The Atlantic*. I sometimes read *The New Republic* and balance it by reading the *National Review*. I just like to read."[2]

Kathleen Parker's feature column appears in more than 300 newspapers. When asked how she comes up with ideas, she says, "I read and read and keep reading until I feel a metabolic shift. I have to feel my blood pressure rise a little bit. The subject, whatever it is, has to evoke some emotion . . . . I have to feel something before I can write. I have to care. No passion in the writer, no passion in the reader."[3]

Anyone who hopes to maintain a steady flow of ideas has to be an omnivorous, gluttonous reader and must read publications that few others read. Ideas may come from the most unexpected sources: professional quarterlies, association newsletters, academic journals, annual reports and almanacs. While they seem boring, such sources often contain the most original thinking and latest developments long before they reach the general public.

Another good way to find ideas is to get out and talk to people. You don't get ideas by staring at a keyboard. Visit unfamiliar places and talk to strangers. Get away from the university and talk to factory workers, taxi drivers and store clerks. Listen to their gripes, problems and stories. Go to a political rally or a Veterans Day observance. The more interest you show for new experiences, the more likely you will find something to write.

The most difficult task that beginning writers face is finding an original idea with a clearly focused angle. Many beginning writers can organize words, sentences and paragraphs using good punctuation and grammar. What most struggle with, however, is coming up with a strong idea that has a chance of being published.

Editors today insist on new material because they know their readers don't want a rehash of what's already out there. *Woman's Day* advises prospective writers in its guidelines: "We want fresh articles based on new material—new studies, new statistics, new theories, new insights—especially when the subject itself has received wide coverage. Any article that could have been published three years ago is not for *Woman's Day*."

Ellen Levine, editor-in-chief of *Good Housekeeping*, advises writers, "Give readers information unavailable elsewhere" and "Strive for exclusive stories."[4] Everything a writer produces needs an original angle supported by information not already in print. Being original means that each article should "smell fresh" when it arrives in front of the reader. It shouldn't sound like it's been pulled from an "article warehouse" shelf somewhere. That's why you can't write an original article simply by recycling and paraphrasing material from existing magazines, newspapers or Internet articles.

Primary Sources Create Original Articles

To create original articles, learn to find and use primary sources. **Primary sources** and **secondary sources** are academic terms that distinguish between information that comes from its original source and that which has been edited through another source. A primary source comes from a person with direct knowledge of an event or a document produced by its original source. Articles from existing publications are secondary sources by definition because another writer has already done the work of gathering, interpreting and editing the information for readers. Secondary sources are necessary in reporting because they help you find an idea, figure out your angle and add context and depth to your material. To get something published, however, you have to find primary sources to provide the "scoop" that no one else gets.

A *Reader's Digest* editor once advised writers: "Bullet-proof your manuscript. When a story is scheduled, our fact-checking department begins its work. Our fact-checkers are second to none. We don't use secondary sources. You can't quote from newspapers or magazines. You've got to go back to the primary sources to confirm that they weren't misquoted."[5]

Here is a list of the best places to get primary sources that will allow you to create original and fascinating stories.

Interviews

Interviews are the writer's stock in trade. Interviews are as important for the writer as the keyboard is for the pianist, the paintbrush for the artist, or the spreadsheet for the accountant. In other words, you won't succeed unless you become an expert at doing them. Learning how to ask questions is important, but not the most important thing about interviews. Great interviews originate with trust. The more you can convey yourself as trustworthy, the more your sources will tell you things that they have never told anyone else. You will learn more about interviews in Chapter 5.

Full Texts of Speeches

Published stories about important speeches summarize and paraphrase those speeches. But if you can find the full text of the original, you have a primary source. For example, visit www.whitehouse.gov and you'll find the texts of the President's key speeches. University and corporate Web sites often contain full texts of speeches or official statements from their officials.

Reports from Companies, Government Offices, Agencies, etc.

These otherwise dull reports may contain gems and nuggets of information. Some internal documents may not be public knowledge until a writer finds them, combs through them and pulls out the "bombshell" that officials hoped no one would notice. A company's or nonprofit organization's annual report is also a primary source since it comes directly from the source.

Original Statistical Data in Tables or Graphs

Many published articles interpret statistical data and serve as secondary sources of "filtered" information. However, a writer who can look at a table of numbers and detect a trend or find unreported news has a special talent. For example, if you can find original statistical data from the U.S. Census Bureau, you may be able to develop a story around a rapid increase in birth rates in your community. The best federal government Web site for statistical data is www.fedstats.gov, which collects data from all federal agencies.

Special Collections

Many libraries contain **special collections** of donated correspondence and papers of celebrities or historically significant figures. These collections serve as excellent sources of primary material when writing articles with a historical slant. For example, we once spent several days at the *Time* magazine archives and Princeton University library going through the papers and correspondence of the founders of *Time* and *U.S. News & World Report*. The material later appeared in articles on the history of those newsmagazines.

Correspondence and Electronic Mail

While electronic mail is a primary source, we encourage you to use it cautiously in feature writing. The "Model Code of Ethics" published by the Associated Collegiate Press encourages writers to verify an e-mail source's identity with a follow-up telephone call. Telephone or in-person interviews always surpass e-mail interviews in the quality of the information that they produce. In your reporting, use e-mail only for obtaining short quotes or facts.

Academic Studies and Scholarly Journal Articles

Although we said earlier that articles from other publications are secondary sources, **scholarly journal** articles containing the results of formal studies are an exception to that rule. Reports on groundbreaking studies from medical journals are frequently published or broadcast in the media. Don't rely on what a magazine story says about a study from *The New England Journal of Medicine*. Go back and find the original article, which is a primary source. You may find a different angle on the same information. Since scholarly journals usually have low circulations, they offer writers the opportunity to publicize the results of groundbreaking studies to a wider audience.

Congressional Testimony

Congressional committees hold hearings almost every day Congress is in session. Topics range from abortion to zymurgy (the home-brewing of alcoholic beverages). These testimonies, which often come from ordinary citizens, can contain interesting anecdotes and original information. Most of them are published on various congressional Web sites. We once quoted from a congressional hearing on identify theft for a magazine article on that topic.

The Feature Values

If you have taken an introductory news-writing course, you're probably familiar with **news values**. These values succinctly express the elements of a story that typically attract readers' attention. The same values can be adapted to magazine and feature writing. In other words, a good magazine article should contain at least one of these elements to be worthy of publication.

- **Novelty or rarity** expresses a one-of-a-kind characteristic. Someone who earns a livelihood through an unusual occupation or pursues a strange hobby could be the focus of a feature profile. For example, an issue of *Popular Science* once carried a story about a new pastime among audio enthusiasts called decibel drag racing. You also have to be cautious because what seems novel or sensational to a young writer may seem common to older readers with more life experiences.
- **Magnitude** relates to the "awesome" aspect of a story. People, things or events may be characterized as the biggest, greatest, largest or oldest. Several magazines and newspapers have written about an Indiana woman married more than 50 times, whose story displays news values of both "magnitude" and "novelty." Magnitude may describe the "extremes" on either end of a range of values such as most or least, largest or smallest and oldest or youngest.
- **Impact** describes issues or events that directly affect readers. **Service journalism** describes a specific type of feature article that provides practical help to readers in some way. (See Chapter 14.) Because magazines tend to cover highly specialized topics with niche audiences, it's important to write about topics that directly affect or interest the publication's target audience.
- **Suspense or tension** is a news value that typically doesn't appear in news-writing textbooks. A good story introduces a problem or an element of mystery or tension at the beginning that hooks the reader. The introduction of tension makes the reader wonder how the story turns out or how the problem is solved.
- **Conflict** may be the most common news value that attracts attention. Journalists are sometimes criticized for exaggerating the degree of

controversy between two parties to create a good story. The human interest value in conflict is why most movies and novels have "good guys" and "bad guys," and literary works have "protagonists" and "antagonists." A positive force needs an opposing negative force to introduce curiosity about the outcome.

- **Humor** is another "news value" that makes any story more appealing. Writing humor is difficult and few people do it well. Writers have to depend completely on their words to make people laugh, while stand-up comics can rely on gestures, volume, tone of voice and timing. You don't have to write a humor story, however, to use humor in many kinds of stories. The use of humorous anecdotes or quotes even in serious pieces can attract and keep readers.

Types of Articles

The first step in writing an article is deciding what kind of article you want to write. While the different types of articles will be explained in detail in subsequent chapters, understanding them now will help you establish a framework to investigate potential ideas. Keep in mind that the boundaries between these categories are not rigid. You can easily find examples of features that blend two or more types.

Foot-in-the-Door Features (Chapter 11)

The best way to break into a publication today is with short, self-contained items that range from 50 words (for a joke) to 600 words (for a mini profile). Readers like "shorts" because they are quick to absorb, less intimidating than a multi-page article, offer variety, can be clipped and saved and play to the current preference for skip-and-scan media.

Profile Articles (Chapter 12)

Interviews produce three types of profile articles: the portrait, the photograph and the snapshot. Chapter 12 will offer tips on creating the well-balanced profile, often called a "warts-and-all" study of an interesting person.

Real-Life Dramas and Stories (Chapter 13)

The real-life drama tells a story that is focused on one person and one event or turning point in his or her life. In some cases, the focus may be on two or three people who encountered a dramatic experience together. A true-life narrative differs from a profile, which describes an individual's personal interests, hobbies, or career.

Service Journalism and "How-to" Articles (Chapter 14)

Service journalism provides useful, practical information that readers can apply in their everyday lives—information that helps them raise their families, prepare for a career, or simply live their lives. They often focus on consumer information such as shopping, health, education or personal finance. Readers are always looking for new ways to save, spend, make and invest money. If you have a creative approach for saving money on taxes, making money in your spare time or finding bargains in unusual places, then you will find markets for your material.

Seasonal and Calendar-Related Stories (Chapter 15)

Most publications look for particular types of articles at special times of the year—Christmas, back-to-school, tax season and so forth. This chapter explains how to tune in to a publication's seasonal needs. It also gives practical tips on writing anniversary stories to commemorate special events, dates and historical celebrities. Popular topics for anniversary articles include Pearl Harbor, school desegregation, the end of the Vietnam War or even historic events within fields of interest that the public may not know about.

Trends and Topics (Chapter 16)

This type of news feature describes some recent trend, phenomenon or issue and quotes experts and participants who give their opinions about it. The distinguishing characteristics of this genre of writing are, first, that it focuses on an issue or trend and not upon a particular person; and second, that you bring together a variety of sources to shed light on an important contemporary topic. These can be "hitchhiker" stories that ride on recent events in the news. Issue and trend stories require a complex blend of analysis, facts, anecdotes and human interest.

Inspirational Writing (Chapter 17)

People need all kinds of encouragement simply to get through life. You don't have to write for a religious publication to write an inspirational article. Hundreds of magazines and feature sections of newspapers look for articles that provide motivation and inspiration toward career success, religious faith or meaning in life.

Business-to-Business Features (Chapter 18)

The main characteristic of this type of article is that it is written for a magazine aimed at a particular job, profession or hobby. This audience has very specialized and narrow interests within a specific field. This type of article can be a news story or feature, a profile, a true-life narrative, a service piece or an investigative story. Many articles in special interest publications are service pieces or profiles of successful individuals. More than 4,000 business-to-business magazines—twice the number of consumer magazines—are published for the trade press. It's perhaps the most profitable and overlooked market for freelance writers.

Internet Articles (Chapter 19)

Internet articles differ from newspaper and magazine articles in two ways: First, they are short and to the point; and second, they mostly focus on news and service journalism. They are similar to magazine articles in that they are targeted to a specific niche audience—often more narrow than special interest magazines.

Choosing a Target Publication

Editors frequently complain that freelance writers don't study their publications before they submit unsolicited ideas and manuscripts. Experienced freelance writers pick a magazine or group of magazines they want to write for before they decide on a story idea. Then they study dozens of back issues at a library. That's because the best source of ideas will come from seeing the types of articles those particular periodicals publish. On the other hand, beginning writers often write their articles first and then try to find a place to publish them.

Here are some advantages to choosing your target publications first and reading through some of their previous issues:

- You know what topics have been covered and therefore can recognize an original idea when you see it.
- You know about current trends within the field of interest you want to write about and can pick a topic related to one of them.
- You can recognize the types of articles most frequently published in these magazines. For example, some magazines never publish profiles, poetry or personal experience articles.
- You become familiar with the writing style, tone and "personality" of the magazine.

Another advantage to reading old issues of some of your favorite magazines is that you can discover their evergreen topics. Susan Ungaro, former editor of *Family Circle*, once said: "Certain 'evergreen' articles are published in every magazine over and over again. For instance, we constantly tell readers different ways to make the most of their money or to take charge of their health. I do a story every spring and fall on spring-cleaning your house, how to get organized, how to deal with clutter in your life. Romance and marriage secrets—how to make your marriage closer, more intimate, more loving—are probably addressed in every issue of every women's magazine."[6]

A Dozen Other Places to Find Ideas

As we've already emphasized, the best way for writers to find an original idea is by reading. Here are a dozen more specific things to read or places to find ideas for your feature and magazine articles.

Yellow Pages of Telephone Books

In his book, *The Freelancer: A Writer's Guide to Success*, Dennis Hensley suggests finding ideas from the yellow pages. He offers these specific tips:[7]

- Send a postcard to all of the associations and organizations listed and ask to be added to their mailing lists for bulletins, newsletters and press releases. "These will give you several news tips," says Hensley.
- Check display ads for businesses ready to celebrate anniversaries and then write profiles of them. Find businesses that offer unusual products or services and write about them.
- Look under the heading "social service organizations" for details on nonprofit organizations that serve the underprivileged.

How to Know if You Have a Great Article Idea

You should answer "Yes" to at least the majority of the following 10 questions:

1. Is this topic so new and original that you can't find any books written on the subject?
2. Is your topic of broad interest to the narrow group who read the particular magazine for whom you are interested in writing? Or will it just appeal to a narrow group within this narrow group?
3. Does this topic deal with basic life issues such as death, love, sickness, money, careers, health—issues that affect millions of people?
4. Do you have a strong, central unifying theme?
5. Can you state your angle in one sentence using an action verb?
6. Does your angle allow you to offer intelligent insight, as opposed to saying something that's obvious, common sense or that readers have already read about many times?
7. Are there elements of drama or conflict that will attract and sustain the reader?
8. Can your topic generate several colorful and compelling anecdotes from your sources? Can you find human-interest stories about it?
9. Does your theme contradict or question what most people seem to think or assume? The best articles call into question the **conventional wisdom** about a subject.
10. Do you have access to the sources you need to write this article? These sources should be participants, keen observers or experts on the topic you are writing about.

You can also browse through the yellow pages for any city in the United States through online services such as www.switchboard.com. This is an excellent resource for finding ideas and sources for articles outside your immediate geographic area.

Newspaper Classified Ads

The best sections of the classified ads to find ideas may be the "Wanted to Buy" and "Personals" sections. People who advertise in the "Wanted to Buy" section are often collectors of unusual types of items. A writer once read a small classified ad looking for "antique Coca-Cola machines and memorabilia." He called the number and found a man who owned three barns full of Coca Cola machines, memorabilia and other items worth hundreds of thousands of dollars. A visit and interview yielded a fascinating cover story full of funny anecdotes and good photos.

Weekly Newspapers

Check local and area newspapers for small news items that you can develop into long feature stories for a magazine. Newspapers are filled with undeveloped stories and announcements of meetings and events that could lead to interesting stories. Look for brief articles about people who have received awards. The award itself may simply be the culmination of an interesting series of events or achievements leading up to it. For example, when an 82-year-old great grandmother earns a college degree from a Florida college, you can be sure there's a story behind it.

Keep in mind that article ideas can't be copyrighted. If you take an article as inspiration and develop it into something else, you haven't committed plagiarism. Plagiarism only occurs when you use words from another article without giving credit.

Bulletin Boards on Campuses or Places of Employment

Bulletin boards frequently contain notices of upcoming events, celebrity speakers or meetings of clubs or organizations that pursue unusual activities. Celebrities who speak at special events may have more time while they're there than they do in their home surroundings. To obtain an interview, simply contact the sponsoring organization for the celebrity's telephone number or e-mail address.

Published Schedules of Meetings and Events

Most newspapers and city magazines publish a calendar of upcoming celebrity speakers, conventions, hobby and trade shows and meetings. They also may publicize meetings of self-help groups and hobby and service clubs with meeting times and contact numbers. For example, support groups exist for families of murder victims, the mentally ill and drug abusers. These groups may allow you to visit if you promise to protect individual identities. Web sites sponsored by city governments and visitors' bureaus contain the same type of information. To find these Web sites, use your favorite search engine and type in "visitors bureau" or "events calendar" for the name of your city.

Television, Radio and Internet News Broadcasts

Find a national news item that you can write about from a local angle. The best way to localize any story is to discuss that issue through a person whom you interview. For example, watch "Oprah" to discover issues on the minds of everyday people and then look for a local angle. Monitor the special interest groups in online discussions on any subject that interests you. For example, go to Google.com, click on "Google groups" and then type in key words for topics of interest to find an online group discussing that topic. David Sumner once used Google groups to find an expert who became the key source for an article on electronic home automation in a nationally published magazine.

Faculty Biographies on University Web Sites

Go to any university's Web site and look for biographical sketches of faculty members. Colleges are the homes of some of the nation's best minds, and the writer who doesn't tap this source of free information is missing a great opportunity. For example, a Florida zoology professor is an expert on alligators and often treks through the state's swamps with a camera and notebook. After getting an idea through reading faculty biographies, you can follow up with a telephone call to the professor. Many otherwise obscure professors are nationally known experts in their subject areas and are flattered by requests for interviews.

To find them, click on the "academic programs" link at any university's Web site, and then find a department that interests you. Most departmental Web sites list the publications and accomplishments of their faculty members along with telephone and e-mail addresses.

Publications that Specialize in Expert Media Sources

Many Web sites offer biographies and contact information for experts on various topics. You can browse through their list of topics for both ideas and sources. Two of the best are: www.allexperts.com and www.yearbook.com.

Association directories are an excellent source for ideas and expert sources. "For every problem you can think of, there is an organization who can guide you to people who have it or have a story to tell. There are support groups for everything you can possibly imagine. There is not a disease or a political cause that is not represented somewhere in some group," says New York-based magazine writer Judith Newman.[8]

Browse through the list of the thousands of professional, hobby and nonprofit organizations in a print or online directory. We recommend *Directory of Associations*, a print source, and the association directory at the Internet Public Library: www.ipl.org/.

A great print resource for ideas and information on current events is *CQ Researcher*, published by Congressional Quarterly Publications. Each issue of this bi-weekly resource contains a balanced discussion and bibliography on a debated issue in current events. Recent topics include cyber security, gay marriage, homeland security, water shortages, prescription drug prices, the SUV debate, movie ratings, abortion and gambling in America.

Old Magazines

Magazines have certain perennial or evergreen topics on which they write stories at least once a year. Look for seasonal articles related to holidays and anniversaries of major events. If you browse through enough issues, you can discover their perennial topics and come up with a fresh angle. Even if you don't think you have a chance for selling that idea to a prestigious magazine, you can send a query on a similar topic to a competing but lesser-known publication.

Suggestions from Friends

Ask a friend, teacher or colleague, "Do you have any friends, relatives or colleagues who are involved in anything newsworthy that I might be able to write about?"

A Dictionary of Clichés

Clichés can provide a ready-made source for an article idea, catchy title and angle by changing a word or two. For example, instead of "Absence makes the heart grow fonder," try doing an article on "Absence makes the heart go wander," describing the difficulty that couples face in maintaining long-distance relationships.

Instead of "An accident waiting to happen," write an article on "An accident waiting to go to court" about staged auto accidents criminals used to commit insurance fraud. To get more ideas, get a dictionary of clichés available in any large bookstore or library.

Write about What You Want to Know, Not What You Know

Curiosity may kill cats, but it creates successful writers. The old journalism maxim "Write what you know" will not take you very far. Reflect on the topics that you're interested in knowing more about and use them to create an idea for a story.

Suggested Activities

1. Spend an hour in the library's newspaper room looking at newspaper stories. Write a one-sentence description for possible magazine article ideas—five from non-wire stories in a local newspaper and five based on national issues or events for which you can find a magazine angle.

2. Look through a telephone directory's yellow pages and find five unusual businesses or occupations that might yield an interesting story. Write a one-sentence description for each of these story ideas that contains a specific angle on that person or business.

3. Go to www.allexperts.com or www.yearbook.com and find five authors who have published a book within the past year. Find out as much information as you can about each book and author. Write a one-sentence idea based on that book's topic for which you could conduct an interview with the author.

4. Start a clip and idea file. For a two-week period, see if you can come up with 25 ideas from reading, Internet surfing, viewing television and movies, listening to music, talking to friends and just thinking. Jot them down and number them in your computer or in a notebook. Revise and edit them before turning them in for class discussion.

Shoptalk

Business-to-business magazine: A magazine whose main purpose is to provide useful information to practitioners of the various professions and trades. About 4,000 trade magazines are published in the United States.

Conventional wisdom: The most commonly held opinions and attitudes about various issues. Many creative and original articles contradict or at least question the conventional wisdom about the topics they address.

News values: Certain characteristics of news and feature stories that make them interesting. The most common news values are novelty, conflict, magnitude, impact, tension and humor.

Primary source: The originating source for specific news and information. Primary source material has not been edited, published or interpreted by other writers. The best primary sources are experts, witnesses or participants in the issues and events you write about.

Real-life drama: The true-life narrative tells a dramatic or inspiring story that usually focuses on one person and one event in his or her life. These articles have a chronological structure with a specific beginning and ending point.

Scholarly journal: Academic publications that publish studies by professors or independent researchers in a specific discipline. Decisions on which articles to publish in scholarly journals are made by a peer review group of professors in that discipline. Because scholarly journals usually have low circulations, they offer writers the opportunity to publicize the results of groundbreaking studies to a wider audience.

Secondary source: A "second-hand" source that stands between the reader and the originating source. Articles appearing in newspapers, magazines or Web sites are usually secondary sources.

Service journalism: Articles written to help readers in their everyday lives. Service journalism articles may help improve readers' health, recreation, finances or careers. "How-to" articles are a special type of service journalism that focus on completing a specific, immediate task.

Special collections: Non-circulating documents held by libraries that often serve as useful information for journalists and researchers. Public officials and celebrities often donate their correspondence and document collections to libraries' special collections.

Endnotes

1. Stephen King, *On Writing: A Memoir of the Craft* (New York: Simon and Schuster Pocket Books, 2000), 150.

2. Interview, Miami, FL, Nov. 17, 1997.

3. Interview, Camden, SC, Oct. 27, 1997.

4. Quoted in Sammye Johnson and Patricia Prijatel, *Magazine Publishing*, (Lincolnwood, IL: NTC Contemporary Publishing, 2000), 193.

5. Quoted in Judy Mandell, *Magazine Editors Talk to Writers* (New York: John Wiley and Sons, 1996), 184.

6. Quoted in Judy Mandell, ed., *Magazine Editors Talk to Writers,* 57.

7. Dennis Hensley, *The Freelancer: A Writer's Guide to Success* (Indianapolis: Poetica Press, 1984), 83-84.

8. Telephone interview, Dec. 11, 2003.

Chapter 3
Strong Angles and Focused Ideas

A successful feature has a strong, focused angle that displays three characteristics: unity, action and specificity. This chapter will explain several ways to determine if your idea is too broad and offer additional suggestions on how to make it more narrow and workable. To achieve these goals, this chapter explains:

- Angles and subject matter
- Characteristics of a strong angle
- Narrowing your topic
- Using the funnel of focus

The most frequent problem that writing teachers find among story ideas from new writers is that they are too broad and unfocused. Some come up with topics they want to write about (such as alcohol abuse or weight loss), but they don't create story ideas that will work. For example, one student wanted to write an article about eating disorders. Her teacher challenged her to come up with a tighter angle on this broad topic. After some conversations with the professor, she decided to focus on treatment and build her story around the experiences of a young woman who had acknowledged her problem and sought help.

Angles and Subject Matter

Meg Grant, the West Coast editor for the *Reader's Digest*, explained how the magazine's editors narrowed a proposed feature article on foster care for children: "We didn't want to do the same piece everybody is reading in their local papers about how broken the foster care system is. We picked a section of the foster care issue that was a smaller piece to chew on, which was about those kids who spend their whole lives in foster care and never get out of the system. We decided to look at one of the programs, and then we found one kid and told his story."[1]

A limited tale told clearly has more impact than a sweeping story that lacks depth and insight. The more frequently that magazines and newspapers cover a topic, the sharper and fresher the angle must be. For example, the following sidebar provides examples of how to narrow the focus of popular topics that are too broad and unfocused:

How to Give a Tighter Angle to a Broad Topic

Too Broad	Tighter Angle
How to Lose Weight	10 Tips for Staying on a Diet When You Travel
Running for Political Office	How to Use Door-to-Door Campaigning in Elections
Improving your Home's Security	Five New Home Security Devices That Cost Less Than $100
Volunteering Brings Rewards	Working with the Homeless Helped John Smith Discover New Purpose
How to Choose a Computer	Avoid Paying for These "Extras" You Don't Need in a Computer

A former *Wall Street Journal* editor put it this way: "Most of us think too big. We try to embrace the circus fat lady, and only well into the effort do we find there is too much of her and not enough of us. The result is a piece impossibly long, or superficial, the reporter frantically skipping from point to point without dwelling on any of them long enough to illuminate and convince."[2]

A focused angle has three characteristics: **unity**, **action** and **specificity**. Let's look at each characteristic.

Unity

Think about the best movies you've ever seen. "The Titanic," for example, was the highest-grossing movie of the 20th century. This movie describes how the famous luxury liner crashed into an iceberg and sunk, while one young couple made futile efforts to survive. The 22 words you just read in the previous sentence sum up this three-hour movie with its three action verbs. It has a simple plot.

If you can't explain your article idea in one sentence, you don't have a workable idea. Dozens of editors and authors we have interviewed echo this "one sentence" rule. Why is it so important? Unity means that everything "hangs together" around a central idea. This central idea creates an organizing principle that helps you determine whom you interview, what you include, what you omit, and what you look for in your research. If you have a sharply focused angle before you begin research, you will save dozens of hours in fruitless, unnecessary research that leads you down the wrong path. A good, clear focus means that the title and introduction let the readers know exactly what they are getting into and a chance to get off if they don't want to go there.

Unity means unity in content, style, voice and approach. Gary Provost says in *Beyond Style: Mastering the Finer Points of Writing*: "Unity, that quality of oneness in your writing, means that everything you write should look as if it were written at one time, by one person, with one purpose, using one language."[3]

It's easy to drift away from your unity. Sometimes you find a fascinating anecdote, and you feel as if you just have to include it. But those paragraphs that interrupt the unity of the article will also jar the reader, so you have to go back and remove them.

Action

Strong, creative articles contain action. They describe people doing things, having fun, suffering injustice or making things happen. A strong action verb in the title or magazine's **cover line** helps attract the attention of the editor and the reader. Go to a newsstand and look at the **teasers** that are placed above the newspaper's nameplate. Both cover lines and teasers are meant to attract readers, which is why they often contain action verbs.

You aren't writing about a person or an organization simply because they exist. For example, suppose you made a trip to Nashville and propose to write an article about the Grand Ole' Opry. What about it? Since thousands of articles have been written about this American music phenomenon, what has happened recently at the Opry that will be news to fans of country music? Most stories originate with an idea about an interesting person or phenomenon or trend, and the trick is to think of a particular way to tell the story. Remember that a story should be a verb, not a noun. It shouldn't just be about a place or an institution. Something should be happening. Chapter 6 will teach some practical techniques on adding action to your stories.

Specificity

Finally, the things that happen include specific dates and places in which they occur. If you can't cite specific dates and places in an article, then it isn't sufficiently anchored. Unanchored articles are vague and make it difficult for the reader to visualize its concepts. Even if your story is on some broad evergreen topic like tax-saving tips, you have to anchor it with people saying and doing things in specific places at specific times.

To see examples of unity, action and specificity, go to a store where magazines are sold and study the cover lines—the little "blurbs" appearing on the side of a magazine's cover. Editors use cover lines and teasers to attract attention from among the hundreds of competing publications on display. Here are some cover lines from recent magazines. Notice that each one contains an action verb.

"Hazing Nightmares: You Won't Believe These Shocking Stories" *(Teen People)*

"What to Do When His Crazy 'Ex' Won't Let Go" *(Teen People)*

"Get Lean All Over: A New Diet and Workout Plan to Max Your Metabolism" *(Shape)*

"Chill Out—How to Calm Your Hot Horse" *(Horse and Rider)*

"Cool Wedding Trends: What Other Couples Are Doing Coast to Coast" *(Bride)*

"How to Avoid the Fat Trap in Fast Food Salads" *(Ladies Home Journal)*

We'll talk more about cover lines in Chapter 14.

Narrowing Your Topic

Here are some questions that will help you determine if your story idea is too broad and unfocused. As an example, let's say you're thinking about writing an article on identity theft.

Can You Find One or More Books on the Subject?

Never write a feature article from re-hashed book content. Editors demand fresh, original stories. They don't want hash that's been ground out of books, the Internet or other articles. A recent search of "identity theft" at www.amazon.com turned up 605 books on the topic, so "identity theft," by itself is definitely too broad of a topic for a feature article.

Is It Possible to Write a Book on the Subject?

Articles can't cover everything because their length usually ranges from 1,000 to 2,000 words. Each story must focus on a small slice of a huge pie. Let's say you narrow your topic to "how to prevent identity theft." Another search on Amazon.com using those terms (in quotes) turns up three books on the subject.

Does Your Title Have Verbs?

Look at the titles of articles in popular magazines. As we mentioned, most have a verb in the title describing something that is happening. It's action that catches and keeps the reader's attention. Never write an article on a phenomenon (or organization, company, etc.) simply because it exists. "Identity theft," of course, has no verbs, and we've already ruled it out as a topic. Similar topics such as "credit card theft," "consumer fraud" or "white-collar crime" are also too broad. Not only that, Amazon searches using these key-word topics yield thousands of books.

So let's look at how five magazines and newspapers recently covered the topic of "identity theft" from five different angles.

1. *Black Issues in Higher Education*: "Education Department Takes Steps To Curb Identity Theft Among Students" (Explains how college students can prevent identity theft using resources from a Web site sponsored by the U.S. Secretary of Education.)
2. *Computer Weekly*: "Businesses Must Foresee the Problem of Identity Theft" (Explains how businesses can take steps to prevent identity theft of their employees' personal financial information.)
3. *Kiplinger's Personal Finance Magazine*: "An Eye For Privacy— Tougher Laws Against Identity Theft" (Reports on the increasing number of states that are adopting strict legislation to prevent identity theft.)

4. *LA Business Journal*: "Online Security Concerns Drive Credit Card Changes" (Explains new technology that helps online shoppers prevent identity theft through stolen credit card numbers.)
5. *Popular Mechanics*: "Encrypting Your E-mail" (Explains new software that encrypts your e-mail and helps prevent identity theft and stolen personal information.)

How can you find a sharp angle on a story? The single best way is to read up on the subject. If you want to write an article on identity theft, for example, we challenge you to read a dozen articles on the subject before you begin writing or interviewing. Then—and only then—will you know what's been covered, what the issues are, where disagreements exist, which questions remain unanswered and what questions to ask. Then—and only then—will you know how to come up with a fresh and original angle on well-worn topics.

While reading about your general topic in other publications is the first step, it only helps you eliminate non-original angles. After that there are no quick and easy steps. There are, however, at least three questions you can ask that will point you in the right direction.

Decide What You Want to Know

First, ask yourself, "What would I like to know about this topic?" One of the biggest myths about writing is the often-repeated aphorism, "Write about what you know." If we only wrote about what we knew, none of us would last more than a week in the publishing business.

Lou Harry, editor of *Indy Men's Magazine*, says that if a magazine editor asks you this question, "What do you know about _____ topic?" then you should always give this answer: "Well, I wouldn't try to pass myself off as an expert, but I think I could ask the right questions."[4] In other words, you don't have to be an expert to write a good story. You simply need to know what it is that you need to know.

Find Unique Sources

Another way of deciding how to focus a topic can be achieved by asking, "What unique or primary sources do I have access to?" A person with expertise or unique experiences in a particular area is a primary source. Maybe you have a famous relative or access to a celebrity. Primary sources also can be court documents, internal reports or other unpublished information. Secondary sources are magazine, newspaper and Internet articles. They are easy to spot because they lack freshness and originality.

Writer and movie producer Nora Ephron advises, "You must come up with some little thing that you know about that others don't. A good journalist figures that out. It means reading everything possible to keep up with what's going on. You can't merely find a subject that may interest a magazine editor. Find a subject on which you have something interesting, surprising or perverse to say."[5]

Find a News Peg

Third, you can ask, "How can I hang this topic on a **news peg**?" A news peg is a current event, anniversary or other event that illustrates the topic you want to write about. For example, the January birthday of Martin Luther King Jr. always offers a news peg to write stories related to civil rights or race relations. It's a way to "get into" or develop a lead for a feature story.

Using the Funnel of Focus

Dr. Gerald Grow, a professor of journalism at Florida A&M University, challenges his students with a "funnel of focus" exercise.[6] The purpose behind this exercise is to begin with a broad topic that could fill a library and focus it into a publishable article topic.

For example, he asks students to begin with a broad topic and then gradually focus it as in the following example:

a) Topic that would fill a library of thousands of books
   Example: education
b) Topic big enough to fill an entire 600-page book
   Example: the history of education
c) Topic for the focus of a special-interest magazine
   Example: the parent-teacher relationship
d) Topic that would fill a whole issue of a magazine
   Example: What parents can do to help their kids in school
e) Topic that would fill several articles in a magazine
   Example: Articles directed to parents helping kids in different grades
f) Topic of one article in a magazine
   Example: How parents can help teenagers with high school math

g) Topic of one article in a particular magazine

  Example: How single, working parents can help their teenagers with high school math

In summary, an angle takes a specific approach to its subject matter. A strong angle can be summarized in one sentence and displays unity, action and specificity. The cover lines on magazines provide examples of focused angles. You can use a step-by-step "funnel of focus" to narrow your topic from one that could fill a library to one for a specific magazine, newspaper or Web site. You can narrow your topic by asking yourself what you want to know and what sources you have access to and by finding a news peg that ties your topic to a current event.

The more narrow your angle, the more likely you will write a creative, original article. The more narrow your angle, the more likely you can find a "scoop" that no one else has written about before. Finally, the narrower your angle, the more likely you will get published. Finding a good angle isn't easy, but the more you read what's already been published, the easier it will become.

Suggested Activities

1. Go to a store where magazines are sold. Write down 25 cover lines and underline their action verbs. Discuss the kinds of topics and "action" that editors seem to like to highlight in their cover lines.

2. Do a "funnel of focus" exercise by starting out with a broad idea and answering the following questions:

- What large topic that would fill a library is your idea part of?
- What is a book-length version of your topic?
- State your topic as the theme of all the articles in a whole issue of a magazine.
- State a magazine-article-length version of your idea.
- Describe your idea as one article in a particular magazine for a particular audience.

3. Pick a hot topic that is currently in the news. Do a database search and find at least 10 articles with different angles on the topic.

Shoptalk

Action: Movement from one place or position to another by a person, entity or phenomenon. The description of change in feature articles makes them more interesting than those without any action.

Cover lines: Short promotional descriptions of articles that appear on a magazine's cover; cover lines highlight the unity, action and specificity of articles.

News peg: A current or recent event related to the topic that you are writing about; a news peg gives timeliness to a feature article.

Specificity: Related to tangible facts or events that can be seen, felt, heard, smelled or observed.

Teasers: Similar to magazines' cover lines, they appear above a newspaper's nameplate on page one to promote stories inside the day's edition.

Unity: The focusing of an article on one main theme using a consistent tone, verb tense and voice.

Endnotes

1. Telephone interview, Nov. 29, 2003.

2. William Blundell, *The Art and Craft of Feature Writing* (New York: Penguin Books, 1988), 24.

3. Gary Provost, *Beyond Style: Mastering the Finer Points of Writing* (Cincinnati: Writer's Digest Books, 1988), 42.

4. Speech, Anderson Public Library, Anderson, IN, Oct. 18, 2003.

5. Quoted in Candy Schulman, "The Idea Ideal," *Handbook of Magazine Article Writing*, Jean M. Fredette, ed. (Cincinnati: Writer's Digest Books, 1988), 25.

6. Gerald Grow, "The Funnel of Focus," www.longleaf.net/ggrow Reprinted with permission.

Chapter 4
Creative Research and Reporting

Successful writers have learned how to report. They know how to find expert sources for productive interviews and how to mine the primary sources of traditional libraries and electronic databases as well as the Internet. Successful writers can combine these resources to yield detailed background information on people, current events and organizations. This chapter teaches you:

- How libraries help you
- Why interviews are essential
- How to use primary sources
- How to conduct background research on people, organizations and current events
- Where to locate useful Internet resources for writers

Many successful nonfiction writers estimate that they spend 80 percent of their time on research and 20 percent on the actual writing. The best writers get out and mingle among people, develop sources, get tips and leads, do many interviews and immerse themselves in research. Good writers also know how to mine the many helpful resources at libraries.

"God is in the details, and compelling color, quotes and detail do not simply materialize," says Jack Kelley, a former *People* magazine editor. "Many of the best magazine writers liken their work to mining. They chip and chip until they extract a nugget. Then they chip some more. They are not embarrassed to keep asking questions," he says.[1]

The best way to narrow the focus of a topic for an article is to read background materials and do research. If you have a general idea of what you want to write about, but are puzzled about the focus, read about it. We suggest consulting at least a dozen books or articles on your topic before you begin looking for interview sources. This background research helps you determine the context, focus and angle for an article. It tells you what's been written, what's been asked, what's been answered and—most important—what hasn't been answered. By discovering gaps and question marks, you can come up with a fresh slant on an old topic.

Good research makes the story trustworthy for the reader and helps you accomplish these objectives:

- Find background material, including small details, useful facts and interesting anecdotes. This adds credibility and human interest to your story.
- Locate up-to-date information on a subject, which adds freshness and timeliness to your subject.
- Find original interview questions, which will distinguish your story from the last 25 written on this subject. Find questions that won't bore your sources.

The first step in research—thinking—is both easy and difficult, but its importance can't be overestimated. Deep thinking precedes creative reporting. If you haven't read much about your topic, you have to do additional background research. After you've consulted numerous sources, ask yourself, "How can I give this subject an angle that hasn't been covered before?" or "How can I say something fresh and original about this subject?" Interviewing should be the last step in the reporting process.

How Libraries Help You

Joe Treen, editor-at-large for *Discover* magazine, says that libraries have three advantages over the Internet: "First of all, they've got books. Second of all, they have people who can help you. Third, they have reliability. I don't always trust stuff I see on the Internet. I think bricks and mortar libraries are not going to go away," says Treen.[2]

Library print sources are also more likely closely scrutinized and fact-checked by professional editors than material you find elsewhere. Academic journal articles are peer-reviewed, which means that two or three experts in the author's field review and approve each article before it appears in print.

You can save valuable time by taking a few minutes to introduce yourself to a librarian. Because librarians enjoy the written word, they find satisfaction in helping writers and researchers. Their job is to make your library work more efficient and productive.

Besides more reliable sources, the library has at least two other advantages. You can browse through magazines and newspapers and read articles in their back issues. Browsing through these publications will help you create ideas as well as locate target markets for your stories. The number-one complaint editors make about freelance writers is that they don't study their publications before submitting a query letter or article. The library is a good place to study old issues of target magazines and really get a "feel" for the kinds of articles they publish.

Second, university libraries subscribe to commercial electronic databases not available on the Internet. Subscriptions to these databases cost anywhere from a few hundred dollars to more than $10,000. For example, *LexisNexis News*, a commercial database available only through libraries, is recognized as the premier research tool for searching full-text articles from thousands of newspapers and magazines. The subscription-only database Science Direct offers access to 900 full-text scientific journals covering such areas as biotechnology, chemistry, computer technology and more. Large libraries pay more than $100,000 a year to subscribe to these databases, but make them available for free to their patrons. While they're always available for free through in-house terminals, many libraries also make the databases available through their Web sites to registered patrons.

Because of the Internet's convenience, most beginning writers first turn there for research. The Internet simultaneously creates both the greatest opportunity and threat to good writing since journalism became a recognized profession in the 19th century. It threatens good writing because Web sites offer unparalleled opportunities for shallow research and plagiarism. You can find hundreds of articles on any topic, rearrange a few facts here, lift a few quotes there and create a 1,500-word "article." This patchwork approach to Internet research is easy to recognize because it smells stale. It's also dishonest and illegal.

On the other hand, the Internet offers a tremendous opportunity to writers because it helps locate expert sources on any topic. It's a great starting point. When properly used, the Internet can offer writers in small towns and out-of-the-way places access to nationally known experts with whom they can follow up with telephone interviews. It offers access to millions of government records that used to require a trip to city hall, the statehouse or the Library of Congress. The Internet offers a "gateway" to the world that can create a national content for articles written for a national audience. But don't do all of your research on the Internet, or you're likely to end up with outdated information.

Why Interviews Are Essential

While background research adds depth and detail to article writing, personal interviews bring freshness and originality. We cannot stress enough the superiority of telephone and face-to-face interviews to online research or e-mail interviews. Face-to-face and telephone interviews cover numerous topics in a relatively short period of time. The time required by e-mail to type onto a keyboard slows down communication and discourages how much information the source volunteers to tell you.

Some people simply can't type, can't type quickly or don't enjoy using e-mail. People in influential positions get hundreds of e-mail messages daily and may brush you off if they reply at all. E-mail can also get lost because of technical problems. It can disappear into cyberspace when a server is down, a power outage occurs or the sender makes a typographical error in the address and it goes to the wrong person.

Sources cannot avoid a telephone call or personal visit as easily as they can an e-mail message. While sources can simply hit the "delete" key for unwanted e-mail, they have to give you an answer when you appear at their door or reach them on the telephone. It's just harder for them to say "no." The more distance you put between yourself and a source, the more information you lose. Think about the lost information this way:

Face-to-Face Interviews

You receive or observe: (a) words; (b) tone of voice; (c) voice inflection; (d) pauses; (e) physical appearance of your source; (f) physical surroundings of your source; and (g) access to nearby family members or colleagues of your source.

Telephone Interviews

You receive or observe: (a) words; (b) tone of voice; (c) voice inflection; and (d) pauses.

E-Mail Interviews

You receive or observe: (a) words. E-mail is useful when you are seeking only brief answers to two or three questions or perhaps you want to conduct a survey of a dozen experts. Some students have been known to conduct e-mail interviews with people who work at the same school they attend.

Myron Struck, editor-in-chief of Targeted News Service, says, "Eight of 10 interns who have come to us over the past four years from journalism programs do not know how to conduct face-to-face interviews and believe that e-mail and perhaps the telephone are far superior." He encourages us to discourage e-mail interviews and "encourage more practice doing face-to-face interviews."[3]

Other Primary Sources

Interviews are the most common primary source used by writers, but not the only one. Primary source material, which we discussed in Chapter 2, originates at its source. Secondary source material in published articles or books has been filtered and interpreted by the writer. In one sense, it's been "censored." Although Internet sources and libraries have mostly secondary sources, both offer some primary sources.

Academic Studies

University libraries subscribe to hundreds of **scholarly journals** related to the academic disciplines that they teach. Some scholarly journals are also published through libraries' commercial databases or on the Internet. Many journal articles focus on obscure topics of little interest to writers or the public. Others, however, contain gold mines of information. Writers serve as an important link in interpreting the findings of academic studies for the public. Writers quote medical journals more often than any other. For example, *The New England Journal of Medicine* may be the media's most widely quoted academic journal. Nevertheless, browsing through scholarly journals in psychology, sociology, political science or business may also give you plenty of article ideas. Since most authors are also professors, you can interview them after finding their telephone numbers through university Web sites.

Listservs

The Internet has thousands of listservs. A **listserv** is an electronic newsletter subscribed to by people with a special interest in that topic. Any subscriber can send questions or comments to all of the other subscribers via e-mail. The primary advantage of listservs is they give you access to hundreds of experts on any topic you choose. For example, Journet is a popular listserv that journalism professors use to indulge in "shop talk" with each other. Almost every occupation, profession or hobby has at least one listserv for its practitioners. You can also find listserv support groups for people with various addictions, afflictions and diseases. Magazine and newspaper writers often subscribe to several listservs related to the beats that they cover. You can find and search for listservs by keyword topics at the Web site www.topica.com. The Web site will also tell you how to subscribe to each listserv.

Newsgroups

When the Internet first developed, "bulletin boards" were its most popular feature. These bulletin boards evolved into more than 10,000 special-interest **newsgroups** on the Internet. Today they're all accessible at Google.com through its "groups" search function. Type in the key word for any topic and you're likely to find comments from hundreds of people discussing that topic in one of the groups.

A newsgroup is like a bulletin board that anyone can read on the Internet, whereas a listserv is like a newsletter that you must subscribe to via e-mail. Because newsgroups are more easily accessible, you also have to approach them more cautiously. Some discuss X-rated topics, but most discuss professional or recreational topics. David Sumner used a "home automation" newsgroup to find and later interview a Minnesota man who owned a "hi-tech" house with dozens of electronic gadgets. He proved to be a great source with lots of interesting comments.

Space doesn't permit us to give you instruction on all the details of using listservs and newsgroups. If you want to learn more, we recommend *The Associated Press Guide to Internet Research and Reporting.*[4]

Congressional Reports and Testimonies

Because of the volume and complexity of its work, the U.S. Congress divides its tasks among approximately 250 committees and subcommittees. They conduct thousands of hearings every year on social, economic and political issues that affect everyone. Testimonies at these hearings come from victims of crimes or accidents to nationally known experts on health and safety matters. For example, Sumner also used transcripts from committee hearings on identity theft for a magazine article on that topic. Consult the government documents department of your library or look for the transcripts of most congressional hearings on the U.S. Senate (www.senate.gov) or House of Representatives (www.house.gov) Web sites.

Statistical Data

"There are lies, damned lies, and then there are statistics," is one of Mark Twain's famous quotes. People can selectively choose and interpret statistics to prove almost anything they want to prove. That's why it's essential for you to get to the original statistical data that hasn't been interpreted or distorted by other writers. When you find the original data, you can report the story using first-hand interpretations.

Despite Twain's claim, statistics add credibility. They describe a quantitative relationship between phenomena and help you prove the growth, decline or magnitude of any issue you write about. The U.S. government spends millions of taxpayer dollars every year to compile statistics on every aspect of American life: economics, transportation, health, crime, public safety, labor, manufacturing, birth and death rates and more. All of these results are available at a Web site (www.fedstats.gov) described as "the gateway to statistics from over 100 U.S. federal agencies." You can search for statistics by keyword, agency, topic or state. This Web site also contains an online version of the annual series *Statistical Abstract of the United States.* Almost every library also has the most recent print edition of the *Statistical Abstract* in its reference section. Over the years, we have used the *Statistical Abstract* as a research reference more often than any other print publication besides *Writer's Market.*

If you want to gain a competitive edge over your peers, learn how to summarize and interpret data using Excel or any other popular **spreadsheet**. Spreadsheets allow you to take a large list of data—such as state-by-state averages on various items—and alphabetize, sort from highest to lowest or find averages. You can also calculate year-by-year averages, percentage changes and fluctuations. One writer we know used www.fedstats.gov and a spreadsheet to compare inflation, unemployment and job growth between Republican and Democratic presidential administrations every year between 1900 and 2000.

Speeches, Reports, Judicial Decisions

The full text of speeches, agency reports, research reports and judicial decisions also provide original information not filtered or interpreted by other writers. Public figures, such as political leaders and company presidents, often place the full text of their speeches on their company's or office's Web site. Professional associations, nonprofit organizations or government agencies may publish the full text of research reports on the Internet. The full text of most judicial decisions at the state and higher levels are available on the Internet. If you're writing about a controversial court decision, for example, go to the Internet and find the full text of the decision so you won't have to rely on other writers' interpretations.

Correspondence and Papers

Original correspondence from well-known people is a wonderful primary source. When famous people die, they often donate their papers to libraries. These "papers" sometimes consist of hundreds of boxes of correspondence and other personal items. The papers of more recent U.S. presidents are contained at their respective presidential libraries where anyone may use them. The enormous size of these collections makes it possible for authors to write dozens of books on them, each with a different angle and sources of information. Many celebrities and public figures donate their papers to the libraries of their alma maters. These papers are contained within a library's **special collections** department. A good place to find story ideas is your nearest library. Ask about its special collections.

The next section explains where to find background research material on people, current events and issues and businesses and nonprofit organizations. For each of these three categories, it offers some of the best: (a) print sources, (b) commercial databases and (c) Internet resources. The commercial databases are available at libraries that subscribe to them or often through the Internet to their registered patrons.

Backgrounding a Person

In cases involving libel, the courts distinguish between public figures and private figures. In backgrounding people, we make the same distinction. Finding published information about public figures is easy. Finding published information about private figures is more difficult but not impossible. In general, print and Internet sources offer plentiful information on public figures, whereas information on private figures may be limited to the Internet. If you are interviewing someone unlikely to be written about, we recommend that you ask for a copy of his or her résumé before you do the interview. Nevertheless, with the proliferation of personal Web sites, **blogs** and newsgroups, Internet research may bring surprising results.

Print Sources

Marquis' Who's Who Series

Most large libraries subscribe to the Marquis Publications' "Who's Who" series, which includes *Who's Who in America?* and specialized titles like *Who's Who in the Media and Communications?*, *Who's Who in Religion?* and regional editions. This series contains information on professors, scientists and leaders of companies and organizations who may not be well known outside their fields. It's the standard reference source about prominent living Americans. Each entry contains a few hundred words with information such as degrees, career accomplishments and sometimes addresses and telephone numbers.

Current Biography

Current Biography is a monthly periodical published from 1940 to the current month. This is an excellent source for emerging celebrities and newsmakers. It contains biographical summaries of newsmakers gathered from numerous media sources.

Contemporary Authors, 1962–Current

Contemporary Authors is a series of more than 100 volumes containing biographies and interviews with current writers in fiction, nonfiction, poetry, journalism, drama, motion pictures and television.

Commercial Databases

Biography Resource Center

This database is the best online source for biographical information. It contains the online full-text version of biographical entries from Gale Group, a well-known publisher of reference books. Results are classified into four categories: narrative biographies, thumbnail biographies, magazine articles and Web sites. For example, a search on "Bill Cosby" yielded narrative biographies from eight sources, thumbnail biographies from four sources, 195 magazine articles and four Web sites about the popular entertainer.

Biography and Genealogy Master Index

This database provides an index to print sources containing biographical information. It doesn't include the biographical information itself. You can enter a name and find all of the biographical dictionaries, encyclopedias or reference works in which their biographical information is included.

Internet Resources

The Internet brings access to tons of information about people—celebrities, public figures and everyday people. "Googling" old friends has become a national pastime. Government agencies publish birth, marriage and death records, property ownership information, criminal records, trial transcripts and much more. Online companies collect as much information about their customers as they are willing to give. The ease with which much of this information is available has raised the concern of privacy experts and advocates. The Electronic Privacy Information Center (www.epic.org) monitors these concerns and advocates for legislation that protects privacy.

Entering someone's name into Google or any search engine won't even come close to yielding all of the available online information about him. Search engines look only for terms appearing as page titles or the superficial levels of documents and Web sites. They don't search the "hidden Web," which consist of documents buried beyond the easily accessible levels. For example, search engines will not retrieve names of people recorded on public documents buried deep in federal and state government Web sites.

It's always best to visit the Web site containing what you think you need and search within it using the site's internal search engine. For example, look for information on anyone you are backgrounding at the city, county and state government Web site where he or she lives. Next, visit the Web sites for companies and organizations with which he or she is affiliated.

Online telephone directories are another useful resource. The Internet contains a large number of national telephone directories, such as www.switchboard.com, www.anywho.com and www.whowhere.com. Use these directories to locate sources mentioned in articles that you read during your background research. For example, if an article quotes an expert from Laramie, Wyo., and you think she would be a good person to interview, you might be able to locate her using these online directories. Then, of course, you can do your own interview.

The most obvious limitation to these searches is that you're more likely to find people with uncommon names—such as Kryszceski. They also do not give you information on cell phone numbers, unlisted numbers or other household members at the same address.

These directories also have yellow pages, which list all businesses by category in any particular city. For example, if you need quotes from several real estate agents in various cities for your story on rising home prices, this would be a good place to find them.

At his popular Web site journalismnet.com, journalist Julian Sher offers an excellent online tutorial in how to find people and do background research on them. We recommend it as required reading and you can find it here: www.journalismnet.com/people/.

Backgrounding Current Events

We use the term "current events" broadly to encompass trends and issues within contemporary society including health, sports, business and politics as well as hobbies and recreation. Chapter 16 explains more about researching and writing trend and issue-oriented articles.

Print Resources

National Newspaper Indexes

Most libraries contain print indexes for national newspapers like *The New York Times, Washington Post, USA Today* and *Wall Street Journal.* These newspapers have searchable online databases; however, they usually charge a fee for articles older than a week and only go back a limited number of years. Libraries' print indexes extend into the 19th century or when the newspaper was founded. *The New York Times* index, for example, begins in 1851.

Reader's Guide to Periodical Literature

This handy guide (published monthly and yearly) indexes articles by topic and names of newsmakers for thousands of magazines. It's better than the Internet for doing topical searches for stories from popular consumer magazines: news, men's, women's, general and special interest. Most of these magazines do not publish their archival information on the Internet. For example, using the *Reader's Guide*, we located some particular types of article examples to use in this book after several unsuccessful Internet searches.

CQ Researcher (Congressional Quarterly Researcher)

This handy resource is a good place to get story ideas. Each issue, which focuses on a specific topic, contains several articles and a balanced overview of that topic. Some recent topics: serial killers, civil liberties, gay marriage, media ownership, cyber security, obesity, combating plagiarism, homeland security, prescription drug prices, SUV debate, abortion debates, gambling in America and medical malpractice. You could, for example, take any of these issues, interview local sources, and give it a local slant for a city or statewide publication.

Editorials on File and *Facts on File*

Editorials on File provides a sampling of opinions from hundreds of newspapers, whereas *Facts on File* compiles the "who, what, where, when and why" of current events into one easily readable article.

Encyclopedia Britannica Book of the Year

This annual publication by the encyclopedia publisher contains summary overviews on all the news from astronomy to law, religion and sports. It also gives brief biographies of major newsmakers and every celebrity who died that year. For example, you can read the "baseball" article in the 2005 book to find a summary of all the major baseball news for that year.

Encyclopedia of Associations

This handy guide contains information on thousands of professional and trade organizations, interest groups and other national associations. Marcia Yudkin, a writer, says that she was trying to determine the number of sunglasses sold every year. She found an answer after locating the Sunglass Association of America in the *Encyclopedia of Associations* and calling its headquarters. "This technique works because one basic purpose of such organizations is to make facts available to the media. In fact, I can't think of any time I turned to the *Encyclopedia of Associations* and struck out," she says.[5]

Commercial Databases

Academic Search Premier

The world's largest academic multi-disciplinary database, Academic Search Premier provides a full text for more than 4,450 scholarly publications, including more than 3,500 peer-reviewed journals. Coverage spans every area of academic study and offers information dating as far back as 1975. The database is updated daily.

LexisNexis

LexisNexis News, which we mentioned earlier, contains full-text articles from more than 5,600 newspapers, magazines and other sources. It includes international, national, state and campus newspapers as well as company and industry news from various business sources. *LexisNexis Congressional* contains the current status and full text of any current legislative proposal in the U.S. Congress, as well as biographical information and voting records for all senators and representatives. "Thomas" (named after Thomas Jefferson) is a free legislative database sponsored by the Library of Congress at http://thomas.loc.gov. It doesn't have as many cool features as LexisNexis, but is still quite useful for tracking legislation. *LexisNexis Legal* allows users to search court decisions by key words and topics. It contains the full text of judicial decisions for most state courts, circuit courts of appeals and federal courts.

Newspaper Source

Newspaper Source contains the full text for U.S. regional and international newspapers, news wires, TV and radio news programs and other sources. It offers abstracts for articles in national newspapers.

Health Source

This database is the richest collection of consumer health information available to libraries. It provides information on many health topics including the medical sciences, food sciences and nutrition, childcare, sports medicine and general health. Updated daily, it features searchable full text for nearly 300 journals.

Internet Resources

Google News (www.news.google.com)

Choose Google's news search tool to search Web sites for hundreds of newspapers and other news services. Google's news alerts provide daily updates on any topics or key words you choose. You can select continuous news alerts or daily alerts, which sends you one e-mail every 24 hours with links to those articles.

Magportal and Findarticles (www.magportal.com and www.findarticles.com)

These two sites offer free searchable databases of magazine articles. You can choose key words and search through hundreds of mainstream and offbeat magazines to find articles on any topic. However, we still recommend the *Reader's Guide to Periodical Literature* as the most comprehensive source for magazine information.

Newsdirectory (www.newsdirectory.com)

Use this Web site to search thousands of newspapers and magazines by topic, country or region of the world.

Individual Newspapers and News Agencies

Although most current news and information on the Internet is free, archived material may not be. But it's often worth the small cost. Many newspapers and magazines allow access to their archived material going back as far as 25 years. *Time, Newsweek* and *U.S. News & World Report* all sell access to their archives. Although using a credit card to pay the fee may be a minor annoyance, these archives may be worth the savings in research time.

Backgrounding a Business or Nonprofit Organization

The best place to start may be with the public relations department of any company or organization. The purpose of these departments is to provide complete and accurate information to the media and the public. These departments also help you connect with experts or appropriate officials within the organization.

Public relations departments can provide you with back copies of the organization's **annual report**. Every public company (one that sells shares of stock in its company as opposed to one that is owned by a family or private individual) is required to publish an annual report for consumers and stockholders. Many nonprofit organizations, although not required to do so, also publish annual reports for their donors and users of their services.

These yearbooks contain detailed information on significant activities and accomplishments, income and expenditures, a directory of officers and explanations of products or services. You can find recent annual reports on the company's or organization's Web sites. Some Web sites, such as www.reportgallery.com and www.annualreportservice.com, contain links to more than 2,000 corporate annual reports.

You won't often find original story ideas in annual reports because their primary purpose is public relations. Every organization wants to put the best possible face on its activities—even when it had a money-losing year. If a company had a bad year, for example, an interesting part of your story may be the "spin" the company tries to put on its dismal performance in its annual report. Annual reports do provide good background information and names and telephone numbers for officers and board members for companies and organizations.

Because public companies are required to publish annual reports, they are significantly easier to background than private companies. For private companies, you must rely on newspaper or magazine articles, online and print directories of companies and any information that company officials are willing to give you.

Print Sources

International Directory of Company Histories

This multi-volume directory has several pages of history for most public and private companies. For each company, it includes useful tables with addresses, Web addresses, number of employees and key dates in the company's history.

Electronic Databases

Business Source Premier

This database contains abstracts and many full text articles from hundreds of scholarly and general business journals.

Regional Business News

This full-text news wire database contains information from businesses throughout the world. It includes A&G Information, Inter Press Service, PR Newswire and more.

Internet Resources

Guidestar

Guidestar.com contains annual reports and background information on thousands of charities and nonprofit organizations.

www.ipl.org/div/aon

This "associations online" component of the Internet Public Library is the best online counterpart to the print *Encyclopedia of Associations* mentioned earlier in this chapter.

Useful Internet Resources for Writers

First, a word of warning. Material placed on the Internet is not free for use by anyone. "It is governed by the same laws that govern its offline use. For example, if it is illegal for one to photocopy a book, it is illegal to digitize the book and make the copy available on the Internet," says *The Associated Press Guide to Internet Research and Reporting*.[6] Attribute any material you use from the Internet in the same way you would a print article.

Portal Web sites

Portal Web sites are resources for journalists created by journalists. They provide fact sheets and background information organized by beat topic, links to national and international newspapers, people-finding Web sites and links to dozens of other Web sites that are useful to reporters doing online research. Here are some of the best gateway sites:

- **www.powerreporting.com**
  Pulitzer-prize winning journalist Bill Dedman, formerly of the *Philadelphia Inquirer*, created this wonderful resource for journalists. It contains links to dozens of people-finders, beat-by-beat categories, company and nonprofit organization information and government resources for journalists.
- **www.journalismnet.com**
  This site, which Google ranks as one of the top three journalism Web sites, was created by Canadian journalist Julian Sher and offers more international reporting resources than Dedman's site. It also offers a unique "people-finding" section with tutorials, which we recommended earlier.
- **www.reporter.org**
  This site offers resources from Investigative Reporters and Editors (IRE), a national organization of investigative journalists based at the University of Missouri School of Journalism. It contains links to 40 journalism organizations, 16 reporter's resource Web sites and eight journalism publications.

Expert and Author Databases

Dozens of Web sites offer databases of experts that are searchable by key words and topics. They have contact information for thousands of experts and book authors on every conceivable topic. Radio and television shows frequently use these sites to find guests. The quality of the experts varies from site to site. Some allow self-selected "experts" who pay a fee to list themselves. The Internet Reference Desk has a page (www.refdesk.com/expert.html) that contains links to 67 Web sites with experts databases. Other recommended sites are: askanexpert.com, yearbooknews.com and allexperts.com. You can also use any search engine with the term "expert database" plus the subject area you're interested in to find more specialized databases.

The Web site www.profnet.com works with public information offices at thousands of academic institutions and nonprofit organizations. After users identify the topic they're writing about, Profnet responds with a list of academic experts willing to discuss that topic with the media. Profnet's main limitation is that it will not respond to queries unless writers identify a specific magazine or newspaper they're writing for. That means they won't help students with writing assignments. However, www.college-news.com, which represents a consortium of 860 experts at 150 leading liberal arts universities, provides an easily accessible database of academic experts that is free for anyone to use.

Federal Government Web Sites

The U.S. government offers the biggest online library in the world. Your tax dollars pay the salaries of thousands of employees who research and collect information that they make available to the public at no cost. Most is available on the Internet and the rest is available from the Government Printing Office at a nominal cost.

The best portal Web sites for federal government information are www.fedworld.gov and www.firstgov.com. Both allow users to search more than 30 million Web pages representing every U.S. government agency. Each federal agency collects public information about its areas of responsibility. It's not only free, but federal information is not copyrighted. That means you don't have to ask for permission to publish or use it. That doesn't mean you can plagiarize it. Just cite the source in your work.

In conclusion, we'll go back to where we started. Consult with a reference librarian because they're paid to know where to look. With so much information out there, it's impossible for anyone to know everything. But reference librarians will most likely direct you to the best print resources, commercial databases and Internet resources.

Suggested Activities

1. Using the Internet resources suggested in this chapter, write a 500-word biography of a company president, university president or other professional who is not a national celebrity.

2. Choose a celebrity and compare the quality and quantity of information you obtain on this person using: a) an Internet search engine, b) the *Reader's Guide to Periodical Literature* (a print source) and c) the *Biography Resource Center* (if your nearest library subscribes to this electronic database).

3. Choose a controversial issue currently in the news and write a 500-word summary of the diversity of viewpoints using *Facts on File, Editorials on File* and *CQ Researcher*.

Shoptalk

Annual report: A publication produced every year by a company or non-profit organization explaining its significant accomplishments and financial activity for the previous year. These reports often contain some biographical information on key officers and board members.

Blog: Web sites usually published by one or two individuals who report on news and personal observations related to their areas of interest.

LexisNexis: A popular subscription-only database offering full-text access to thousands of newspapers and magazines, press releases, corporate information, court decisions and government records.

Listserv: An electronic special-interest newsletter subscribed to by people interested in that topic. Any subscriber can send e-mail questions or comments to all of the other subscribers.

Newsgroup: Online discussion group on topics of special interest that anyone can read and contribute to. They differ from listservs, which have subscription-only access. Newsgroups can be accessed using Google's "group" function.

Scholarly journals: Journals whose content deals with academic disciplines and sub-disciplines whose authors are typically college professors. Most articles are based on extensive research and must be reviewed by several academic experts prior to acceptance and publication.

Special collections: A library department that acquires and organizes non-published resources that often come from private donors. These resources may include collections of letters and papers, photographs, unpublished reports, manuscripts and works of art.

Spreadsheet: A computer program that allows users to enter data and text in rows and columns and perform numerous statistical calculations on the data. Spreadsheets can create charts, tables and graphs.

Endnotes

1. Jack Kelley to author, Nov. 29, 2003.

2. Telephone interview, Nov. 21, 2003.

3. Telephone interview, Aug. 30, 2004. Mr. Struck was formerly editor-in-chief for States News Service.

4. Frank Bass, *The Associated Press Guide to Internet Research and Reporting* (Cambridge, MA: Perseus Publishing, 2001).

5. Marcia Yudkin, *Writing Articles About the World Around You* (Cincinnati: Writer's Digest Books, 1998), 113.

6. George Galt, "Copyright on the Internet," *The Associated Press Guide to Internet Research and Reporting* (Cambridge, MA: Perseus Publishing, 2001), 143.

Chapter 5

Interviews: Moving Past the Predictable

Good interviewers know how to ask the right questions of the right people at the right time. Preparation and the ability to adjust to unexpected situations are essential. Anything can happen in an interview . . . and often does. Key elements in this chapter include:

- A checklist of interview tips
- Problem scenarios you may face
- How to use direct, indirect and partial quotations
- Guidelines for choosing the right attribution

Ask a professional writer to share the "secret" to a successful interview and you're likely to get a one-word reply—preparation. Obvious advice? Yes, and equally obvious are the follow-up tips: Writers should do extensive research on the people they interview—the previous chapter gave you ways to track down these people and immerse yourself in their areas of expertise. Writers should compile a list of thought-provoking questions based on library and Internet research. Writers should phrase their questions in a way that their interviewees can't possibly respond with simple yes/no answers; writers should . . . . And the suggestions go on and on. We include a checklist of familiar interview tips on the next page.

Barbara Walters once told an interviewer: "I really do a lot of preparation. I write all of my questions out on three-by-five cards. I write each question individually. I have lots of them; I can do 200 of them."[1]

Checklist for Successful Interviews

1. When setting up an interview, alert your interviewee to the topic you are researching but don't reveal the exact questions you plan to ask.
2. Request a specific amount of time for the interview—an hour is usually sufficient—and limit the interview to that timeframe.
3. Do extensive research about your topic and your interviewee before you meet.
4. Prepare a long list of questions based on your research.
5. Phrase your questions in a way that encourages the interviewee to offer opinions and feelings.
6. Include a few questions that will elicit anecdotes from your interviewee.
7. Use a tape recorder unless you are pressed for time and won't be able to transcribe the interview session.
8. Listen to each answer that your interviewee gives; prepare to ask follow-up questions that might not be on your list.
9. Take notes on your interviewee's body language.
10. If you plan to ask questions that might anger or alienate your interviewee, save those until you have established a rapport.

Preparation means defining a clear purpose for the interview. What kind of information do you hope to obtain? Is your purpose learning about your subject's personal life or obtaining information about his or her professional expertise? Just as every article needs a clearly defined angle, so does each interview. All of the questions you ask should be focused on that purpose.

For all the preparation that you will do as an interviewer and writer, you will never master the art of interviewing. The reason is simple: The writer controls only half of an interview. The interviewee controls the other half, and the writer can never be certain what the interviewee will do or say. Although the advice on the opposite page is valid, be aware of another, less predictable secret to a successful interview. You should be willing to move past your preparations and beyond your script if, in the course of the interview, an unexpected but equally interesting story angle surfaces. In short, writers should enter an interview situation with a meticulously detailed roadmap that, when followed, will lead to the information they need. But they also should be flexible enough to investigate surprise twists and turns that pop up in the course of the interview and take writers into uncharted territory that other writers haven't explored.

John Riddle, author of 34 books and founder of "I Love to Write Day,"[2] learned the importance of flexibility early in his career when he talked with Robert Reed, the actor who played TV dad Mike Brady on the 1970s' sitcom "The Brady Bunch." Reed was performing in a play near Riddle's Delaware home, had time on his hands and agreed to an interview with Riddle even though the young writer had no firm assignment from an editor.

"The night before our talk, I typed up a long list of questions, all based on Reed's TV career," recalls Riddle. In spite of his good intentions and careful preparation, the interview got off to a dismal start. Reed seemed bored, and "it took all of two minutes to run through 30 questions. He kept saying things like, 'No comment' or 'I'd rather not talk about that.' My heart sank, as I realized I probably wasn't going to get enough information for a publishable article."

That all changed when the telephone rang and Reed took a call from the drama teacher at a nearby high school. His mood improved and he began to smile as he scribbled notes on a scrap of paper. When he returned to Riddle, he explained that he had just accepted an invitation to talk with local students about live theater. He added that he had been trained as a Shakespearean actor, theater was his first love and he never passed up an opportunity to discuss it.

"A light bulb went off," says Riddle with a laugh. "I realized that I should forget the TV questions and ask him about his career in the theater." Good decision. Reed "came alive, and for the next 45 minutes he talked nonstop about his various roles onstage and how he had auditioned for 'The Brady Bunch' figuring that the show would only last a few months. When it turned out to be a hit, he was forever typecast as TV's father figure, which made it hard for him to get serious theatrical roles."[3]

Insights vs. Information

An interview is a conversation with a purpose. It's not a casual visit that meanders from one topic to another without an obvious direction. But what direction should it take? As an interviewer, you hope to leave an interview with enough insights and information to turn out a good feature story. If you plan to write a profile of a person—as John Riddle did—you want to tune into the person's character and personality. You want his opinions and feelings. If you are gathering material for an article about a timely issue, you're looking for statistics, facts and explanations. You also are hoping to gather an interviewee's unique perspective on the issue.

Open-Ended Questions

Blended carefully into an interview, open-ended questions can serve a couple of purposes. Depending on the question you ask, you can tap into interviewees' whimsical or humorous sides or you can pick up on clues to their personalities and characters. Most veteran interviewers keep a list of favorite open-ended questions in reserve and use them only after the question-and-answer session is well under way and the interviewee seems relaxed. Be aware that some open-ended questions—especially tired ones such as "How would you like to be remembered?"—invite the person either to launch into a sermon or serve up a generous helping of corn. Here's a starter list of five open-ended possibilities:

- What was the most serious mistake you almost made?
- What is your number one pet peeve?
- What would you most like to change about yourself?
- Describe your idea of a perfect day.
- What makes you laugh? Cry?

Well-known interviewers such as CNN's talk show host Larry King know the importance of keeping the focus on the person answering the questions and not on the person asking the questions. The word "interview" is misleading because "inter" means "between" and "view" means "thoughts" or "ideas." That suggests an exchange of thoughts and ideas between two people. But that definition doesn't work in feature writing because readers aren't interested in a writer's thoughts and ideas. Readers care about the interviewee. In his book *Anything Goes*, King writes that "The show has never been about what I think and feel; it's about how the major players in an issue think and feel. That's why it works."[4]

Whether you're a beginning writer as John Riddle was, or a veteran like Larry King, you will likely take the same steps in preparing for and conducting a successful interview. In addition to considering the tips we offered you on an earlier page, you must decide on the **"voices"** that deserve a place in your story. You also must think on your feet as you implement your plan for your question-and-answer session.

Identifying the "Voice of Authority"

If your assignment is to produce a **profile** article, your central interview is going to be the person you are profiling. That "voice" will dominate. Secondary interviews, sometimes called "support" interviews, will be interviews with sources who can offer different perspectives—a best friend, spouse, employer, co-worker, roommate or parent. (See Chapter 12.) If your goal is an article that probes an issue or tracks a trend, your list of likely interviewees will include at least one **voice of authority**, plus people who have differing opinions on the issue and one or two people who are caught up in the trend. (See Chapter 16.)

Topical features on issues and trends generally have two types of sources: the **expert** and the **participant**. The expert is the voice of authority who has career or educational credentials in the subject you are investigating. The participant is someone who has first-hand experience in the subject you are writing about. The questions that you put to the participants will be more **open-ended** than those you direct to your authority sources. Participants will often add colorful anecdotes and quotes to your story, whereas the experts give it the voices of authority and enhance credibility.

It is better to schedule the interview with the expert first. This person commands respect and can offer credible insights and information because of experience, education, position or title. For example, if you are researching obesity in children, your expert may be a pediatrician or a nutritionist; your participant will be a child or parent of a child who has successfully overcome obesity. If your assignment is to investigate alcohol abuse among college students, your expert might be a psychologist or an addictions counselor; your participant will be a college student who is willing to talk about his or her experience with alcohol abuse. You might ask the addictions counselor, "What are five or six indicators of substance abuse?" You might ask the student, "Describe for me the moment when you realized that you had crossed the line between social drinker and problem drinker."

The more impressive your source's credentials, the more credible your article will be. A hierarchy exists. A doctor has more clout than a nurse; a professor's comments pack more punch than an instructor's observations; the president of a company gets more attention than a department manager. Readers often are skeptical, so you need to provide information from sources with impact.

In addition to the voice of authority, other interviewees help explore the issue from a variety of angles. For the article about obesity in children, you'll want to hear from teenagers who are teased by peers because of their appearance. For the alcohol-abuse story, you'll want to hear from students who have observed excessive drinking and can provide anecdotes that move the story beyond statistics, advice and warnings.

Get Ready, Get Set

One of the dangers of interviewing sources who have impressive credentials is that you may feel intimidated when you sit down and begin the question-and-answer process. Control is everything. As an interviewer you need to control the direction the interview takes and the information the interview produces; you also need to have the confidence to cut off responses that ramble, and you should doggedly restate questions that the interviewee wants to avoid. The best way to show who's in charge is by exhibiting professionalism the moment you pick up the telephone and request an appointment. Identify yourself, explain your writing project, tell your source how he fits into your research and estimate the amount of time you need. Usually an hour is enough for an in-depth interview; a half hour works well for a secondary interview. Instead of asking, "Would you be willing to talk with me?" ask, "When would be convenient for us to meet?"

As you prepare for the session, make use of every available resource. Do a crash course in the topic that you plan to cover in your story and the people you plan to interview. In addition to doing online research, remember that every hospital, university and business of any size has a public relations staff whose job is to deal with media requests. These people operate under different names. In the entertainment industry, they're called publicists; in the military, they're public affairs officers; in the business world they're corporate communications specialists. Whatever the job description, a PR person often is a writer's best friend. One of America's most gifted interviewers, *The Washington Post*'s Bob Woodward once characterized PR people as "generally excellent" when it comes to getting writers the information they need to write a story. They're also valuable in setting up interviews and providing background on the person you are interviewing.

Off to a Strong Start

Just as the lead sentence in a story either grabs a reader's attention or causes him to yawn, so does the first question in an interview either capture the interviewee's interest or prompt him to nod off. You want to appear friendly but not casual, confident but not cocky, assertive but not pushy. Your opening question needs to be an original, stimulating one. It should show that you've done your homework, and you're not going to waste time with questions that you could have answered by doing a little research.

For example, a local homemaker has announced plans to run for the state legislature. Thinking she would make an interesting subject for a story about the changing face of American politics, you set up an interview with her. Which of these questions is most likely to send the message that, as an interviewer, you know what you're doing?

- Have you ever run for office before?
- Almost 52 percent of the voters in our state are female, yet only 14 of the 100 members of the House of Representatives are women. In your opinion, what are the reasons for the imbalance?

The first question is weak for three reasons. First, the interviewee can answer it with a yes/no response. Second, you could have found out the information by reading her campaign brochure. Third, her reply isn't likely to yield an interesting or insightful comment. The second question shows that you've taken time to log onto your state's Web site and have done a gender count. As a reward, you will probably get a thoughtful reply that you can work into your feature and, simultaneously, you will earn the respect of the candidate. She knows she can't shift into automatic pilot and merely repeat the facts from her official biography. She's going to have to frame her comments carefully because her words may influence the way voters feel about her.

As important as it is to avoid an opening question that lulls your interviewee to sleep, so is it essential to avoid making him angry. Save the negative questions until the final few minutes, after you've established a rapport. Even then, be careful not to phrase the questions in such a way that he feels you've turned against him. A good way to distance yourself from a delicate question is to precede it with a phrase like, "Some of your critics say . . ." or "Some people say . . ." and end with "How do you respond to that criticism?" For example, if you are interviewing an athlete who has just signed a multi-million-dollar contract, don't ask, "Why do you think you're worth this much money when teachers, police officers and firefighters barely scrape by on their salaries?" Instead, ask, "Some critics say that professional athletes are overpaid. How do you respond to that kind of comment?"

But What If . . . ?

As an interviewer, you have to be able to think on your feet. Although no one can prepare you for all the interesting (and sometimes bizarre) situations you may experience before, during or after an interview, some of these situations are predictable. Listed below are a dozen scenarios that you are likely to encounter in your writing career. Put yourself in the situations, consider your options and decide how you would handle them.

1. You're assigned to interview a very busy executive. His assistant agrees to arrange the meeting but says that her boss prefers that you FAX your questions in advance. It will save time, says she, and he'll have the opportunity to pull together information from his files that might help you write the story. What are the pros and cons of such an arrangement? Should you say yes?

2. You've requested an interview with a local attorney to discuss a legal issue that you plan to cover in a Sunday feature. Before he schedules an appointment, he asks how much he'll be paid for the interview. Time is money, he says, and he typically makes several hundred dollars an hour. What's your response? Should you ever pay someone for an interview?

3. Five minutes into an interview your interviewee is called out of the room. You depress the "pause" button on your tape recorder and proceed to review your notes. She comes back and the interview continues. She gives you great information, and just as the session winds down you notice that you never released the pause button. You have about 10 minutes before your time is up. How should you use those remaining minutes?

4. You're interviewing someone who obviously is nervous about being quoted in print. When you set your tape recorder in front of her, she freezes. What can you say to help her relax so she will give you the information that you need?

5. You are set to interview a person who has been well coached by his public relations staff. You know that he has a list of **talking points** that he will keep dredging up regardless of the questions you ask. How can you cause him to leave his script and answer your questions with spontaneity?

6. You're set to interview a person who has been at the center of some controversy at some point in his life. You've jotted down a long list of questions, and you know some of them are very sensitive and personal. How do you handle the interview so he doesn't walk out?

7. Your editor wants a profile article of about 2,500 words. The problem is that circumstances require you to conduct the interview on the telephone, and the person gives you short, clipped answers. You don't have the benefit of describing his body language or the setting. You

only have words . . . and not enough of them. What kind of additional research can you do to salvage the story?

8. You've identified a key source to interview for a feature story you're researching. You call her, she agrees and then asks two quick questions: Where shall we meet, and how much time will you need? The success of your story might hinge on your responses. What do you say?

9. You're having a great conversation with a source who is giving you colorful quotes and strong anecdotes. The trouble is, your interviewee keeps saying, "By the way, that was **off the record**." The material that is **on the record** is predictable and boring. What do you do?

10. At the end of a very successful interview your interviewee thanks you and says, "When will I be able to read this before you turn it in to your editor?" How do you respond?

11. You've just had a great question-and-answer session with a very quotable source. You want to stay on his good side because you might want to feature him in future articles. What are some things you can do to build a strong professional relationship?

12. Three days have passed since you conducted a very candid interview. You get a call from the interviewee who has had second thoughts about a couple of the comments she made. She asks you to please not include them since they could cause her a great deal of trouble. You haven't written the story yet, so it's not as if she's asking you to edit something that is part of your story. What do you do?

Time to Switch Roles

Interviewing sources is only part of a feature writer's job—the part that casts you in the role of researcher and reporter. Now you have to switch roles and become the writer. This means that you need to figure out what you're going to do with the material you've gathered from your interviews. You're certainly not going to use every comment uttered by every source. Which quotations are strong enough to warrant inclusion in your article? Are you going to use **partial quotations**? Are you going to use **indirect quotations**? Are you going to paraphrase some of the comments that you've collected? Are you going to tighten or "clean up" any of your interviewee's answers? If the person you've interviewed occasionally makes a grammatical error, should you fix it? If the person has the habit of saying "you know" too often, can you delete that phrase?

Here's what we suggest: After you've completed an interview, go through your notes (or transcript if you've taped the conversation) and underline or highlight those comments that are likely to spark an emotional reaction from readers. Look for words that might surprise, amuse, anger or shock your readers. Look for ideas, opinions and insights. These highlighted sentences or parts of sentences will probably make the strongest quotations. If you have to cut through a lot of rambling words to get to the core of an interviewee's comment, consider using a partial quotation. Pull out the heart of the statement, put quotation marks around those words, and paraphrase the rest of the sentence. Likewise, if you understand a key point that your interviewee made but he didn't articulate it very well, consider paraphrasing it.

Aim for a 50-50 balance between **direct quotes** and paraphrases of what your subject says in your article. Don't try to quote everything or paraphrase everything. The more articulate your subject, the more you can use direct quotes. If your interviewee is less articulate, you will need to use more paraphrasing. In general, too many quotes make it more difficult for the reader to comprehend the information, and you can do the reader a favor by paraphrasing some of it. Table 5.1 presents some guidelines about when to quote and when to paraphrase.

Here are some examples of certain words that should never be encased in quotation marks.

- Empty comments: "It's a pleasure to be here," said the speaker.
- Clichés: The scientist said he likes to think "out of the box."
- Statistical information: "I am married and have two sons," said Smith.
- Obvious observations: "Whichever team has the most points at the end of the game will win," said the coach.

Table 5.1. When to quote and when to paraphrase

Use direct quotes when the comments:	Paraphrase when the comments:
1. Give a concise, revealing anecdote	1. Offer biographical or factual information
2. Cluster words in a colorful or entertaining manner	2. Present numbers or statistical data
3. Establish an emotional connection with the reader	3. Are long or redundant and you can re-write them using fewer words
4. Emphasize a significant point or display the subject's expertise	4. Give information that is already public knowledge (which you may not include at all)
5. Reveal the subject's personality, character or values in a unique way	5. Offer dull but essential information to the story

He Said, She Said: Words With an Attitude

Before you begin to integrate quotations into a story, you'll need to decide if you are going to write your **attributions** in present tense or past tense. For example, "My first celebrity interview didn't go well," <u>admits</u> John Riddle (present tense). "My first celebrity interview didn't go well," <u>admitted</u> John Riddle (past tense). Whatever your decision, be consistent throughout the article.

Some words of attribution carry little if any "baggage." They don't influence the reader's perception of the speaker or add any color to the speaker's comment. Among them:

Said	Mentioned
Commented	Added
Responded	Remarked
Stated	Observed
Explained	Noted
Clarified	Pointed out

Other words have an attitude. They either suggest the emotional state of the speaker or offer clues to the speaker's personality. Some people call these "loaded words" because they are loaded with unspoken meaning. A few examples are:

Insisted	Swore
Argued	Proposed
Blurted	Whispered
Stressed	Shouted
Asserted	Whined
Revealed	Begged
Affirmed	Cried
Confided	Grumbled

Note: The only words that a person can legitimately "hiss" are those with a string of "s" sounds. ("Stop being so silly," she hissed.) Avoid attributions such as laughed, giggled, gulped, sniffed and smiled. Remember, it's impossible to "smile" words or to sniff and speak at the same time. (Try it!) Wrong: "Let's go out," she giggled. Right: "Let's go out," she said with a giggle. Above all, don't allow your sources to "share" words. It suggests that your interviewee is dealing out words: one for you, one for me. ("Skiing is my favorite form of exercise," she shared.)

It's not a good idea to include quotations from two different sources in the same paragraph. This confuses readers. Instead, give each source a separate paragraph.

Publications often have policies regarding "cleaning up" quotations. Most editors don't object to a writer deleting an occasional "you know" phrase or correcting a minor slip in grammar. The important point is that a writer should never tamper with the meaning of an interviewee's comment. If you are uncertain about the meaning, you should contact your source and ask for clarification.

And this brings up two final suggestions. First, a good next-to-the-last question to put to an interviewee is this: "Have we missed anything that you feel is important?" Second, the last question before you turn off your tape recorder or close your notebook is: "Where can I reach you by phone in the next few days in case I need to clarify or double check your comments?"

Suggested Activities

1. Read a feature article of at least 1,500 words published in either the Sunday lifestyle section of a newspaper or in a favorite magazine. How many people did the author interview? Identify the voice (or voices) of authority. What credentials do these sources have? How did the author establish the sources' credentials? Note how the sources vary in age, gender, geographic location and background. Are there any clones that repeat information or add nothing to the story?

2. Identify someone you would like to interview—famous, infamous, living or dead—and come up with 10 questions you would ask the person. Arrange the questions in the order that you would ask them.

3. Create a list of a dozen open-ended questions that you can adapt to almost any interview situation.

Shoptalk

Attribution: Words that identify a speaker as the source of information. Most news articles use forms of the verb "said" (said Jones, says Smith). In a feature story the writer has the freedom to use other verbs of attribution (explained Jones, insisted Smith).

Direct quotation: Exact words spoken by an interviewee and placed within quotation marks, and included in the body of an article. ("I grew up in the South during the turbulent 1960s," said Jones.)

Expert or voice of authority: An interviewee who, through experience or education, is a credible source of information about a particular topic.

Indirect quotation: Words spoken by an interviewee but not placed within quotation marks. (Jones said that he grew up in the South during the turbulent 1960s.)

Off the record: A comment meant to help the writer understand something but not meant for publication.

On the record: A comment intended for publication.

Open-ended question: A question that cannot be answered with "yes" or "no" and strives to elicit an interviewee's insights.

Partial quotation: Part of a sentence spoken by an interviewee and placed within quotation marks. (Jones said he grew up in the South "during the turbulent 1960s.")

Participant: Someone with first-hand experience in dealing with the subject you are writing about. Participants are "experts" by virtue of their experience.

Profile article: Feature that looks in depth at one person.

Talking points: Key information that an interviewee is determined to work into an interview regardless of the questions asked.

Voices: The people who are quoted in a feature article. Ideally, each "voice" adds something different and important to the story.

Endnotes

1. Jack Huber and Dean Diggins, *Interviewing the World's Top Interviewers* (New York: Shapolsky Publishers, 1993), 128.

2. "I Love to Write Day" is a grassroots effort to encourage people of all ages to become better writers. Each November more than 12,000 schools plan special writing events and activities to celebrate written communication.

3. Interview, April 26, 2004.

4. Larry King and Pat Piper, *Anything Goes* (New York: Warner Books, 2000), 114.

Part II
Writing Feature Articles

Chapter 6
Action-Packed Writing

The most interesting writing contains action. Action originates in people, organizations or other phenomenon that bring change to the world to one degree or another. This chapter teaches you how to use the tools and techniques that create action-packed writing:

- Use the building blocks of writing
- Use people to tell stories
- Write with action verbs
- Find concrete words
- Introduce tension

In the movie and book *A Beautiful Mind*, MIT professor John Nash's life begins to deteriorate as he suffers the debilitating effects of schizophrenia. After several hospitalizations, he begins to progress toward recovery and success. He returns to teaching at Princeton, and the true story concludes with his trip to Stockholm in 1994 to accept the Nobel Prize for economics. The steady pace and action throughout the story make it riveting and engaging.

How many times have you started watching a movie but just couldn't get interested? The pace seems slow and the plot takes too long to develop. You begin to wonder if you missed something. Don't underestimate your viewing sophistication. It's probably just another boring movie.

Similarities exist between boring writing and boring movies. Boring writing lacks action. Action scenes and strong characters propel a movie and hold viewers' attention until the end. "Every viewer knows how boring a talky or purely scenic movie can be; it's the action that makes it interesting," said Benton Patterson in *Write for the Reader*.[1] Action scenes and strong characters also propel good writing and hold the readers' attention until the end.

The purpose of this chapter is to teach you how to create action-packed stories. Feature writing uses specific principles to make your writing livelier and more interesting. It doesn't matter whether you're telling a dramatic story or explaining a current issue or a recent scientific breakthrough. Colorful, action-packed writing of all genres has some common characteristics. Let's look at these ideas in more detail.

The Building Blocks of Writing

All types of writing consist of four basic building blocks: **narrative**, **dialogue**, **description** and **exposition**. That includes magazines, newspapers, novels, encyclopedias and even textbooks. For example, novels use mostly dialogue and narrative, while encyclopedias and textbooks use mostly exposition.

Compare narrative and dialogue with a car's engine, frame and tires. They give it the power to race down the highway. Think of description and exposition as the body, chrome and trim. They make the car pleasing and attractive to the eye, but they aren't essential to get you from Point A to Point B.

Narration moves the story from Point A to Point B and finally to Point Z. Dialogue brings characters to life through their speech. Description creates a sensory reality for the reader, while exposition provides the background and context necessary to understanding the story.

For examples of each of the building blocks, we have chosen excerpts from the chapter "Alicia" in *A Beautiful Mind*. It describes how John Nash met his future wife Alicia Larde while she was a graduate student and he was a young professor at the Massachusetts Institute of Technology during the 1950s.

Narrative describes things happening; it tells a story; it's always moving from Point A to Point B. The more narrative you include in your writing, the more it will hold readers because it creates movement and propels the action in the story. For example:

> He was surprised to see a young woman who had been his student the previous year standing behind the librarian's desk. He had encountered her in the library from time to time before, but now it seemed she was . . . work-

ing there. She too had seemed a bit startled when she saw him come in, but had given him a sweet smile and had greeted him by name.[2]

Dialogue introduces people into a story, and people always make a story more interesting. Dialogue recreates conversation with two or more people. For example:

> Nash took no notice of her, but Alicia was quite prepared to woo him. All that year, she would seek him out. "Come with me to the music library, Joyce," or "Come with me to Walker Memorial. I want to see Nash." "She set her cap for him," Joyce recalled. "She had a campaign going."[3]

Description means what it sounds like. It paints a word picture of the environment in which these events happen. The best stories create an experience of the senses. A reader doesn't only learn something from a good feature story; he feels it, sees it, smells it and hears it. While description can enhance some scenes in your writing, keep it brief. For example:

> There was only a handful of coeds at MIT at the time, and the 21-year-old Alicia Larde glowed like a hothouse orchid in this otherwise drab, barracks-like environment. Delicate and feminine with pale skin and dark eyes, she exuded both innocence and glamour, a fetching shyness as well a definite sense of self-possession, polish and elegance.[4]

Exposition illuminates concepts, ideas and background information. Exposition does not show; it explains. While often necessary, it's the least interesting style of writing. For example:

> It was marvelous being an MIT coed in the early 1950s, an era famous for its celebration of mothers and dumb blondes, because the coeds were so special and had . . . the best of both worlds: it was serious, but there were lots of men.[5]

The difference between narration and exposition is that narration shows people doing things while exposition conveys facts and concepts. Narration is specific and concrete while exposition is usually more abstract, which makes it more difficult for the reader to conceptualize.

Use People to Tell Stories

In the early 1970s, the editors of *Time* magazine discovered through audience research that the "People" department was the most-read part of the magazine. This department contained brief news about celebrity relationships, weddings, gaffes, controversial quotes and other human-interest tidbits. That discovery led to the company's launch of *People* magazine in 1974, which grew to become the most profitable American magazine by the 1990s.

The moral of the story? People like to read about people.

Joe Treen, a *Discover* magazine editor who formerly worked at *People* for 12 years, says, "The key to *People* that gets ignored all the time is that it isn't just about celebrities. It's also about ordinary people. The celebrities will sell the issue at the newsstand, but it's the ordinary people that they all read about and talk about afterward."[6]

Behind every new product, controversy, piece of legislation, economic situation, scientific breakthrough or sociological trend are people. Use people to tell these stories because people invent products, create controversy, introduce laws, buy and sell stocks, discover cures and popularize a new fad or hit song. The bright, informative or entertaining story must bring those people into the spotlight because readers are more interested in people than in things.

Anecdotes—little stories and examples about people—are important for three reasons. First, they take a general statement and demonstrate it to the reader through a specific situation, therefore making it easier to grasp. They create a real-life example of an abstract concept. Second, anecdotes show people doing things so readers can see them, empathize with them and imagine themselves in the same situation. And third, anecdotes not only make articles more interesting, but add credibility and believability. Readers will more readily believe your ideas or arguments if they can visualize them occurring in a specific setting with real-life people. We will say more about anecdotes in Chapter 8.

Write with Action Verbs

The best verbs are strong, **action verbs**. Using strong verbs will generate more improvement in your writing than any other single technique. Avoid the weakest verbs in the English language—"is," "are," "was," "were" and other forms of "to be" because they don't describe any action.

All verbs perform one of three writing functions:

1. Display concrete action performed by the subject (**action verbs**)
   Examples: crash, eat, jump, race, breathe, scream, die
2. Express the subject's feelings or attitudes (**state-of-being verbs**)
   Examples: believe, hope, feel, have, expect, consider

3. Link the subject to an object with a form of "to be" (**linking verbs**)
   Examples: be, is, are, was, were, will be

Action verbs strengthen writing more than state-of-being verbs, which are stronger than linking verbs. Don't confuse "action verb" with "active voice verb" because they're not the same. "Active" and "passive" describe verb constructions that any of these three types of verbs may take. An action verb describes specific, tangible action taken by human beings, nature or machinery. **An action verb can be written in active voice or passive voice.** Read the previous sentence again because it contains an action verb (write) using a passive voice construction (can be written). Of course, action verbs in active voice always create the best writing. Here's the same sentence in active voice: **You can write an action verb in active voice or passive voice.**

Here are some examples of weak verb phrases followed by revised versions with a strong verb:

- they are different—they differ
- used in combination with—combined with
- their conclusion was—they concluded
- came up with—created
- made an adjustment to—adjusted to

When you are tempted to strengthen a weak verb with an adverb, try to think of ways you can eliminate the adverb and use a stronger verb. Any word ending in "ly" is a suspect adverb and may be unnecessary with a strong verb. Here are some examples of adverbs and weak verbs followed by a stronger verb:

- walk purposefully—stride
- walk aimlessly—wander
- give generously—bestow
- read thoroughly—absorb
- stop quickly—halt
- drink slowly—sip
- spend carelessly—waste

Avoid Dead Constructions

Another way to ensure that you use action verbs is by avoiding a **dead construction**. Here are some examples of dead constructions: there is, there are, there was, there will be, it is, it was, it will be. These constructions display no life and convey no action. The pronouns "there" and "it" are on life support, used only because the author can't find a more colorful noun. The linking verbs—various forms of "to be"—lead your writing to the graveyard and the reader to the next article.

This rule has no exceptions: You can always improve a sentence beginning with a "dead construction" by rewriting it. The following sidebar displays some examples of "dead constructions" followed by recast sentences with an improved action verb structure.

How to Replace Dead Constructions with Strong Nouns and Action Verbs

Poor   There will be a meeting of the Equestrian Club next Wednesday night.

Improved The Equestrian Club will meet next Wednesday night.

Poor   There is no finer writer in American literature than Ernest Hemingway.

Improved Ernest Hemingway deserves more accolades than any American writer.

Poor   It is imperative that all Society of Professional Journalists members attend the next meeting.

Improved All Society of Professional Journalists members must attend the next meeting.

Poor   There were tears in her eyes as she accepted the "Outstanding Editor" award.

Improved Tears came to her eyes as she accepted the "Outstanding Editor" award.

Poor   It was a dark and stormy night.

Improved The skies thundered while rainstorms filled the moonless night.

Use Active Voice

"Voice" is a confusing term because writers and journalism teachers use it in three ways. First, voice describes the manner in which writers reveal their own personalities through their writing. Chapter 12 will talk more about this meaning of the word. Second, "voice" describes whether the author uses a first person, second person or third person viewpoint. Third, it describes verb structure—active voice and passive voice—that determines the relationship between the subject of the sentence and its object. If the subject acts upon the object, then the sentence is active voice because the subject is active. If the subject is acted upon by its object, then the sentence is passive voice because the subject is passive. Confused? Here's an example to clarify.

Active: Dr. Mayer misdiagnosed Jared's respiratory problem. (the subject—Dr. Mayer—acts)

Passive: Jared's respiratory problem was misdiagnosed by Dr. Mayer. (the subject—Jared—receives the action)

"Use active voice and not passive voice." You will hear this rule over and over again from teachers and editors for the rest of your career. Active voice creates better writing than passive voice for three reasons:

1. Active voice sentences emphasize who performs the action.
2. Active voice sentences use fewer words than passive sentences.
3. Active voice sentences clarify the "who did what to whom" relationship.

You can always use these three tips to identify a passive voice sentence:

1. The subject of the sentence receives the action from a direct object.
   Example: Jared's respiratory <u>problem</u> was misdiagnosed by Dr. Mayer.
2. The sentence uses a verb phrase containing a "to be" verb such as "is," "are," "were" combined with the past perfect tense of another verb.
   Example: Jared's respiratory problem <u>was misdiagnosed</u> by Dr. Mayer.
3. An actual or implied preposition such as "by" follows the verb.
   Example: Jared's respiratory problem was misdiagnosed <u>by Dr. Mayer</u>.

Like most English language rules, exceptions occur. You can or must use the passive voice in two types of situations.

1. When the people or forces responsible for actions are unknown. For example: "The airplane's cargo was damaged during the flight." You don't know who or what caused the damage so you have to use passive voice.
2. When the recipient of the action is more newsworthy than the actor. For example: "The mayor was arrested by FBI agents on embezzlement charges." In this case, a prominent local official is more newsworthy than unidentified FBI agents who arrested her.

Finally, don't confuse a verb's voice with its tense. The verb's tense describes when the action occurs. The verb's voice describes whether the subject of the sentence is the actor (active) or the subject is acted upon by its direct object (passive). Verbs have six tenses: past, present, future, past perfect, present perfect and future perfect. You can write each tense in active or passive voice.

Find Concrete Words

Specific is the opposite of abstract. Specific words describe particular qualities that your senses perceive: details of appearance, sounds, smells, textures, tastes. "Concrete" is similar in meaning to specific. Abstract words refer to concepts that can be perceived with the mind but not with the senses.

"The trick in writing is using specifics. You don't say the person went to school; you say the person went to Kent State," says Joe Treen, editor-at-large at *Discover* magazine. "You don't want to write about 'crime in America.' You want to write about a specific crime, such as identity theft. And then you write about one person who lost his identity. Make him emblematic of the whole problem. Specificity makes it work."[7]

Here is an example of making an abstract word more specific:

Abstract: Vegetation

More specific: trees
Even more specific: oak, pine, birch

More specific: vegetables
Even more specific: corn, beans, broccoli

More specific: flowers
Even more specific: lily, sunflower, zinnia

Can you create a visual image of "vegetation"? That's difficult. What about corn? Of course you can. That's the whole idea behind using specific instead of abstract words in writing. Don't say trees when you can specify pine, hemlock, maple or hickory. If a dog came snarling up to the screen door in your story, tell the reader whether it was a German Shepherd or a Collie.

Learn to fill your articles with colorful, specific details, and editors will love you. Give readers visual, auditory, olfactory, gustatory and tactile descriptions that will captivate their imaginations.

Here are some examples of replacing an abstract sentence with a specific sentence:

Vague: The audience enjoyed the concert.
Specific: The crowd gave the performers two standing ovations.

Vague: He makes a fortune singing and playing the guitar.
Specific: In 1991, his gross income from concerts and albums was $16 million.

Vague: Mary had a lousy day, and everything went wrong.
Specific: Mary's car had a flat tire, and she lost her purse today.

Introduce Tension

Mystery novels and movies that follow this principle of creating tension will always attract a following. An unsuspecting person discovers a body, reports it to police and—presto—there's the plot. You begin wondering "Who did it?" while investigators spend the rest of the time following clues and interviewing suspects. The story ends when the suspect is arrested, convicted or sent to jail. The good guys win and the bad guy loses.

That's great, but it's not that easy to create suspense or **tension** in a service article about how to choose the best refrigerator. You might begin, however, with an anecdote about a father who doesn't have enough storage space in the refrigerator for the graduation party he's planning for his daughter. Make the reader ask, "How will this problem be solved?" or "How will this story end?"

The problem-solution structure is only one of many you can choose from. The theme of overcoming failure, challenges, obstacles and roadblocks to achieve eventual success, however, is a sure-fire way to hold your readers.

Jon Franklin in his famous book *Writing for Story* calls this the **complication.** "A complication is any problem encountered by any human being; it's an event that triggers a situation that complicates our lives, which is where it got its name."[8]

Another structure that creates and holds reader interest is the conflict-consensus model. This structure works best for issue-oriented articles. Here's what a mini-outline looks like:

- Introduce a problem that people disagree about
- Present different viewpoints and proposed solutions
- Summarize consensus points that everyone agrees on

We'll talk more about complication-resolution and conflict-consensus models in Chapter 9.

The book *A Beautiful Mind*, written by journalism professor Sylvia Nasar, exemplifies all of the characteristics of action-packed writing.[9] Focusing on Nash and his wife, Nasar creates suspense by detailing the uncertain outcome of his illness, their divorce and eventual reunion. As the dramatic narrative unfolds, she reports the conversations that occurred between Nash and his intimate circle of family members, professional colleagues and doctors. Her writing bristles with action verbs, active voice, narrative and dialogue.

While not every story is so inherently interesting, you can make any story more interesting with concrete words, action verbs, active voice and narrative. In conclusion, get moving!

Suggested Activities

1. Write five sentences that begin with the constructions "there is," "there are," "there was," "it is" and "it was." Then re-write the same sentences eliminating the dead constructions.

2. Find five feature stories from newspapers, magazines or the Internet. Summarize the angle of the stories in one sentence using action verbs.

3. Take a notebook on a half-hour walk around a neighborhood or college campus. Make a list of the 10 most vivid impressions coming from sight, hearing or smell. Be specific and detailed using strong nouns and concrete verbs.

Shoptalk

Action verbs: Verbs that describe visible, tangible action taken by people or things.

Active voice: A form of verb structure in which the subject of the sentence is the principal actor in the sentence.

Complication: The central problem encountered by the central character of a story. The process of solving or overcoming the complication forms the plot for the story.

Dead construction: A lifeless pronoun-verb combination at the beginning of a sentence such as "there is, there are, there was, there will be, it is, it was, it will be," etc.

Description: Details about a person's appearance, clothing or surroundings that help reveal the person's character and personality.

Dialogue: The description of conversation between two people that occurs at a specific time and place. It differs from quotes that simply involve the reporting of later reflections and observations from one person.

Exposition: Factual material in a story that explains needed background or context. Expository writing usually lacks people or action and should be limited.

Linking verbs: Forms of "to be" verbs such as is, are, was, etc., that link a subject to a similar object.

Narrative: A story with a chronological structure that proceeds from one event to the next.

Passive voice: A form of verb structure in which the subject of the sentence is the recipient of the action from another object in the sentence.

State-of-being verbs: Non-action verbs that describe a person's attitudes, thoughts or feelings.

Tension: The introduction of an unsolved problem at the beginning of a story that writers use to attract and sustain readers' attention.

Endnotes

1. Benton Patterson, *Write for the Reader: A Practical Guide to Feature Writing* (Ames: Iowa State University Press, 1986), 15.

2. Sylvia Nasar, *A Beautiful Mind* (New York: Simon & Schuster, 1998), 190.

3. Ibid., 197.

4. Ibid., 190.

5. Ibid., 194.

6. Telephone interview, Nov. 21, 2003.

7. Ibid.

8. Jon Franklin, *Writing for Story: Craft Secrets of Dramatic Nonfiction* (New York: Penguin Books, 1986), 72.

9. Sylvia Nasar, *A Beautiful Mind* (New York: Simon & Schuster, 1998).

Chapter 7

Strong Beginnings, Satisfying Endings

Leads and endings serve as the bookends of articles. They hold everything together. The lead hooks readers' attention, introduces the topic and indicates the direction of the article. The closing paragraph is the destination toward which all previous paragraphs aim. This chapter offers you examples of:

- Nutgrafs and billboards
- Leads that often fail
- Leads that usually succeed
- Endings that come full circle

Feature articles, like airplane flights, are most vulnerable to crashes during takeoff and landing. At least that's the observation of one of our writing colleagues who uses the dramatic comparison to underscore the importance of strong beginnings and satisfying endings to stories. His point: an article can contain great information, but if the opening paragraph (the "takeoff") doesn't grab and hold readers' interest, the material that follows the introduction may remain forever unread. The ending of an article, like the landing of an airplane, should be smooth rather than abrupt, fast-paced rather than delayed or prolonged. Like pilots who know their destinations before taking off, writers should identify their endings before beginning their articles. Otherwise they risk getting lost, taking detours or wandering in circles as they try to decide how and when to stop.

not necessarily

The No-Frills Approach

Unlike reporters who cover **breaking news** events and must get to the point of their stories quickly, feature writers have the luxury of setting up their articles with one or two engaging paragraphs. They may choose the no-frills **summary lead** that answers basic questions—who, what, where, when, why and how—but shouldn't limit themselves to this straightforward approach.

Summary leads have taken a lot of criticism in recent years. They were the predictable way of getting into a story for so long that a backlash was inevitable. "Boring!" claim their critics. Maybe so, but what summary leads lack in creativity, they make up for in information. Here's an example of a get-to-the-point summary lead that might appear on page one of a newspaper or as the lead story of a radio or television newscast:

> Tornadoes darted across Oklahoma last night, zigzagging through neighborhoods and claiming 10 lives in their wake. Meteorologists blamed an unlikely mix of weather conditions for causing an estimated $5 million in property damage.

The 16-word opening sentence contains, in a nutshell, the essence of the story. It answers five of the six basic questions. Who? Tornadoes. What? Darted. Where? Oklahoma. When? Last night. How? Zigzagged through neighborhoods. The only question that it doesn't answer is the "why." The second sentence fills in that blank. Taken together the two sentences give an abbreviated version of what happened in Oklahoma the previous night. If readers or viewers choose not to absorb the rest of the story, they know the highlights.

A summary lead can work equally well for a feature story. For example, when the Smithsonian Institution assembled a traveling exhibit of historic Fourth of July magazine covers, Holly Miller, one of the authors of this book, explained the project this way:

> In a burst of patriotism following the attack on Pearl Harbor, American magazine editors collaborated on a campaign to boost morale and show their support for the U.S. war effort. The project was called "United We Stand," and its goal was to feature the Stars and Stripes on the covers of magazines nationally circulated in July 1942.[1]

This two-sentence summary lead contains 57 words and answers all of the basic questions. Who? Magazine editors. What? Collaborated on a campaign. Where? In America. When? July 1942. Why? To boost morale and show support for the war effort. How? By featuring the Stars and Stripes on the covers of their national publications.

Some feature writers, bogged down by **writer's block**, create summary leads as a way to get a few words on their computer screens and achieve some momentum. After their writer's block starts to lift and their articles begin to unfold, they often go back to their summary leads and top them off with more creative leads. However, they don't delete the summary paragraphs. Instead, they keep them as their second or third paragraphs, often called **billboard paragraphs** or **nutgrafs**. Such a paragraph, which we also discuss in later chapters, tells readers, in a nutshell, what the story is about. Many editors expect every article to contain a nutgraf or billboard paragraph. So, in the case of the article about the patriotic magazine covers, an alternative version might begin this way:

> Donald Duck, dressed in a military uniform and carrying a flag, marches across the cover of *Walt Disney's Comics*. Meanwhile, a mother and daughter duo unfurl the Stars and Stripes on the front of the *Ladies Home Journal*. Over at *House & Garden*, a white-columned mansion features a waving Star-Spangled Banner on its cover. Coincidence? No way.
>
> In a burst of patriotism following the attack on Pearl Harbor, American magazine editors collaborated on a campaign to boost morale and show their support for the U.S. war effort. The project was called "United We Stand," and its goal was to feature the Stars and Stripes on the covers of magazines nationally circulated in July 1942.

The second paragraph served as the lead in the first version of the story and as the nutgraf or billboard in the later draft. Either introduction is an acceptable way of getting into the article. Writers sometimes create several alternative opening paragraphs before they choose the ones they like best. These are the ones that find their way into print.

Leads, Introductions, Hooks

Writers typically use three terms for the opening of an article. Each term is slightly different but equally appropriate in meaning. The **lead** is a fitting description because an effective opening paragraph leads readers into the story. The **introduction** is a logical label because an opening paragraph should introduce readers to the topic and tone of the story. The **hook** is an appropriate term because a strong opening paragraph hooks readers' attention and prompts them to read on.

Whatever the terminology, the beginning of a feature article must serve three purposes:

- Capture the readers' attention
- Introduce the main idea of the story
- Pull the reader into the story

Writers know this, and they often labor over their opening sentences for hours. They fine-tune, add, delete and exchange words until they are satisfied. Some writers tell us that they can't move forward with articles until they have the leads exactly as they want them. Other writers prefer to forge ahead, complete their rough drafts and then return to their opening paragraphs to do the fine-tuning, adding, deleting and exchanging of words. Whichever process works best for you is the process you should follow.

11 Questionable Leads

In our opinion, few rules are unbendable when it comes to feature writing. Whereas sentence fragments prompt most grammarians to cringe, we believe that the occasional fragment can add great style to a feature article. Another stretching of the rules involves feature writers' fondness for inventing phrases when the dictionary fails to provide them with the perfect words. The results can be very creative. For example, columnist and radio personality Paul Harvey came up with "bumper snicker" when "bumper sticker" didn't quite do the job for him. Lead sentences invite similar flexibility. As professors, we caution students against using certain leads that are usually ineffective. At the same time, we acknowledge that exceptions exist. A gifted writer can make almost anything work. The leads that we classify as "questionable" include the following categories.

Encyclopedia Lead

Writers sometimes use statistics-laden sentences to introduce an article. An **in-flight magazine** topped off a feature about Rhode Island this way: "Nestled between Massachusetts and Connecticut, Rhode Island is the nation's smallest state, comprising only 1,231 square miles. The longest distance north to south is 48 miles; west to east, just 37 miles."[2] These sentences seem more at home in an encyclopedia or a guidebook for New England-bound travelers.

Luggage Lead

This is the summary lead gone wrong. In an effort to give readers all the important facts of a story, the writer squeezes everything possible into the opening paragraph. The lead turns into a catchall, much like a piece of luggage. Rambling on and on, it may contain dates, ages and other specifics that the writer would be wiser to save and weave into later paragraphs. For example, "Linda Brown, 45-year-old wife of John Brown and mother of Sue, 8, Jay, 6, and Bill, 2, launched a campaign in December to clean up the three-mile stretch of beach that edges her family's property on Long Island that is littered with trash from weekend campers who failed to observe the 'no trespassing' signs that Linda posted in July." Huh?

Pun Lead

Too cute for words, these leads often elicit groans instead of chuckles from readers. One of the worst ones this writer ever created was an introductory paragraph to a profile article about cartoonist Jim Davis: "Forget the nine-lives theory. Garfield, the fat cat in the orange and black glad wags, the one with the droopy lids, the thoughts that bite and the paws that refresh, is within a whisker of turning nine."[3] Years later, the groans persist.

Personification Lead

Giving human characteristics to inanimate objects can create some funny pictures in readers' minds. For example, "If walls could talk, these would speak of five generations of a farm family trying to survive the tantrums of Mother Nature." The problem here is that readers know that walls can't talk and although Mother Nature is capable of some wild weather, she doesn't throw tantrums.

Twenty Questions Lead

Trying to engage readers by asking them a question may work, but asking a barrage of questions usually wilts readers: "Do you have a teenager who is approaching dating age? Are you worried by all the stories you've heard about kids making bad choices when they're out with friends? Are you wondering what you might do about it? Are you willing to carve out some quality time to address the issue?" As a reader, are you tempted to turn the page?

Seriously, Folks, Lead

Public speakers as well as feature writers are sometimes guilty of this one. They've uncovered a very funny story that is sure to grab their audience's attention. The problem is that the funny story doesn't exactly relate to the topic of the speech or the article. They can't resist, and so they use it anyway. After telling the funny story, they make a clumsy transition to their topic. This leaves readers bewildered and possibly resentful. The humorous opening story causes readers to think that the entire article will be amusing. Suddenly the tone changes and the writer is delivering a serious message. The readers feel they have been tricked. And they're right.

Minutes-of-a-Meeting Lead

Sometimes called a chronological lead, this introduction reads like a recording secretary's notes. The article unfolds in precisely the order that the action occurred. For instance, "The concert began at 8:10 p.m., after the arena's maintenance crew fixed a problem with the sound system. The audience applauded the back-up musicians when they came on stage. The cheers grew louder as the lead singer of the group took her place in front of the microphone. She cleared her throat and nodded to the drummer. He gave the countdown to the first song."

Quote Lead

Rarely are a speaker's words so riveting, dramatic or outrageous that they deserve to be the opening sentences of a feature story. Predictable comments—"It's a pleasure to be in Spokane," said the presidential hopeful—aren't worthy of inclusion anywhere in an article, and certainly aren't candidates for the lead. Of course, exceptions exist. Quotation leads can work if they fulfill the following conditions:

- They are brief and concise.
- They capture the article's main idea.
- They are provocative.

Freak Lead

The purpose of this lead is to surprise readers. We call it a "freak" because it sometimes begins with a sound rather than a word: "Brrrr! Jumping into icy lake water in the middle of January may not be everyone's idea of sport, but for residents of one Michigan community it's a highlight of the winter season." Not bad, you say? We agree, but we suggest that writers should use freak leads sparingly. Too many stories that begin with a gimmick word and an exclamation point—"Ouch!" "Oops!" "Wow!"—lose their power . . . fast!

Back-Door Lead

A feature article should never begin with the words "It was" or "There is." This is like slipping into a house through the back door. It attracts no notice and has little impact. For example, "There is a man in Syracuse, N.Y., who has built a career around his passion for Coca-Cola memorabilia." A better version: "A resident of Syracuse, N.Y., has built a career around his passion for Coca-Cola memorabilia." Sometimes the back-door lead is called a dead-construction lead. Either way, the connotation is negative.

Hypothetical Lead

Feature writing, like news writing, is based on truth. A hypothetical lead is fiction and has no place in the media. Don't resort to concocting scenarios or creating people who don't exist, such as. "A college student, undecided about his career goal, might change majors five times before leaving school without a degree." Instead, find a real person who faced the dilemma that your article explores. A better example is, "Joe Smith, a sophomore at UCLA, changed majors five times before leaving campus last June without a degree." See the difference?

Leads that Succeed

If you avoid—at least most of the time—the 11 leads mentioned above, what leads should you consider for your articles? Of the many options available, we'll describe six that work well. In each example, we'll quickly outline the article assignment and the challenge that the writer faced in completing the assignment. Recalling these challenges was easy in some cases since we were the writers who wrestled with the assignments.

Scenario Lead

By accurately recreating a place, the writer allows readers to "see" the backdrop against which the story unfolds. The key to making this lead work is to avoid too much description. Don't include every detail; use a light hand in sketching the environment. Let the reader's imagination take over from there and fill in the gaps.

Assignment: An informational article about America's tribal colleges and the important role they play in higher education.

Challenge: To communicate the financial and physical needs of these schools without portraying them as inferior to wealthier state universities.

> Janine Pease-Pretty On Top, president of Little Big Horn College in Montana, points with pride at the plaques displayed on campus to honor those persons responsible for the school's physical growth. The benefactors are not wealthy alumni showing their gratitude, but building-trades class members exhibiting their skills.[4]

Shock Lead

Lead paragraphs that shock or surprise readers are likely to grab and hold readers' attention at least for a little while. They succeed if, in the course of doing research, the writer uncovers a truly surprising bit of information. Chances are, the information that surprised the writer will also surprise the readers.

Assignment: An article that introduces readers to a new tourist opportunity in Washington, D.C., called the Spies of Washington Tour.

Challenge: To recap the colorful history of espionage in the nation's capital without getting bogged down in dates and other details.

> Francis Gary Powers, Jr., admits that it was difficult growing up as the son of an American spy. "How high were you flying, Dad?" he used to ask his father, the U-2 pilot who was shot down deep in Soviet territory in 1960, interrogated for four months, and then imprisoned by the Russians for espionage.
>
> "Not high enough, Son," was his dad's favorite response.[5]

✸ Blind Lead   *good lead*

This lead raises readers' curiosity by omitting a key piece of information. The omission causes readers to continue reading until their curiosity is satisfied. The lead is "blind" because it doesn't identify by name the people who are the subjects of the articles. That important fact remains a mystery until the second or third paragraph. In the following example, the "they" of the story are not identified by name until the fourth paragraph.

Assignment: A feature article about President Ronald Reagan's former aides who planned his funeral far in advance of his death.

Challenge: To tell a story of love and dedication without letting it become overly emotional.

> As Washington hotshots in their 20s and 30s, they pulled all-nighters, crisscrossing the globe to build the crowds and choreograph the most enduring moments of Ronald Reagan's presidency . . . . Then they went their separate ways . . . . But over the years, Mr. Reagan's advance men—pioneers in the stagecraft revolutionized by the actor-turned-politician—stayed in touch, quietly planning their boss's grand finale under the code name "Operation Serenade."[6]

Indirect Quote Lead

Earlier in this chapter we cautioned against using quotations as leads for articles. An alternative to a direct quotation is an indirect quotation. This works well if you want to capture the essence of what someone said but you don't want to use all of the words just as the person spoke them.

Assignment: A profile article about one of the world's best-selling romance novelists.

Challenge: To accurately portray an author who is genuinely unaffected by her success.

> The trouble with writing at home, says author Janette Oke over the din of her dishwasher, is the ever-present lure of housework. It's always there, tugging her away from her computer, beckoning her from her research and causing her to leave her characters fending for themselves, mid-plot, somewhere out on the Canadian prairie. "Once a housewife, always a housewife," she adds with a shrug that lets you know she wouldn't have it any other way, thank you.[7]

Direct Address Lead

This lead invites the reader to participate in the story. How? The writer speaks directly to the reader by using the word "you" in the opening paragraph. The resulting lead is much like a conversation between writer and reader. In the example below, the article's author and the readers share a common interest: running.

Assignment: A feature story aimed at serious runners who are looking forward to a break in the winter weather.

Challenge: Bringing something fresh to a familiar topic.

If you live where there are four real seasons, then you already know that the year contains four absolutely must-run days. The runs on these days are of the cut school, skip work and get a sitter for the kids variety. In summer, it's when you get to run through a misty rain. In fall, it's the first day with a bite to it, when you think about buying a new pair of tights.[8]

Anecdote Lead

Anecdotes make excellent leads when they truly illustrate a major point of the entire article. Unlike the "Seriously, Folks" lead that we described earlier in this chapter, the anecdote serves as a smooth introduction to the article because it is a little story that relates directly to the topic at hand.

Assignment: Informational article about the difficulties that new pastors face as they make the transition from their seminary training to their first church assignments.

Challenge: Point out the obstacles that new clergy must overcome without blaming seminaries for not adequately preparing their former students for what they will encounter in their professional lives.

Ten days into his first pastorate in rural upstate New York, the Rev. Jim Gertmenian faced the challenge of conducting a funeral for a member of the parish that he served. He had recently earned a master of divinity degree at a large urban seminary, but his theological education hadn't included instruction in how to prepare such a service. What's more, he had attended only two funerals in his life. Geographically removed from professors and peers, he resorted to the telephone for long-distance guidance. He survived the experience, and 30 years later admits he was an "extreme example" of a young pastor who entered professional ministry with a gap in his hands-on skills.[9]

Endings that Satisfy Readers

Many feature writers tell you that the most important words of an article are the opening sentences, and the second most important words are the closing sentences. Once you have created the lead paragraph and the closing paragraph you have the equivalent of bookends. Then you must arrange the contents in some logical order between the bookends. This is no easy task, of course, but the lead paragraph should give you a direction, and the closing paragraph should give you a destination.

Some writers like to put a "gold nugget" at the end as a way of rewarding those who read an article through to its conclusion. It can be an interesting tidbit, a shocking fact or a revealing quote from one of the sources. Many of the devices that work for the lead also work for an ending, especially an interesting anecdote or a compelling summary statement. The main requirement of an ending is that it gives readers a sense of emotional closure or finality.

Bringing an article in for a smooth "landing" is more of a challenge for the feature writer than for the news reporter. The traditional **inverted pyramid** organization is still acceptable for a news story. The reporter clusters the most important facts of a story in the opening paragraph. Subsequent paragraphs flesh out details in descending order of importance. The rationale for this kind of organization is that a reader can stop reading at any point and still know the highlights of the story. Or, an editor, pressed for space, can cut the article from the bottom without fear of discarding important information.

The feature article requires more thought and planning. A good article can "crash" in its closing paragraph if the author makes one of these mistakes:

- Repeats information in an effort to re-emphasize a previously stated point
- Supplies conclusions that the writer wants the reader to draw from the article
- Leaves key questions unanswered
- Allows the story to dribble off without a sense of closure

Often the best way to identify an ending for an article is to revisit the lead paragraph. You may be able to bring the story full circle by returning to a question you raised in the lead, by quoting the same person you quoted in the introduction or by revealing the ending to the anecdote that you used to open the article.

Identifying the Bookends

If three writers tackled identical assignments and interviewed the same sources, they would likely come up with three different articles with three different leads and endings. There is no single "right" way to start a story, organize its major points and bring it to a conclusion.

As you scan your notes and transcripts, try to identify several possible leads and potential endings. Don't stop with just one lead or one ending;

give yourself several choices. From these choices, select the lead that you like best and type it onto your computer screen. Next, select the ending that seems most appropriate and type that paragraph onto your screen. With your "bookends" in place, you can return to your notes and determine how best to arrange the material between the bookends.

If getting started is a struggle for you, try constructing a basic summary lead. You can always go back and replace it later. Creative writers recognize that they have several options, and they allow themselves plenty of time to experiment before completing their final drafts.

Suggested Activities

1. Read the opening paragraphs of several feature articles in a major magazine. Try to categorize them. Does a particular category of lead seem to dominate?

2. Select and read a feature article in a current magazine or in the lifestyle section of a large newspaper. Create at least three alternative leads—one a scenario, another an anecdote, a third a question—for the article. Which do you prefer?

3. Conduct an in-class interview; write the lead paragraph and the ending paragraph of a profile article based on the interview.

4. After you have created the lead and ending for your in-class interview article, write a nutgraf and place it after your lead.

Shoptalk

Billboard paragraph: A paragraph, often placed after a lead, that tells "in a nutshell" what an article is about. Some journalists call it the "nutgraf." Similar to a summary lead, it often serves as the opening of a story.

Breaking news: Newsworthy events that are unfolding right now. The reporter's challenge is to collect and verify the facts and relay them to readers quickly and without embellishment.

Hook, introduction, lead: The opening sentences or paragraphs of an article, designed to capture readers' attention and interest.

In-flight magazine: A publication produced by an airline and available at no cost to passengers aboard one of the airline's flights.

Introduction: See **Hook** above.

Inverted pyramid: A way of organizing an article; the writer places the most important material first and then arranges subsequent information in descending order of importance.

Lead: See **Hook** above.

Nutgraf: See **Billboard paragraph** above.

Summary lead: An article's opening sentences that answer the essential questions about an event: who, what, where, when, why and how.

Writer's block: A "condition" claimed by many writers when words don't flow and sentences don't find their way onto paper or computer screen.

Endnotes

1. Holly G. Miller, "United We Stand," *Columns* (Fall 2003), 5.

2. Nathaniel Reade, "Focus on Rhode Island," *US Airways Attaché* (June 2004), 78.

3. Holly G. Miller, "Jim Davis: He's Got The World By The Tail," *The Saturday Evening Post* (November 1984), 52.

4. "Helping Tribal Colleges Build A Legacy of Learning," *Lilly Endowment Inc. 1999 Annual Report*, 7.

5. Holly G. Miller, "A Star-Spangled Fourth," *The Saturday Evening Post* (July/August 2001), 74.

6. Jacob M. Schlesinger, "Operation Serenade: Laying Groundwork for Reagan's Funeral," *The Wall Street Journal* (June 10, 2004), 1.

7. Holly G. Miller, "Janette Oke: The Prairie's Own Companion," *Ink* (December-January 1994/1995), 20.

8. John Bingham, "Opening Day," *Runner's World* (April 2004), 66.

9. Holly G. Miller, "Easing the Transition," *Congregations* (January/February 2002), 11.

Chapter 8
Anecdotes: The Color of Writing

Anecdotes are little stories that illustrate big ideas. Use them as leads and endings. Scatter them throughout articles to clarify and humanize data. Uncover them during interviews. Shape them into short, specific and memorable examples. This chapter will introduce you to:

- The techniques of storytelling
- Characteristics of anecdotes
- Places to look for anecdotes
- Questions that lead to the discovery of anecdotes

The story goes this way: Two pals, Jack Canfield and Mark Victor Hansen, assembled a book of more than 100 heartwarming anecdotes that they felt certain would lift the spirits of readers. They offered their collection to 123 publishers, none of whom shared their enthusiasm for the project. Undaunted, the authors visited a booksellers' convention in California and convinced an editor from a small Florida press to read a few pages on his flight home. The editor opened the package in an airport lounge and soon had tears streaming down his cheeks. The result? Hansen and Canfield had a deal, *Chicken Soup for the Soul* had a publisher and America had a bestseller. With 85 million copies of their books now in print, the authors have ladled chicken soup for the woman's soul, the baseball fan's soul, the bride's soul, the Canadian's soul, the writer's soul and the list goes on and on.

We retell this familiar success story for two reasons. First, the phenomenal sales of the *Chicken Soup* series prove that readers love little stories, especially those that are dramatic, inspiring or humorous. Second, the story about Canfield and Hansen is an example of an anecdote. It's an anecdote about anecdotes.

Creating a Scene

Most editors will tell you that the best feature articles are those that connect emotionally with readers. That's what makes a feature story memorable. "Editors see tons of 'sermonic' articles," says Mary Ann O'Roark, a former editor at *Seventeen*, *McCall's* and *Guideposts*. "In those articles, the writer says, 'Here's my wisdom, and I impart it to you.'" The result is a "stuffy lineup of information." Instead, she says, "Editors want good stories prepared in ways that engage readers. An article must entertain before it can educate and enlighten."[1]

One way that a writer can create engaging and entertaining articles is by learning to identify, write and place anecdotes. These tightly written mini-stories are delicious little morsels that one editor describes as the "chocolate chips" of articles. They are as much at home in speeches, sermons, comedy monologues and books as they are in feature stories. They work well as leads, endings or illustrations scattered throughout a manuscript. They humanize dry data. For example, an article about a major medical breakthrough may contain all sorts of important information, but the article becomes memorable when the author inserts an anecdote about a patient whose life is saved because of the medical breakthrough.

People want to read about other people. Long after readers forget the surprising statistics, compelling details or key points of a story, they remember the colorful anecdotes that showed rather than told the significance of the key points.

Techniques of Storytelling

Fiction writers are skilled at creating memorable anecdotes. They know the techniques of building drama, painting word pictures and describing characters so realistically that readers understand and care what happens to the characters. For this reason, book publishers occasionally hire novelists to serve as writers or ghostwriters for nonfiction books. The publishers want their nonfiction books to have the same color, impact and readability as a good novel. That's not to say that they want the writer to fudge on facts or embellish the truth. Absolutely not. Accuracy is the top concern of all writers of nonfiction, even novelists recruited for nonfiction projects.

What fiction writers bring to nonfiction assignments is something that goes beyond the essential ABCs—accuracy, brevity and clarity—of good journalism. They have mastered the art of storytelling. They know how to use little stories to illustrate big ideas. They have the ability to describe real people and actual events in compelling ways. They recognize when a piece of writing is starting to lose momentum, and they understand how to pick up the pace by inserting a poignant or humorous true story. They have the skill to add dabs of color to what might have been a black and white documentary.

Characteristics of Anecdotes

You don't have to be a writer of fiction to craft memorable anecdotes. Successful feature writers follow these five pieces of advice.

Keep Them Short

Anecdotes should never overshadow the points they support or the topics they illustrate. They should not be so long or so strong that they pull readers' attention away from the subject of the article. This means that writers, after creating anecdotes on their computer screens, read and reread the sentences aloud, zapping words and deleting punctuation as they go. They take note of adverbs and adjectives and remove those whose presence they can't defend. After they have reduced the story to its bare bones, they edit the remains.

This search-and-destroy mission is a familiar process that skilled writers have followed for centuries. An example: The Irish poet and playwright Oscar Wilde once arrived at a party complaining of exhaustion. His host asked why he was so tired. "All day I worked on one of my poems," explained Wilde. "In the morning I took a comma out, and in the afternoon I put it back in."

Make Them Relevant

We include the 51-word anecdote about Oscar Wilde because it illustrates the point that the previous paragraph made—that good writers constantly tinker with their copy, even spending time debating the need for a comma. The Wilde story was relevant to the topic. We included the longer anecdote about *Chicken Soup for the Soul* at the beginning of this chapter because it introduced the discussion of anecdotes in general and underscored the idea that little stories are popular with readers. Again, it was relevant to the topic.

An anecdote must have a purpose; otherwise, it only adds clutter to an article. As we said in Chapter 7, anecdotes often make effective lead paragraphs. Used as a lead, an anecdote can fulfill two important purposes:

- It can provide a colorful introduction to the topic of the article by piquing readers' interest and luring readers into the article.
- It can create an emotional bond with readers by describing a familiar situation. This prompts the reader to respond, "I've been there; I've felt that same way."

Some anecdotal leads serve both purposes. They introduce a topic and, at the same time, build a bond with readers. As an example, anyone who has ever suffered from homesickness can relate to this anecdotal lead to a newspaper feature article:

> Two years ago, college freshman Amy Ransom cried every night and counted every day until she could go home to Coshocton, Ohio. Her mother offered long-distance pep talks, her little sister kept the cards and letters coming, and her dad counseled her to hang in there, Honey, Thanksgiving isn't so far away.
>
> Somehow she made it.[2]

The pivotal third sentence—"Somehow she made it"—hints at a happy ending. The reader knows that something good happened to this college student to help her settle into campus life. The opening paragraphs set the stage for a profile article about a young music major who was discovered by a Grammy-winning alumnus and now is on her way to a recording career.

A strategy that often strengthens the bond between writer and reader is the inclusion of the word "you" in the lead anecdote. In the previous chapter we called this the direct-address lead. By using "you," a writer reaches out as if to say, "Hey, reader, pay attention! I'm talking to you!" In the example below, the common bond between writer and reader works only if the reader is of a certain age and thereby can relate to the situation that the lead describes.

> You're downsizing. After so many years at the same address, you've decided to make your move. Florida, maybe. Or perhaps a smaller, more manageable place close to home with less lawn to mow and driveway to plow.

Your friends recommend the laid-back life of a condo community. Sounds inviting. Whatever the choice, only one thing stands between you and your new digs. The attic.[3]

This lead introduced a how-to article that helped readers separate trash from treasure as they cleaned out attics and basements and prepared to relocate. It obviously was geared to older readers. The lead, only one paragraph in length, contains 65 words. Five of those words are a form of "you." Taken together, the sentences describe a problem that "you" faced—getting rid of a life's accumulation of stuff. Subsequent paragraphs resolved the problem and provided the end of the anecdote. To qualify as an anecdote, readers need to know the solution that "you" discovered.

Stress the Specific

A powerful anecdote gives readers a tightly focused example that illustrates a general idea. It has one or two specific people doing specific things at a specific time and place. The more specific you are, the more impact the anecdote has. As an example, which of the following sentences do you prefer as the lead paragraph to an article about teen runaways?

- A Texas teenager ran away from home last winter because she was tired of her parents' arguments. She's still missing.
- Three days after Christmas, Meg Jones, 13, stuffed a pair of jeans and a T-shirt into her backpack and ran away from her parents' split level in a posh suburb of Houston. She couldn't tolerate their bickering any longer. They still haven't found her.

Whenever you add specific information to a story you also add words. This results in a dilemma: Should you be brief or should you be specific? The answer is that writers should be brief <u>and</u> specific. Most writers include a range of anecdotes in their articles. They want variety. One anecdote might be of the bare bones variety and contain only two or three sentences. Another may be more fully fleshed out and offer several details. The writer decides the degree of development that each anecdote deserves. If an article runs long, the writer looks for anecdotes to trim or delete. A good test to give a manuscript is to remove an anecdote and then read the manuscript from beginning to end. If the article flows well and is interesting, the anecdote was unnecessary.

Give Them a Beginning, Middle and an End

If an anecdote lacks all three elements, it doesn't qualify as a little story. As we indicated in Chapter 7, writers often create scenarios that serve as backdrops to their stories. These scenarios are colorful, but they don't tell a complete story. Instead, they set the scene for a story. Here's an example of a scenario:

> Long before the borrowed white limo delivered its very important passenger to the entrance of the Bowling Green, Ky., Holidome, word went forth to expect someone special. The clue was Room 168. Flowers had arrived at 11; a fruit basket followed at noon. By 12:30, green punch, wheat crackers and a cheese ball under plastic were arranged smorgasbord-style on the boguswood credenza.[4]

This opening paragraph gave readers a sense of how people in a small town prepared to welcome a celebrity guest, in this case, Miss America Sharlene Wells. It describes a place, complete with flowers and fruit. Until something happens to someone, it's not an anecdote. Later in the same article, the writer offers readers an anecdote:

> A few days after winning the Miss America title in Atlantic City, Wells was interviewed and photographed by a words-and-pictures duo from *People* magazine. She had the sniffles, her eyes were bleary and, besides that, her feet hurt. The photographer assured her that the picture he wanted was the heads-and-shoulders variety—she had no reason to put on her shoes. She acquiesced, secured the crown to her blonde hair, arranged the folds of her reptile-patterned dress and assumed a regal pose.
>
> Imagine her shock the next week when the picture was published full frame—her stocking feet revealing a full complement of Dr. Scholl's medicated disks. Ouch. The California designer Mr. Blackwell promptly named her to his infamous worst-dressed list and said she looked like an armadillo in corn pads. "Wasn't that cute?" she asks. "I learned never to trust a photographer."[5]

These paragraphs do more than create a scenario. They tell a cause-and-effect story. Something happened to Miss America and that "something" qualifies it as an anecdote. A photographer duped her into posing for a picture (cause). She was embarrassed after she saw the picture in print (effect). At the end of the anecdote she is a slightly different person because she has learned something from the experience.

In the case of a **split anecdote**, the beginning of the anecdote serves as the article's lead, and the end of the anecdote, separated by many paragraphs, concludes the article. Readers have to complete the entire article to find out what happened to the person introduced in the opening paragraph. For example, suppose you are writing an article about the dangers of not wearing a seatbelt. You interview someone who was almost killed in an automobile accident, and you decide to use half of the story as your lead. It might sound like this:

> Bill Ryan never thought it would happen to him, but last Valentine's Day the unthinkable occurred. He hadn't snapped his seatbelt in place because he was only driving a few blocks to pick up his son after swim practice. He saw the van approach, clearly out of control. He heard the screech of brakes, felt himself lifted from the driver's seat and catapulted forward. Then everything went blank.

You stop short of telling readers the rest of Bill Ryan's story. Instead, you continue your article. You offer statistics about seatbelt usage and include comments and advice from various experts whom you interviewed. Not until the last paragraph of your article do you return to Bill Ryan and answer the questions that your lead raised.

> Ryan was one of the lucky ones. He limped out of the hospital—pins in both legs—four weeks after his car's head-on collision with the van. The doctors who patched him up say that with six months of physical therapy he'll be as good as new. He claims he'll be better than new because, "Now I know how fragile life is, and I'll never put mine on the line again."

Place Them Strategically

You can overdo a good thing. If you have uncovered two great anecdotes that support the same point, don't use both. That's like assigning two people to do one person's job. Select the story you like the best and file the second for possible use in some future writing project. An overabundance of anecdotes can turn an article into a disjointed collection of random stories.

Deciding where to drop in an anecdote is a skill that all feature writers should cultivate. Too many writers, aware of the power of a good story, grab readers' attention with colorful anecdotal leads but then consider their jobs done. They follow the anecdotes with paragraph after paragraph of dry facts. In the process, they risk lulling their readers to sleep. Anecdotes, strategically placed throughout an article, can give readers a "time out" from information overload. A colorful illustration can offer a welcome pause in an article's narrative, insert the human element and underscore a point.

As an example, midway through an article about body language—"How to Read Between the Lines"—author Holly Miller feared her article contained too much advice and was beginning to sound sermonic. She tucked in an anecdote to give readers a break and to illustrate the effectiveness of strong body language. The little story added humor and color as it described a meek secretary's confrontation with a gruff executive. To lead into the anecdote, the writer quickly explained the background of the story: A secretary had been asked by her boss to pull together a report. On the day it was due, her boss wasn't around, and she needed someone to approve what she had written before she mailed it. This led to a face-to-face standoff with a man several rungs above her on the corporate ladder. The article's author let the secretary tell the story in her own words.

> "The executive looked at me and growled, 'What do you want?' I explained I was on a tight deadline and politely asked him to read my report to make sure it was correct. The man bellowed, 'I don't have time!' I marched across his office, planted my feet firmly in his carpet, and folded my arms as if to say, 'I'm here to stay.' He put his head down, shuffled his papers and tried to ignore me. But I never stopped staring at him. After a few minutes he looked up, grumbled, and reached for the article." Not until she had left his office with the wad of approved pages tucked under her arm did she begin to shake. "I couldn't believe my boldness," she said.[6]

The vivid scene, complete with "he-said-she-said" dialogue, makes a point and creates a bond with readers who identify with the secretary. The article's writer could have made the same point by simply stating, "strong body language has the capacity to empower a powerless person." Instead, the writer chose to use an anecdote to illustrate the fact and to add some zest to the article.

Searching for Anecdotes

The best anecdotes are those that you discover in the course of your interviews. This ensures that the colorful little stories you include in your articles haven't appeared in dozens of other articles. In a pinch, you can always find memorable anecdotes in published collections or on Web sites such as www.anecdotage.com. These anecdotes typically deal with historical events and famous people. They may lack freshness. The anecdotes about Oscar Wilde and the *Chicken Soup* books, told earlier in this chapter, are examples of often-repeated stories.

Hal Karp, a contributing editor who writes frequently on auto safety for *Reader's Digest*, says that finding good anecdotes is difficult but essential. "I often spend two or three days or even a whole week trying to find one anecdote," he admits. Where does he look? He makes telephone calls to "points of contact" related to the type of anecdote he's seeking. "For example, if I'm looking for accident victims, I ask, 'Where are all the points of contact for an accident victim?' Victims come in contact with paramedics, police and emergency room doctors. So I start going down the list. I call fire departments, paramedics and law enforcement officers."[7]

The way you phrase your questions during interviews can determine your success in drawing out new and memorable anecdotes. Let's review four of the anecdotes included in this chapter and try to guess the questions that brought forth the stories.

Questions for College Freshman Amy Ransom

1. Describe your emotions and your behavior during your first week on campus.
2. What did your family do to help you through the adjustment period?
3. Recall for me the telephone conversations that you had with your dad. What words did he use to comfort you?

Questions for Miss America Sharlene Wells

1. What was the first mistake you made after winning the pageant?
2. Describe the interview that led to the embarrassing picture in *People* magazine.
3. Recreate the moment when you first saw the published photograph. How did you react?

Questions for Accident Victim Bill Ryan

1. Beginning with the time you got into your car, recount the drive that led up to the accident.
2. What went through your mind as you saw the van coming toward you?
3. Describe the scene when you first regained consciousness in the hospital emergency room.

Questions for the Secretary Who Confronted Her Supervisor

1. What circumstances led to your standoff with the corporate executive?
2. Recreate those few moments when you were at an impasse in his office.
3. What went through your mind as you stood your ground and waited for his response?

Most people speak in generalities. They gloss over major moments with simple statements such as, "I was homesick," "I was embarrassed," or "I was scared." Beginning interviewers accept the generalities and move on to their next questions. Sharp writers recognize the potential drama behind such statements, zero in for details and don't stop asking questions until they have the whole story, told in living color.

Suggested Activities

1. The opening anecdote in this chapter—the *Chicken Soup for the Soul* story—contains 140 words. Edit the story to less than 100 words.

2. Ask a friend to describe a specific moment of victory or defeat. Through follow-up questions, try to pull out as many colorful details as you can. After you have collected the information, shape it into an anecdote of three sentences. Review the material and flesh out the story to a paragraph of about 150 words. Split the anecdote in half in a way that the first half might serve as the lead of a feature article and the second half might serve as the ending of the article.

3. Locate an article in a magazine or newspaper that has an anecdotal lead. Read the lead to friends and see if they can discern the topic of the article. Does the anecdote serve as a smooth and colorful introduction to the subject that the article examines? Read the article without the opening anecdote. Which do you prefer?

Shoptalk

Split anecdote: A story that is cut in half and separated by paragraphs containing other information. Often the first half of the anecdote serves as an article's lead and the second half brings the article to a conclusion.

Endnotes

1. Lecture, July 29, 2004.

2. Holly G. Miller, "Poise, Spirit, Voice=Star Quality," *The Anderson Herald-Bulletin* (Jan. 24, 1988), B-1.

3. Holly G. Miller, "Treasures in the Attic," *Columns* (Spring 2004), 7.

4. Holly G. Miller, "On The Road With Miss America," *The Saturday Evening Post* (May/June 1985), 42.

5. Ibid., 43.

6. Holly G. Miller, "How to Read Between the Lines," *Today's Christian Woman* (October-November 1991), 76-78.

7. Telephone interview, Aug. 2, 2004.

Chapter 9
The Structure of Writing

Structure is how the parts of a story—such as facts, quotes and anecdotes—are put together in a way that is most clear, logical and easy to read. In all types of writing, the research must be analyzed and the information must be synthesized into a coherent whole. Rather than prescribing certain rules of organization, this chapter suggests ways to think about your material and sensibly present it to the reader. The key points of this chapter are:

- Unity and coherence
- The billboard paragraph
- Analysis and synthesis
- Writing without notes
- Seven structural models

Writing a magazine or newspaper feature is similar to constructing a building. First comes the foundation and then the frame, flooring, walls, windows, doors, ceiling, roof, plumbing and electrical wiring. Building a story proceeds in a similar fashion. Every story begins with a foundation and a framework. The way you build your story—its **structure**—demonstrates your logic and ability to link pieces of information together coherently. You really have to think about structure and figure out how to present the facts and details so they will make the most sense. Without this **coherence**, readers become frustrated and move to something else.

Unity and Coherence

Unity and coherence are important qualities of any story. Unity means that a story focuses on one topic and one topic only. It demonstrates that it was written for one purpose using one voice, tense and tone. Coherence results from logically organizing the pieces of the story so they make sense to the reader.

The way that you organize the parts of a story—the pieces of information resulting from your research—creates its structure. Just as the structure of a home may consist of wood, brick, limestone or laminated siding, a story may consist of different types of structure. This chapter will explain several different types of structure and ways to build united and coherent stories.

Jane Harrigan, former editor of the *Concord (N.H.) Monitor*, tells a story about a writer friend of hers. "One day as I was climbing the stairs to her apartment, she yelled down a warning: 'Watch out! I'm in the middle of a piece, and the place is a mess.' Inside, her writing room looked just like mine, piles of paper covering every horizontal surface. Then something on the windowsill caught my eye. It was an index card with a single sentence written on it.

"'What's that?' I asked.

"'That's the point,' Sue replied. 'I put it there so I always know where to find it.'"[1]

Summarizing a story's central idea in a single sentence is a time-tested principle of writing. It's also a time-tested principle of organization. If you don't know what you're writing about, then you certainly won't know how to organize it. Without that sentence, an article has no unifying theme, focus or compelling message. That focus prevents all of the bits and pieces of information you have collected from sprawling into an incoherent mess.

The Billboard Paragraph

Everyone knows what a billboard looks like and what it does. It makes a big announcement while you're driving down a highway. The billboard paragraph announces to readers where you plan to take them.

The billboard is an expansion of that one-sentence theme; it's simply a paragraph that appears early in your piece and sums up what your article is about. It tips readers to your theme, guides them on their way and enables them to decide if they want to continue. Most editors want to see a billboard paragraph within the first five or six paragraphs. In general, the shorter the article, the higher the billboard should be.

"The biggest mistake that many writers make is that they omit the billboard or they hide it deep down in the story," says *Discover* magazine editor-at-large Joe Treen.[2]

Sometimes the billboard paragraph doubles as a summary lead because it simply summarizes what the article is about. It guides your research, saves time and helps you stay focused.

A weak story structure has certain red flags that let you know it still needs work.

They include:

- When you read the story, it feels unwieldy, choppy or unorganized.
- It lacks smooth transitions and logical development from point to point.
- Some parts seem shallow and hurried.
- Related types of information are not grouped together.
- Detailed or technical information that could be in **sidebars** slows down the pace.

Analysis and Synthesis — *apply to Profiles* *interpretation of person*

Getting organized may start with staring out the window while you think about what you're doing. Writing isn't simply typing words and letters into a keyboard. Writing requires thinking, which includes analyzing and synthesizing ideas. **Analysis** occurs when you divide something into its component parts, then examine each part—one at a time. This book, for example, analyzes 22 components of feature and magazine writing in individual chapters.

Analysis tries to impose some order on the mess your research notes resemble. Look for significant groups of ideas and related concepts. Then determine whether you have two, three or four kinds of ideas or topics and explain what characterizes each kind. That's **synthesis**, which is the opposite of analysis. For writers, synthesis involves choosing the most significant parts and interpreting what they mean in relation to the whole.

Here are 10 specific writing tasks that involve analysis and synthesis:

- Sifting through research to decide which facts are most interesting or newsworthy
- Comparing and weighing conflicting bits of evidence
- Deciding when to verify questionable information with more research

- Deciding whether each piece of information contributes to your main theme
- Choosing related pieces of information and grouping them together
- Discarding interesting information that's irrelevant to the purpose
- Deciding when to quote directly and when to paraphrase
- Deciding if you need to find more anecdotes to make it more interesting
- Organizing format, structure and tone for internal consistency
- Organizing the material so that it unfolds logically in the reader's mind

Always keep your central purpose in mind when you go through this analyzing and synthesizing process. If you always pay attention to the main theme, you will save time during the organizing process.

Writing without Notes

Hiding your notes as you start to write can save you from becoming a victim of details. This suggestion may surprise you after everything we've said about analyzing and synthesizing research results. But after you've done that, many writing teachers and coaches recommend writing the first draft without notes. This forces you to put down on paper only those fresh ideas that are at the top of your thinking. It also helps you write with a conversational style.

If you remember these ideas off the top of your head, then they are probably going to be the same ideas that readers find most interesting and compelling. After you've written the first draft, you can go back, verify facts and fill in the details from your notes. Writing from memory helps you see the forest; then you can go back and take care of the trees.

Does that mean you shouldn't use a tape recorder for interviews? We've heard opposing arguments among writers about the usefulness of tape recorders. Critics of tape recorders say that they can make you the "victim of details" by focusing too much on them and not enough on the big picture. Transcribing interviews also adds another time-consuming step in the writing process. Furthermore, tape recorders make some people nervous and less likely to speak candidly.

Nevertheless, we believe that the advantages of tape recorders outweigh their disadvantages. Their main advantage is accuracy. No one can write as fast as people speak since most people average about 170 words per minute. Therefore, writers end up filling in the blanks of their notes with re-created quotes and what they think their subject probably said.

Our advice remains the same, however. What you remember from an interview "off the top of your head" is usually the most interesting information. You can write the first draft without notes and without your tape recorder. Go back and transcribe the interview later to get the precise words of what your subject said.

Seven Structural Models

The following types of structure offer methods to organize your material. They give you ways to think about material and determine when you have a coherent story. The model that works best depends largely on the type of story you are writing. Some stories require a combination of two or three types of structure.

Full-Circle Technique

One of the simplest and most effective structural models can be combined with almost every other technique. The split-anecdote or full-circle technique may begin with an anecdote that illustrates the main purpose of the story. For example, one writer wrote a story about how microchips on pet collars have drastically reduced the frequency of lost pets. The story began with an anecdote about a dog owner whose dog ran away. The dog owner placed "lost and found" ads in the newspaper for two weeks before getting his dog back. The concluding anecdote quotes from the same pet owner who purchased one of these chips for his dog's collar to prevent it from happening again.

You can see how the author "circled back" to the same incident, which helped give the story unity and coherence. Another option is to start with a useful anecdote from one source and conclude with another anecdotal example from the same person.

The full circle structure isn't limited to leads and conclusions, however. You can use a strong anecdote with vivid quotes about a real-life problem throughout the article to illustrate the larger theme. The specific real-life example is woven throughout the fabric of the larger issue under discussion. It's very effective in holding the reader's attention.

Neither is this structure limited to using anecdotes. If you begin with a startling fact in the lead, repeat it at the end to bring the reader back to the same idea.

Chronological

The chronological structure is also simple and effective. It demonstrates how "this happened," and then "this happened" and then "this happened." It's effective because it uses narrative to reveal action in an unfolding series of events. It works successfully with many types of stories ranging from profiles (Chapter 12) to real-life dramas (Chapter 13) to trend-controversy stories (Chapter 16). You can use a chronological structure within another structure such as "problem and possible causes" by explaining a series of events leading to the larger problem you are discussing.

One study found that a chronological structure was by far the most common type of structure among 25 Pulitzer Prize-winning feature stories between 1979 and 2003. Among those 25 stories, 19 used a chronological structure either solely or combined with another structure.[3]

Scene-by-Scene

The scene-by-scene structure is like a movie: Your writing describes the story as it unfolds from one scene to another. This structure must be used with material containing a lot of narrative, dialogue and description. It won't work with issue-oriented stories containing mostly exposition and facts. Scene-by-scene structures are usually combined with chronological structure, but may break the chronology with flashback scenes or other expositional information.

Person-to-Person

The person-to-person structure works when you interview several people who contribute opinions or facts to a roundup or issue-oriented story (Chapter 16). Quoting one person at a time before moving on to another is generally good advice. That's because readers become easily confused as to who said what if you jump back and forth among interviewed sources.

For example, suppose you write a story about airline safety. If you're quoting an airline pilot, an airline executive and a Federal Aviation Agency (FAA) official, the reader evaluates the credibility of each source partly by the job title and professional qualifications. However, if all the writer says is "Smith says," and "Jones says," the reader has to remember whether Smith is the pilot or the airline executive and Jones is the FAA official or the pilot. By keeping the quotes grouped together according to source, it's easier for the reader to evaluate and interpret each set of remarks.

Problem and Possible Solutions

While sticking to one person at a time is a good idea, it won't always work when the focus is on an issue such as airline safety. You may have to use the "problem and possible causes," "problem and possible solutions," or "comparing and contrasting of viewpoints" structure.

For example, one of the hotly debated issues following the Sept. 11, 2001, terrorism attacks in the United States was whether airline pilots should be allowed to carry guns on flight duty. Here's one way to outline this problem.

> **Problem:** hijacking of airlines by terrorists
> **Solution 1:** Allow the senior pilot on any flight to carry a gun
> **Solution 2:** Allow any pilot who wishes to carry a gun to do so as long as it's a legally registered weapon
> **Solution 3:** Allow some pilots to carry a gun if they apply for a special permit and undergo supervised FAA training

Now, of course, the pilot, airline executive and FAA official may have different opinions about each possible solution. So you have to group their quotes by categories of solutions instead of by person. Incidentally, Congress eventually passed "solution 3," allowing pilots to carry guns after undergoing supervised training.

The study of 25 Pulitzer Prize-winning feature stories mentioned earlier found that five used a problem-solution structure combined with a chronological structure.

Problem and Possible Causes

Life isn't simple. Some problems don't have identifiable causes, and solutions appear remote, if they exist at all. Many stories—both in print and on television—explore "possible causes" when looking at human and social problems. A few years ago, ABC Television produced a "20-20" program narrated by Diane Sawyer on learning-challenged children and adults. The central character in the story was a 35-year-old woman who functioned at a child-like level. The story followed a "problem and possible causes" structure by interviewing eight medical experts from prestigious universities. The experts concluded that while some learning problems are genetic, they sometimes result from an infancy deprived of adult interaction. They emphasized the importance of a close parent-child bond and a stimulating play environment during infancy.

Persuasion and Argumentation

The goal of persuasive writing is to make the reader think and adopt a new viewpoint. Magazines, unlike newspapers, don't pretend to be objective. If you're a liberal, you read *The Nation* or *The New Republic* and filter the news of current events through its lenses. If you're a conservative, you read *The Weekly Standard* or *National Review* to do the same. A print or Internet magazine writer can display opinions in a feature article. The opinions can be explicit or subtle. Effective persuasive writing, however, supports its opinions with evidence.

The basic outline of a persuasive article is simple:

- Lead
- Billboard paragraph stating argument
- Supporting evidence number 1
- Supporting evidence number 2
- Supporting evidence number 3
- Refutation of opponents' arguments
- Summary and conclusion

The supporting evidence should include quotes from experts, statistics and factual research. Charles Krauthammer, who writes a monthly column for *Time* magazine, emphasizes the importance of factual evidence in persuasive writing: "I marshal facts. I like to make arguments and, of course, you need facts. So we go to the Library of Congress, libraries, bookstores, to get them from books, newspapers and the Internet, of course. We'll call the Congressional offices for information and we will contact the partisans on any issue to get their propaganda."[4] Krauthammer earned an M.D. from Harvard Medical School before deciding to pursue a career as a writer. He says his medical training helped him learn to analyze and synthesize evidence and contributed to his success as a writer.

Organizational Tools

Before concluding, we'd like to mention three other gadgets in the writer's box of tools that help writers organize their material and readers to more easily comprehend it: numbered and bulleted lists, sidebars, and tables and graphs.

Numbered and Bulleted Lists

You may have already noticed the frequent use of numbered and bulleted lists in this book. Numbered and bulleted lists are analytic devices that provide at least four advantages to readers because they:

- Emphasize the main points
- Help the reader organize and remember the information
- Improve the graphic appeal of a page by allowing more white space
- Summarize complex information concisely

Lists are a remarkably compact way to deliver factual information. You can avoid the need for a lot of wordy transitions simply by listing items. The time to find list information is during your research, not when you begin to write the article. List information results from analyzing—and breaking down—complex information. Whenever you can take a complex concept and break it down into three or four tangible statements, you help the reader understand the concept more clearly.

Sidebars

Editors love **sidebars.** Readers love sidebars. When readers scan pages of a publication, sidebars catch their attention and pull them into the article. They bring to the page what graphics experts call "points of entry." A sidebar is a summary of an article's related information presented outside the main body of the article in a separate space.

While most sidebar information can be written into the story, sidebars have a number of advantages, some of which they share with numbered and bulleted lists:

- Attract readers' attention by allowing points of entry
- Enhance graphic appeal of a page with contrast and emphasis
- Summarize complex information concisely
- Help writers organize their material
- Place technical data or details outside the text

The Wall Street Journal profiled the small southern coastal town of Fairhope, Ala., which it described as a "home to artists, writers—and now retirees." A sidebar titled "Fairhope at a glance" included a list of pertinent facts about the town: population, population density, average annual

A Sidebar of Sidebar Ideas

1. The practical, useful list
2. The quirky, interesting list
3. A quiz for readers
4. A glossary
5. For more information, go here
6. This one just didn't fit anywhere else

rainfall, average January low temperature, average July high temperature, cost-of-living index, median home value, unemployment rate and state income tax.[5] The "useful list" like this is probably the most common type of sidebar.

Travel stories or reviews of performances frequently include an "if you go" sidebar with times and admission prices, travel directions, related Web sites and telephone numbers. Service journalism articles about choosing products or service providers may include a "questions to ask" sidebar to help you make an intelligent decision.

Sidebars don't have to be limited to lists or service journalism information. They can present an "it happened to me" first-person account or a question-and-answer interview with an important source from the article.

Tables and Graphs

If you have a story that involves numbers or data, find a way to present them in a table or graph. This visual display of quantitative data is especially important if you use those numbers to demonstrate or emphasize a point. Readers can more quickly grasp the impact of numbers displayed in a table than read through the text and pull them out of the article. You can use the table or graph to quickly display "what" happened and explain how and why it happened in the text. This visual presentation may be especially helpful in trend-controversy stories (which we'll discuss in Chapter 16) that depend on increases or decreases in certain phenomena to make their point.

A popular television program sends a team to someone's house to clean up and organize one or two cluttered, messy rooms. The first thing the team does is help the family decide their purpose for the room. Do they want it to be a den, recreation room, home office, bedroom or what? Then they help them organize a garage sale to get rid of at least half their stuff. The team proceeds to transform the space into a neatly organized, clutter-free room that fulfills the family's purpose for it.

In other words, you have to start with the purpose before you decide how to organize your material. Maybe your apartment looks like that of Jane Harrigan's friend, which she described at the beginning of this chapter: ". . . piles of paper covering every horizontal surface." Maybe that's the way your desk looks when you sit and stare at the computer. If you don't remember anything else from this story, remember this: the index card with a single sentence written on it.

"'That's the point,'" she said of the index card. Let the point—the billboard paragraph—be the guiding principle of organization, and everything else will fall into place.

Suggested Activities

1. Read one of the Pulitzer Prize-winning feature stories available at www.pulitzer.org. Identify and analyze the types of structure that are evident in the story.

2. Read five stories from five different magazines and write a one-sentence description of each. If you have difficulty doing that with any of them, analyze the story's structural unity and why the one-sentence description is difficult.

3. For the next article you write, do as much background reading as possible and then write a 500-word summary of your topic without using notes. Analyze the summary to figure out what's missing and what types of sources you need to interview to complete it.

Shoptalk

Analysis: The process of thinking through the topic you are writing about and breaking it down into smaller pieces. Research results also must be broken down into smaller pieces.

Coherence. The unity of a story that results from logically organizing its facts, anecdotes and quotations. The component parts fit together in a way that makes sense to the reader.

Narrative: A story with a chronological structure in which one scene follows another.

Sidebar: Lists or pieces of related information presented outside the main body of the article in a separate space.

Structure: The way the parts of a story—such as facts, quotes and anecdotes—are put together that is most clear, logical and easy to read.

Synthesis: The process of thinking about the "small pieces" of information resulting from your research and figuring out how to best summarize and present them in the final story structure.

Endnotes

1. Jane Harrigan, "Organizing Your Material," in *The Complete Book of Feature Writing*, Leonard Witt, ed. (Cincinnati: Writer's Digest Books, 1991), 100.

2. Telephone interview, Nov. 21, 2003.

3. Edward Jay Friedlander, "Teaching Magazine and Feature Writing By Example: Twenty-Five Years of Pulitzer Prize-Winning Stories in the Classroom." Paper presented at the annual convention of the Association for Education in Journalism and Mass Communication, Toronto, August 2004.

4. Interview, Washington, D.C., Oct. 27, 1997.

5. Nicole Harris, "Southern Charms," *The Wall Street Journal* (June 28, 2004), R10.

Chapter 10
The Art and Style of Writing

This chapter looks at ways to improve the style and literary quality of your writing. Style results from an effective combination of voice, viewpoint, rhythm, tone and humor, which this chapter describes in detail:

- Voice—The personality of writing
- Viewpoint—The perspective of writing
- Rhythm—The music of writing
- Tone—The attitude of writing
- Humor—The fun of writing

John Steinbeck once said, "A writer lives in awe of words; they can change meanings right in front of us. They pick up flavors and odors like butter in a refrigerator."

One of the things you learn to do as a writer is look at every word under a magnifying glass. You enlarge the image, look at the word and ask yourself: Is this word doing a job that no other word does? Does it have greater clarity than any other word? Is this the shortest and simplest word I can use? Does this word make an impact on the reader? If the answer to any of these questions is no, then you hit the delete button and look for another word. And you do this for every single word, whether it's a 1,000-word article or 100,000-word book.

Mark Twain's many quotes that remain familiar to the public are a tribute to his eloquent style of writing. **Style** is the quality that makes your writing fun to read. Stylish writing results from always choosing the right word—not the almost-right word. Stylish writing also results from the right combination of voice, viewpoint, rhythm, tone and humor.

The easiest way to achieve clarity is to write with short sentences, short paragraphs and everyday words. Numerous studies have concluded that readers comprehend short sentences more easily than long sentences. They understand two-syllable words more easily than four-syllable words. And they comprehend three-sentence paragraphs more easily than 10-sentence paragraphs. Short sentences and paragraphs give readers more places to pause and think about what they read.

The best sentence range in journalistic writing is 10 to 20 words, and the best paragraph range is two to five sentences. Every sentence with more than 25 words can be re-written with two shorter sentences.

Voice—The Personality of Writing

Voice primarily refers to how writers reveal their personality in their writing style. Magazine editors like stories with voice and personality in them more than newspaper editors. Except for columnists, newspapers typically rely on an objective style of reporting in which the writer remains out of sight.

The best way to describe voice is to compare it with music. Some artists have a unique, strong voice. As soon as you hear them on a radio or CD, you immediately recognize the voice. The enduring popularity of Elvis Presley, for example, is a tribute to the clear, mellow voice recognized by almost everyone who hears his music.

Writers can have a unique voice, too. You can read an article and recognize the writer without seeing her byline. Voice is how you put yourself in your writing. A strong voice can be achieved using a first-person, second person or third person viewpoint. Some writers with a strong voice may never use the pronouns "I" or "me" in their writing.

Voice is also your natural way of producing words. It's the power behind your words that evolves from your unique way of seeing the world. It gives your writing a special strength, forcefulness and believability that sets it apart from weaker, uncompelling stuff.

If style is the external way in which you execute and dress up your writing, voice is the unseen force that drives your narrative and comes from deep within. The writer's voice cannot be separated from the writer's core values. If you have a clear sense of identity—who you are, what you believe and your direction in life—then you will more likely display that same strong voice in your writing.

While objectivity may be the cardinal rule for reporting news stories, it isn't necessarily for features. Voice means giving the reader some interpretation of the material you are presenting. You let the facts govern your interpretation, however, and not the other way around.

William Blundell, a former editor of *The Wall Street Journal*, stresses the importance of the reporter's voice in this colorful way: "A feature story without the reporter in it, without his strong presence in interpretation and conclusion, without his calling a spade a spade instead of bringing in someone from Harvard to declare it a 'long handled personal earthmoving implement,' is a weak, flaccid story." Blundell goes on to say that the interpretive reporter "steps in to make conclusions that cry out to be made. He gives self-serving puffery short shrift. He may make observations of his own from time to time because he is the reader's agent . . . . When all this is done, the reader gradually becomes conscious of a guiding intelligence within the story working for his benefit, the close and warming presence of a fellow human being conversing with him in print . . ."[1]

No one can teach you how to use voice. You have to develop it through a lifetime of experience. Here are some suggestions to point you in the right direction.

First, write in a conversational style. Some writers like to "blow it all out" on the keyboard, go back, and do the editing and revising later. Don't worry about how your writing looks and sounds the first time around. Just write. Try to explain a topic in the same way that you would explain it to a friend.

Second, trust your instincts. Don't try to report what is appropriate or acceptable. Report exactly what you see and hear. If you think an obscure detail is significant to the story, then trust your instinct and report it. If your gut tells you that the angle your editor suggested is not the real story, then go with your gut and get the facts you need to report it. You can convince your editor later.

Third, the proper display of the writer's interpretation in feature stories should be subtle and guided by common sense. Ask yourself, "How would the reasonable person react to this set of facts I've discovered?" Your interpretation can guide how you organize the material and whom you choose to quote. If your article takes a position on a controversial issue, then it should be honestly revealed and consistent with the editorial policies of the publication for which you are writing.

Viewpoint—The Perspective of Writing

First person? Second person? Third person? Most writers of most feature and magazine stories use third-person **viewpoint**. The writer is the narrator. The writer tells an objective story about other people or reports a set of facts. The words "I" or "you" occur infrequently. For many reasons, the third-person viewpoint is also the safest route to go for both beginning and advanced writers.

Beginning writers want to use first person because it's the easiest to use. They think it requires less research and on-scene reporting. That perception of first-person viewpoint also makes it the most difficult kind of writing to do successfully.

First-Person Viewpoint

First-person articles are easy to write but difficult to write successfully. "The number one mistake that most beginning writers make is to write in the first person automatically just because it feels comfortable when the fact is that the reader doesn't know you and doesn't care about you," says Art Spikol, a *Writer's Digest* columnist.[2] It creates the impression that the writer thinks himself more important and influential than he really is. Readers are not interested in the personal experiences of writers they don't know.

Only three types of articles merit a first-person viewpoint. First-person is appropriate if the writer is the most interesting character in the story. If you're the least interesting, then keep yourself out of the story. Readers are interested in hearing the first-person stories of people who have achieved great success or overcome dramatic obstacles. If these people aren't writers, then writers can help them write their stories in the "as-told-to" format.

Second, when the article explains a topic of wide public interest, the writer can share occasional personal insights not possible in third-person. When you see the first-person viewpoint in feature stories in well-known magazines like *The New Yorker* or *Atlantic Monthly*, the writer's personal experiences are not the point of the stories. When they do appear, their purpose is to describe situations or incidents that the writer personally observed. This situation or incident cannot be fully explained unless the writer shares his or her insights. The purpose of sharing these insights is not to draw attention to the writer, but to shed more light on the topic of wide public interest that he is discussing.

The third appropriate use of first-person is in service journalism articles whose purpose is to help readers with practical information. Writers can use first-person viewpoint when they are experts on the topics they are writing about. Used in this way, first-person can enhance both credibility and rapport with readers. However, the writer's credibility as an expert must be clear. You have to establish yourself as an expert by mentioning formal credentials or experiences that qualify you to write authoritatively about this topic or by including a separate "**author's bio**" at the end of the story.

If you choose to write a feature story in first-person viewpoint, then follow this advice. First, use it sparingly—not every paragraph, but perhaps once every three to six paragraphs. Second, use it only when it originates in "on the spot" reporting. When used carefully and sparingly, a first-person approach can lend credibility to on-the-spot reporting and create more rapport between the reader and the writer. It demonstrates that you were there and know what you are talking about.

Third, use it consistently throughout the story. The writer's viewpoint can't suddenly appear without seeming invasive. It has to appear consistently throughout the story. Finally, don't use it in interviews to report, "I asked so-and-so" and "she told me." To readers, this type of attribution is annoying, cluttered and unnecessary. Instead of writing, "I asked so-and-so," you can write, "When asked about . . . . so-and-so said . . . ."

Second-Person Viewpoint

As we wrote in Chapter 7, second-person writing using the "you" voice can create a personal relationship between the writer and the reader. It enables the writer to speak to the reader as if one friend were speaking to another. Second-person viewpoint is also effective in service journalism and "how-to" articles. It can be combined with first-person viewpoint when the writer is an expert on the topic.

The second-person viewpoint has three limitations, however. First, it can annoy readers when the writer uses it to create a false familiarity that doesn't exist with the reader. It's sort of like strangers and clerks who call you by your first name the first time they meet you. Don't assume you "know" the reader; don't assume you know exactly what readers like, dislike or what they have experienced.

Second-person viewpoints can annoy the reader if they describe a situation that some readers can't relate to. For example, what if an article starts with this lead:

> When you're in a bar and a sloppily-dressed guy comes over and offers to buy you a drink, what do you say?

Male readers and female readers who don't go to bars will be annoyed by this lead. You can't assume that readers have had this particular kind of experience unless you are writing for a magazine with a young female audience who enjoys going to bars.

A third disadvantage to second-person writing is the writer's vulnerability to appearing presumptuous or "talking down" to the reader. Second-person works best when it comes across as one friend talking to another, not as an expert telling a beginner how to do something. If there is any hint of arrogance in the writer's tone, readers will detect it.

Third-Person Viewpoint

Third-person is the most common viewpoint in magazine and feature writing. It follows the typical "he," "she," "it" and "they" approach to reporting. It's also the best approach for beginning writers. If you do good research and reporting, then all you have to do is tell the reader what you discovered. Good, solid, factual reporting can—and will—speak for itself.

Rhythm—The Music of Writing

An appreciation of music can teach you about **rhythm** and how to listen to the pace of your writing. "Writers use music in many ways," according to Roy Peter Clark, a senior scholar at The Poynter Institute for Media Studies in St. Petersburg, Fla.[3] These include:

- To set a tone or a mood
- To create contrast
- To establish a rhythm
- To strike a chord
- To end on a high note

When Clark asked some journalists in one of his seminars about their favorite music, he received some interesting responses. Jonathan Dube of MSNBC.com said he likes "Start Me Up" by the Rolling Stones: "Listening to this song is like getting a shot of adrenaline in the arm—again and again and again. I can feel it moving through my body each time Keith Richards strokes his guitar, flooding me with bursts of energy," said Dube.[4]

Stephanie Crockett of BET.com said she likes "Back in One Piece" by Aaliyah and DMX. "I always choose a hip-hop or R&B song to move me before I write. I'm suggesting this song because it is both. Hip-hop, with its racy lyrics and questionable subject matter, reminds me to always write my truths."[5]

Reading your writing aloud helps you determine whether it is smooth and harmonious or choppy and off-key. Many of the nation's best-known writers do this. For example, Ellen Goodman, a Pulitzer Prize-winning columnist from *The Boston Globe*, says, "I think you have to listen to your own work. When I was working in the city room, everybody used to joke about me moving my lips while I was writing. I was putting it through my own ear. You have to really learn that. If there's a clang in your ear, then that's bad."[6]

Leonard Pitts, another Pulitzer Prize-winning columnist, says, "I think a great deal about rhythm. Some of my biggest fights with editors were over changes that they wanted to make, which to me disrupted the rhythm. It's such a difficult thing to explain. I am talking about the rhythm and the way it sounds. It's indispensable in good writing—that sense of propulsion, the sense of ebb and flow and moving and different pulses."[7]

One way to improve rhythm is by varying the length of sentences and paragraphs. A writing style characterized by sameness in sentence length, type and structure produces a monotonous rhythm that may bore even the most enthusiastic reader. This is particularly true when all of the sentences are either very long or very short.

Another way to improve rhythm is to use **parallel structure**. Parallel structure offers ideas to the reader using the same patterns of grammatical structure—the same verb tense or phrase or clause structure. If you use compound elements in a sentence, make sure both are nouns, both are verbs or both are adjectives. Make sure verbs are in the same tense and voice.

For example:

- **Without parallel structure:** Both candidates said they would make sure property taxes go down, but that social services would be increased and new industries would come as a result of their effort.
- **With parallel structure:** Both candidates promised to decrease property taxes, increase social services and attract new industries. (In this example each verb appears in simple present tense.)

The lack of parallel structure in writing means sentences are longer, more convoluted, confusing or difficult to read. The use of parallel structure gives your writing a poetic flow and makes it sound better to the reader's inner ear.

Tone—The Attitude of Writing

Think of **tone** as the attitude with which you approach a topic. The tone may be humorous, satirical, light-hearted, heavy, sarcastic, whimsical, persuasive, argumentative, self-deprecating, disparaging or respectful.

Joe Treen, editor-at-large for *Discover* magazine, says consistency of tone is important: "You need to work around one single tone. You don't want to switch your tone around. As another editor once said to me, 'What gong do we want to be hitting here?' You only get to ring one 'gong' in a story."[8]

New York-based writer Judith Newman, author of *You Make Me Feel Like an Unnatural Woman*, advises writers to be careful with tone, especially sarcasm. "If magazines are infected with any disease, it's the disease of snarkiness and sarcasm for its own sake. Snarkiness means trying a little too hard to be hip without much thought behind it. If you're going to treat something skeptically, then really be thoughtful about it. It's easy to not treat people's concerns sensitively."[9]

Humor—The Fun of Writing

It's easier to tell a story and make the listeners laugh than it is to put it on paper and make readers laugh. Stand-up comedians have at least six advantages over humor writers. To make their audiences laugh, they can use: (1) tone of voice, (2) voice volume, (3) hand gestures, (4) eye expression, (5) timing and (6) body movement. Humor writers have words at their disposal—nothing else.

If you can make people laugh, especially with your writing, you have a wonderful gift. Use it every time you can, even in "serious" writing. Nothing, least of all this book, can teach you to write humor. Humor is the most difficult type of writing to consistently or successfully achieve. You must have an innate sense of humor before you can become a writer of humor.

The danger with humor writing is that if it fails, it causes readers to roll their eyes and makes the writer look dumb. While we encourage you to sprinkle humor in your writing, we also encourage you to proceed with caution. There are no rules. If it makes people laugh, then it works.

If you're just starting your writing career, voice, viewpoint, rhythm, tone and humor may seem like too much to conquer all at once. And they are. Writers with decades of experience still struggle with learning their proper use. At this point, conducting in-depth research and writing with clarity are the most important skills you can master. Eloquence and style will accrue with experience.

Suggested Activities

1. Choose at least one article each from magazines aimed at younger, middle-aged and older readers and discuss their differences in style.

2. Write a short article based on a humorous personal experience without using first-person viewpoint.

3. Listen to some music by your favorite artist. Write down all the terms that describe it that could also be used to describe a writer's style.

Shoptalk

Author's bio: Two or three sentences about the author's background that appear at the conclusion of an article.

Parallel structure: The use of the same verb tense, phrase and clause structure in sentences and paragraphs.

Rhythm: Variety in the movement or pace of writing. Strong rhythm results from varied sentence and paragraph length with frequent use of action verbs and active voice.

Style: A broad term describing the combination of voice, viewpoint, rhythm and tone in an author's writing.

Tone: The writer's attitude displayed in an article. Common tones are humorous, satirical, light-hearted, sarcastic, whimsical, persuasive, argumentative or respectful.

Viewpoint: The role the author takes in writing an article. First-person makes frequent use of the "I" viewpoint, whereas second-person uses the "you" viewpoint frequently. Third-person primarily uses "he," "she" or "it" viewpoints.

Voice: How writers reveal their personality and identity in their writing styles.

Endnotes

1. William Blundell, *The Art and Craft of Feature Writing* (New York: Penguin Books, 1986), 64.

2. Art Spikol, *Magazine Writing: The Inside Angle* (Cincinnati: Writer's Digest Books, 1979), 109.

3. Roy Peter Clark, "The Songs of Writers," The Poynter Institute, Poynteronline (www.poynter.org), accessed Dec. 11, 2004.

4. Ibid.

5. Ibid.

6. Personal interview, Boston, MA, Dec. 18, 1997.

7. Personal interview, Bowie, MD, Dec. 19, 1997.

8. Telephone interview, Nov. 21, 2003.

9. Telephone interview, Dec. 11, 2003.

Part III
Creating Different Types of Feature Articles

Chapter 11
The Wide, Wide World of Shorts

Readers like short items they can absorb quickly. Editors solicit these "shorts" to add variety and color to their publications. New writers often ease their way into the publishing world with fillers, blurbs and little features. This chapter will help you understand:

- The differences between fillers and "shorts"
- Where to find material for brief items
- A formula for list articles
- Ways to recycle blurbs and anecdotes

An aspiring young writer, bound for his first trip to Europe, mailed a flurry of query letters to newspaper and magazine editors offering them lengthy articles about every stop on his itinerary. Using a bulleted format sometimes called a **gang query** because it includes multiple story ideas, he tossed out three possible titles:

- "Barging through Burgundy"
- "Jack the Ripper's London"
- "Prague's Incredible Flea Markets"

The ideas were creative enough, yet all but one editor responded with a standard thanks-but-no-thanks rejection note. The lone encourager was a staff member at one of the giant New York-based travel magazines who scrawled across the bottom of the query: "Sorry, foreign assignments only go to our senior contributors." Then the editor added as an afterthought, "But I notice you're from Ohio. Anything going on out there?"

What the beginner didn't realize was that some national publications—

not just travel magazines like this one—produce as many as four or five regional editions. The cover story and most of the main features in an issue don't vary, but a certain number of pages are dedicated to editorial material about people and places within a specific region. For example, magazines shipped to the West Coast might contain a one-page story about a small family winery in California's Anderson Valley; readers in the Southwest won't see the winery story but they'll be alerted to a new bed-and-breakfast inn near Santa Fe. Midwest subscribers won't have access to either the wine or the inn stories, but in their absence might read a feature about an upcoming exhibit at the Rock and Roll Hall of Fame and Museum in Cleveland, Ohio.

Regional editions make sense for a couple of reasons. First, Americans are eager to learn about people close to home and about things they can do and see on a tank of gasoline. The publication that offers a steady stream of ideas for regional attractions is likely to build readership and retain subscribers in those locations. Second, advertisers are more apt to buy space in publications that feature stories linked to their service area. A small airline that schedules daily flights in and out of Key West, Fla., might be interested in placing an advertisement in a publication that features "The Cuban Cuisine of Key West."

Editors who operate out of offices in New York City, Los Angeles or Chicago need to know what is new and interesting in out-of-the-way places around Key West, Fla.; Santa Fe, N.M.; and yes, Cleveland, Ohio. The editor who asked the Ohio freelancer, "Anything going on out there?" was dead serious. The smart writer should have taken the hint, forgotten about the barge in Burgundy and checked out the riverboat docked near Cincinnati.

Fillers, Shorts and One-Pagers

The length and range of fillers, shorts and one-pagers are broad and include everything from 50 words for a joke to 600 words for a mini-profile. Readers like **shorts** because they are quick to absorb and less intimidating. They offer variety, can be clipped and saved, and they play to the current preference for skip-and-skim media. Art directors and layout editors welcome short items because they add color and energy to a page. They can be clustered, boxed, set at an angle or dropped as an attention-getter onto an otherwise gray page. Editors value short items because they ensure flexibility. If a major feature article runs long, an editor can remove a short to accommodate the need for extra inches. If an advertiser decides at the last minute not to buy space in an issue, the editor can retrieve a self-contained short from a file and plug it into the open page without disrupting the rest of the publication.

Writers should embrace shorts because they seldom require a query letter (we'll explain queries in Chapter 21), and they serve as foot-in-the-door features that eventually can lead to major assignments, internships or—best of all—permanent jobs. The student journalist who feeds a New York editor a constant stream of brief but bright items from Ohio, Oregon or North Carolina may earn a place in the publication's stable of trusted contributors. The editor lets the writer know about major stories slated for future publication, and the writer responds with related shorts that help expand the articles into **editorial packages**.

For example, say an editor plans a feature about a new crop of young entrepreneurs—recent college grads who take risks and start their own companies rather than join established corporations. A writer from Michigan hears about the project and offers a 500-word mini-profile of two sorority sisters who have launched a successful catering service out of a Detroit storefront. The article, "Tea for 200," adds an element of humor as well as geographic and gender diversity to the 3,000-word package that is dominated by males who have built businesses around their high-tech skills.

Before long, the back-and-forth communication between editor and writer results in a professional relationship that yields big benefits for both parties. The editor's network of writers grows, and the publication takes on a national flavor, thanks to fresh voices reporting stories from rural and urban areas of the country. Who knows, the writer may even earn a place on the publication's **masthead** as a **contributing editor** or, more specifically, have the distinction of being its West Coast, Midwest or Southeast **regional correspondent**. This usually doesn't translate into a salary (a token honorarium is the best that a contributing editor can hope for), but it ensures that any story idea the writer submits will be accorded serious consideration. It also means that when an editor has an important assignment, he will look first to his list of contributing editors. Before long that writer from Ohio may have a firm assignment to take a barge through Burgundy, shadow Jack the Ripper around London or scout bargains at Prague's flea markets.

The Wide, Wide World of Shorts

By definition, shorts are interesting, informative and relevant nonfiction items of various lengths. Don't confuse them with **fillers**, which suggest items that have little purpose other than to take up space. Years ago, many newspapers and some magazines kept on hand a supply of random fillers to dust off and drop into a story that didn't quite fill the space allotted it. It was possible for a reader to finish a profile article about a Washington politician or a Hollywood celebrity and then be informed, "The capital of Nevada is Carson City" or "The average person uses 123 gallons of water a day."

Fortunately, fillers are rare these days. Editors no longer fear white space; in fact, they welcome "air" because it allows a story to "breathe." Computer technology also now permits an editor to eliminate small amounts of unwanted air by slightly adjusting the space between lines and words.

Unlike fillers, shorts are a planned, not a random, part of a publication's content. They might take the form of humorous anecdotes such as you see in *Reader's Digest*. They might be recipes, appropriate for a magazine such as *Woman's Day*. They might be brief inspirational stories that fit perfectly into the pages of *Guideposts*. They can be 300-word how-to articles— "Five Steps to a Great Mid-Career Résumé"—for a July issue of a business magazine or the business pages of a daily newspaper. Or they might offer a quick compilation of shower gift ideas for the bride-to-be for the front page of almost any newspaper's feature section in June. They might occupy a box, a column or an entire page. All are tightly focused and self-contained, and they never include the line "continued on page . . . ."

Tracking the Salable Short

The amount of research necessary to produce a marketable short varies. For the story about shower gifts for the bride-to-be, the writer might browse the specialty shops of a mall, taking notes on unusual items that a young couple would unlikely purchase for themselves. Two or three brief interviews with retail buyers about what's hot this season provide insider tips from experts who have a handle on trendy merchandise.

Sometimes a single interview with an expert source provides enough information for two or three shorts. For example, a college journalist might research a profile article about a literature professor for the campus newspaper and come away with three ideas to pitch to larger publications. The professor mentions, during the course of the interview, that many teenagers lose interest in recreational reading during their middle-school years. The journalist picks up on the comment and asks the professor to expand on it. The writer then poses several follow-up questions such as:

- What should parents look for when they buy books for their kids?
- How do contemporary books like the Harry Potter series compare with the "classics" like the recently revived Nancy Drew mysteries that adults remember?
- How can you tell if a child is ready for a book that deals with serious themes?
- Are comic books bad for kids?

From this conversation come these three shorts:

- "How To Keep Your Kids Reading This Summer"
- "The Five Best Kids' Books of the Year"
- "When Harry (Potter) Met Nancy (Drew)"

The same three story ideas also might spring from a report, issued by experts and reported in the media, that says that the reading skills of American teenagers are rapidly diminishing. The sharp writer, always on the lookout for breakthrough studies conducted by reputable researchers, clips the news story and contacts a credible expert—that same literature professor—for comments. The resulting interview doesn't have to be long because it is tightly focused on ways that parents can reverse a disturbing trend. Depending on the angle that the writer chooses to take, the shorts are appropriate for publications aimed at parents, grandparents, librarians and educators.

Expandable List Articles

One of the article possibilities cited above—"The Five Best Kids' Books of the Year"—could be packaged as a **list article**. Many editors welcome list articles because these features can be expanded or reduced as space allows. As an example, prolific freelance writer Dennis Hensley once created a list of 20 tasks that an airline traveler can accomplish when stranded by an unplanned layover in an airport. He got the idea, as you might guess, when he was delayed for several hours by a flight cancellation. The resulting article reaped multiple sales because it was an evergreen (always in season) and it appealed to a broad audience. But here's the interesting part: One publication that was pressed for space printed 12 tasks that a traveler can accomplish during a layover. Another editor, with even less available space, pruned the list to 10 tasks.

Along these same lines, David Sumner, co-author of this textbook, once had his luggage delayed by more than a day when he was scheduled to

25* Gifts You'll Love to Give and They'll Love to Get! (*or as many as space allows)

Are you tired of giving predictable presents—those ties that blind, cookies that "settle" during shipment, electronic gadgets that supposedly streamline life but clutter closets? Why not consider the following list instead? Some gifts are homemade, others are tailor-made; they range in price from free to inexpensive. But they're all guaranteed to be ones your recipients will never forget!

For Teens Who Like to Do Their Own Thing

Treat them to an inexpensive night on the town. Buy a gift certificate for their favorite fast food (Pizza? Pasta? Burgers?), then add a couple of movie passes. Top it off with coupons for an after-the-show treat at the local ice cream shop.

For the College Student

Buy (or make) an oversized laundry bag; stencil his name on the front in bold letters. Fill the bag with bottles or boxes of detergent, fabric softener and bleach. Include a roll of quarters for the washing machine and a couple of magazines to help him pass the time while his jeans tumble dry.

For New Grandparents Who Live Out of State

Buy a small photo album and label it "A Day in the Life of . . . ." (Fill in the baby's name.) Record on film all the events in baby's typical day, such as taking her morning bubble bath, eating breakfast, walking in the park, playing, greeting daddy after work, being rocked to sleep. Plan to replace the photos a couple of times a year as baby becomes more active and her "day" is more eventful. Variation: Although not as portable (grandparents never leave home without their snapshots), a videotape with baby as the star makes an animated alternative to this gift.

For the Office Exchange Gift

Make sure your coworker's coffee breaks at home are more leisurely than the ones you share at work. Choose a pretty mug with an appropriate message, then add a small bag of flavored coffee or tea, a homemade coffee cake and a book.

For Adult Children Who Have Left the Nest

Buy an address book and enter the names, phone numbers, addresses, birthdays and anniversary dates of family and friends. The book will save you from sounding too motherly ("Don't forget to send Uncle Fred a card next Tuesday!") and help them assume responsibility for writing thank-you notes, building a Christmas card file, compiling invitation lists and remembering friends on special occasions.

For Young Parents

Offer to keep their children overnight once a month for a year. Arrange to pick up your young houseguests in mid-afternoon so Mom can relax as she prepares for her evening out (or in) with her favorite "date."

---

make a speech at a major convention. He was forced to give his talk in the same casual clothes he had worn on the flight the previous night. But, he told his audience, he came away from the experience with a new idea for a short feature: "Ten Must-Have Items For Your Carry-On Bag."

List articles usually follow a two-part formula. First, you need an introductory paragraph that sets up the article by explaining the purpose of the list. Since these articles are straightforward, the introduction should be brief and to the point. Second, the list is presented in either bulleted or numbered format. For example, "25 Gifts You'll Love to Give and They'll Love to Get!"[1] is an evergreen article that its author has sold several times. A version of the story has appeared in a December issue of a women's magazine, a digest-sized publication and even in a holiday idea book. The article qualifies as a short because an editor can easily trim the text to fit any space that is available—a column, a half-page, a full page. (See the sidebar for an abbreviated version of the article.) The wise writer who recognizes that an article might be marketable more than once takes care to sell only **first rights** to a publication. We'll clarify copyright questions in Chapter 22.

Personal-Experience Shorts

Some editors solicit short items pulled from a writer's personal experience. These anecdotes are often either humorous or inspirational, but not complex enough to support a full-length feature. They have maximum impact on readers when the author distills the "message" rather than dilutes it with a lot of description and background information.

Good examples of inspirational shorts are the little stories contained in a standing column in *Guideposts* called "His Mysterious Ways." (Examples of these are posted on the magazine's Web site.) Each anecdote comes from the writer's personal experience, recounts an incident that cannot be explained by logic and has the capacity to raise gooseflesh on readers. At the center of each story is an unforeseen turn of events that skeptics would call "luck," and religious believers would call a "God thing." For example, an unpredicted shower drenches a burning house where young children are sleeping unattended. No one else in the neighborhood experiences the rain, and the pavement around the house remains perfectly dry.

As popular as "His Mysterious Ways" is with readers, the column almost didn't get off the ground. Editors at *Guideposts* kept rejecting "miracle stories" because they didn't fit into the magazine's mission to equip readers with practical tools to help them face and overcome life's inevitable obstacles. After all, a reader who struggles with a problem similar to the one recapped in the magazine cannot expect a duplicate miracle to provide a happy ending. Only after these "miracle" submissions continued to pour into their offices did the editors decide to group them under the common label of "His Mysterious Ways" and offer them as unexplainable stories of faith. That was years ago. Since then, the column has evolved into a mainstay of the magazine and typically tops the list of subscribers' favorite features.[2] Its popularity supports the notion that people like "short reads" that stir emotions.

Recycling Anecdotes

One of the best places to look for shorts is within articles you've already written. Most stories contain anecdotes, and many anecdotes can stand on their own merit. The editors at *Reader's Digest* survey scores of magazines in search of stories within stories that meet the *Digest's* high publication standards. For example, a 2,000-word profile on perennial television host Dick Clark, published in *The Saturday Evening Post*, yielded a 100-word nugget about how Clark quietly integrated the popular "American Bandstand" TV show several decades ago. The anecdote probably caught the eye of the *Digest* editors partly because it was an interesting little story tied to a national issue (discrimination) and partly because the average age of the *Digest* readers is 49, and people who are 49 grew up watching Dick Clark and, possibly, "American Bandstand." The lesson here is that demographics are important, even when combing your copy for small, salable blurbs.

Anecdotes don't have to tell about celebrities to enjoy a second life as a short. Some publications compile stories about non-celebrities under a title that clearly identifies the common element that unifies the content. *Reader's Digest* compartmentalizes 100-word stories into columns with labels such as "Humor in Uniform," "Life in the United States," "All in a Day's Work" and "Laughter, the Best Medicine." The *Digest* encourages contributors to submit their anecdotes to the editors by typing them directly onto its Web site.

Typically, magazines solicit submissions about people who reflect the magazine's readers. A publication geared to runners will welcome blurbs about interesting people who share that passion. A magazine for career women may look for anecdotes that fit into a monthly feature called "Timeout" that offers ideas on how to reduce job stress. A magazine for teachers solicits brief stories about educators who have developed creative ways to deal with universal classroom challenges.

Beyond the Blurb

The longest short is the one-page story that, depending on the publication's format, usually contains no more than 500 to 600 words. The one-pager is a challenge to write because the author has to prune every unnecessary word from the text. This means the article that emerges can have only one focus. If it's a profile article, it zeros in on a lone aspect of the subject's life; if it's an essay, it centers on a single key point. A one-page travel article would never try to embrace the entire city of Nashville but might transport readers to a historic pub in Music City where wannabe singers take turns at an open microphone.

Regardless of whether you want to submit 50-word jokes or 600-word articles to a publication, the steps that lead to success are the same.

- **Do your homework.** Survey several publications and determine if they use short items. Pay particular attention to the table of contents, where you'll find a listing of departments and standing features. When a magazine such as *Reader's Digest* lists a standing feature called "Humor in Uniform," you know the editors are obligated to come up with a certain number of military-related anecdotes every month. If you have a good story that is linked to the armed forces, you just might earn a byline. Tip: Review back issues to ensure these departments and features are present in every edition.
- **Analyze several short items.** What seems to be the preferred length? Are they clustered under a common title? Do they carry bylines? If so, do the bylines belong to regular contributors or members of the staff? In other words, does a newcomer have a chance of breaking into print?

- **Keep up on trends.** The best shorts are timely items. Often editors cluster nuggets that are linked to trends, new research, innovations and recently released statistics.
- **Keep your eye on the calendar.** Editors love to drop in seasonal shorts: "Three Causes of Holiday Depression" (December); "Quiz: How Compatible Are You?" (February/Valentine's Day); "A Checklist for Winterizing Your Garden" (September). We talk more about seasonal features in Chapter 15.
- **Be patient.** Remember that short items with long shelf lives are always in demand. The problem is that editors aren't always sure when they will have just the right place for them. If an editor tells you he wants to hold your short for possible use in the future, be willing to wait.

When it comes to creating feature material for newspapers and magazines, the smart writer thinks small—at least at first.

Suggested Activities

1. Survey several national magazines and take note of those that publish regional editions. On a map, draw a 50-mile circle around the location of your home and look for five points of interest within that radius. Select the one that is most appealing and write a 300-word story. Submit it to a magazine or a large-city newspaper that publishes a regional edition that includes your location.

2. Take a profile article that you have written and isolate an anecdote that might stand alone as a short. Pare it down to as few words as possible without forfeiting any of its impact.

3. Assuming that your profile article (mentioned above) is at least 1,000 words, rewrite it, cutting its length by at least half.

Shoptalk

Contributing editor: A title sometimes given to writers who frequently write for a publication but are not on staff. Often they earn a higher rate for their work and are assigned to major stories by staff editors.

Editorial packages: A feature article plus its sidebars, graphics and other related elements.

Filler: An item that has little purpose other than to fill space on a page.

First rights: Author gives a publication the right to publish an article the first time; after the article appears in print, ownership of the article returns to the author, who, in turn, can sell "second rights" to another publication.

Gang query: A letter of inquiry, written by a freelancer, that proposes more than one story idea to an editor.

List article: A brief article that contains information presented in a 1-2-3 format.

Masthead: Often positioned near a magazine's table of contents, it lists editors and other personnel affiliated with a publication.

Regional correspondent: A writer responsible for generating articles from a specific geographic region of the country. These contributors live in the region and usually work out of their homes.

Short: Interesting, informative and intentional nonfiction items of various lengths.

Endnotes

1. Holly G. Miller, "25 Gifts You'll Love to Give and They'll Love to Get" was first published in *Today's Christian Woman* (November-December, 1995), 86-87.

2. Van Varner, *His Mysterious Ways* (New York: Ballantine Books, 1988), xi.

Chapter 12
Picture This: The Profile Article

A well-balanced profile article gives readers an honest look at an interesting person. Strategies for gathering fresh material include shadowing the person for a day and asking probing questions of friends and associates. This chapter shows you:

- Three approaches to profile articles
- The benefits of conducting support interviews
- Ways to recycle profiles
- How to use a profile to put a "face" on an issue

Wander through the portrait gallery of any major museum and you'll see familiar faces—former presidents, world leaders, members of royalty and high society—smiling (or glowering) down at you from their gilded frames. You recognize them, of course, but just barely. The portraits are likenesses of people on their very best days. Gone are the wrinkles, blemishes and other imperfections. The artist has thickened the hair, whitened the teeth, bobbed the nose, flattened the ears and trimmed the tummy. Misty colors and soft brushstrokes have embellished the gifts of nature and eliminated the ravages of time. If the subject of the portrait had a well-known flaw in character or appearance, the artist has either ignored it or downplayed it. The womanizer gazes adoringly at his wife; the undersized warrior appears larger than life on his majestic steed; the matron with the ample hips looks positively svelte with her precious children filling her lap.

You ask: Were these people *really* as attractive in life as they appear on canvas? Answer: Probably not. Wealthy folk throughout history have spent hundreds of thousands of dollars to have artists portray them as they *wished* they had looked in their prime.

See No Evil, Speak No Evil

Some editors prefer profile articles that are written versions of these see-no-evil portraits. Their magazines publish only favorable likenesses of people, taking care to eliminate all mention of human shortcomings and failures. If a profiled person has had a well-publicized problem that the publication must acknowledge or lose all credibility, the writer downplays the problem with carefully chosen words. Inappropriate behavior becomes "playfulness," run-ins with the law shrink to "skirmish" status, multiple marriages emerge as "broken relationships" and periods of drug abuse euphemistically are downgraded to times of "unwise lifestyle choices." If these esteemed icons smoked marijuana in their college days, they certainly didn't inhale it.

Writers who write these profiles and editors who publish them don't intend to be dishonest or mislead readers. They merely subscribe to the old advice: If you can't say something nice about a person, don't say anything at all. They aren't in the business of criticizing or even scrutinizing their subjects. The results of their efforts are profile articles that put subjects on pedestals for readers to admire. These stories are most at home on the pages of fan magazines, religious publications, internal newsletters and other **sponsored periodicals**.

Superficial as they are, idealized profiles can be dangerous to a magazine, to its readers and writers and even to the personalities who serve as subjects for stories that gush. Here are three reasons why overwritten profiles are not as harmless as they may seem.

First, most readers are savvy enough to know that no one is perfect, and they question the honesty and ethics of a publication that perpetuates such a myth. The public will not take the magazine seriously and may categorize its writers as lightweights. If the publication is sponsored, the writers risk acquiring the label of **spin doctors**.

Second, readers who believe the pumped-up portraits that they read often feel in awe of the people who are profiled. These readers measure themselves against the featured personalities and, compared to perfection, they always come up short. A working mother feels guilty when she reads about the super mom who successfully balances home, career, family, friends and community service. The high school student loses self-esteem when she reads about the teen-age rock star who manages to get great grades, wears a size 4 and just signed a movie contract.

Third, people who fall off pedestals sometimes never recover from the injuries they sustain to their reputations. This is especially true of highly visible Christians who too often are depicted by religious/inspirational magazines as downright flawless. If the personality slips and makes a human error, the Christian world is devastated and the secular world responds with a loud "Aha!" The "sin" may be as common as getting a divorce or as innocent as an inspirational vocalist "crossing over" to the pop charts. Whatever the problem, the blame rests less with the personality and more with the publication for holding her to an unattainable standard of perfection.

Black Plus White Equals Gray

As a writer, you are not writing to please your subject; you are writing to inform your reader. For that reason, many editors stipulate they don't want portraits, but "warts-and-all" profiles. This simply means a story that is a written version of a black-and-white news photo that hasn't been "touched up" in the darkroom or manipulated on the computer screen. It's an honest representation of the person, flaws (warts) and all. Ironically, when black (a personality's negative qualities) mixes with white (the person's positive qualities) the result may be gray, but it certainly isn't neutral or bland. The profiled person seems normal, real and worthy of readers' respect.

Striking the right balance between a person's positive and negative qualities requires skill. Just as the writer and editor want to avoid elevating the personality to sainthood, so do they want to avoid discrediting or embarrassing the person. The goal is honesty, but the transition from creating word portraits to crafting word photographs can be clumsy at first. The tendency is for writers to mention one human shortcoming and then tout five attributes to offset it. Some writers attempt to humanize their subjects by passing off a positive quality as a negative one. For example, "He admits to being overly generous with his family" or, "She can't say 'no' to a good cause, especially if it involves children."

Tuning into a subject's "humanity" is as simple as using your power of observation and asking the right questions during the interview portion of your research. **Shadowing** the person for a day provides insights into the way he relates to co-workers, family, friends and even pets. Does he dominate conversations? Is he shy? Formal? Are people relaxed when they are in his company? Ride in his car with him. Does he drive too fast? Is he often late for appointments? Is he constantly on his cell phone? What kinds of music does he like? (Check out his tape or CD collection.) Take note of his personal space (office, home, dorm room). Is it messy? What pictures hang on the walls? Do you see any indication of a hobby—a motorcycle helmet, tennis racquet, computer games, guitar? As your tape recorder captures his words, your notebook becomes a receptacle of colorful, but unspoken, details.

If your interview includes a meal in a restaurant, how does he treat the waitress? What does he order? Is he watching his weight? Is he a vegetarian? Does he have a weakness for hot-fudge sundaes? These are the interesting observations that you can explore in your conversation with him. If he's on a diet—and who isn't?—he is on common ground with a lot of your readers. If he admits to an addiction to chocolate, there's another connection.

Connect the Dots

During a formal interview (as opposed to the casual conversation that takes place during the shadowing experience), follow up on the various clues that you've gathered. If you spotted a guitar in the corner of his office and you know that country music dominates the CD collection in his car, ask about it. Your reward might be a great anecdote about how he once spent a summer in Nashville trying to make it as a studio musician. By including the story in your article you let readers know that your subject has had lofty dreams and has experienced disappointments. With one brief anecdote you succeed in humanizing him and making a link with your readers.

In "Almost Famous," a semi-autobiographical film by journalist-turned-screenwriter Cameron Crowe, a teenager attaches himself to a rock group for the purpose of writing a profile article for *Rolling Stone* magazine. In the course of the story, 15-year-old "William" (played by actor Patrick Fugit) comes of age as a person and as a writer. His first draft is a superficial "portrait" that the editors at *Rolling Stone* promptly reject. His next attempt, an honest portrayal based on personal observations, several days of shadowing and a variety of interviews, earns praise and launches Cameron/William on a successful career. The published article exposes the band members' flaws but also captures their strengths. They emerge as very real and likeable characters.

If you fear that the material you are gathering for a profile article por-

Just Say No

Sometimes the people you profile will assume that, of course, they will have the opportunity to "preview" your article before you send it to the editor. How do you respond to such a request? Just say no, politely. Their intentions are probably good—"I can check for accuracy," they might say—but the results can be disastrous. What if they have second thoughts about a certain comment they made? What if they add and delete words? Tamper with your descriptions? Rearrange your commas? Suppose they decide they don't like the story at all and insist that you not publish it? A profile article is *your* interpretation of a person whom you have studied. It is not a joint project of interviewer and interviewee.

Here's the rule: When a person agrees to be interviewed, he is saying that he trusts your skills as a writer. If he persists in his request to see your story before publication, assure him that:

- As you organize the material you may come across information that needs clarification—statistics, proper names, unfamiliar terms. If this happens, you will call and read him those parts of the article that you question. This is a check for accuracy, not a request for approval.
- Most magazines employ fact checkers whose job is to telephone everyone quoted in a story and double check names, titles, dates and quotations. So, if he is concerned about accuracy, this serves as another safety net.

Exception to the rule: If you write for a sponsored publication that an organization's public relations staff produces, your article will be routinely routed to the interviewee for his approval. In this situation you are not an objective journalist; you are a member of the organization's publication team and your message is subject to certain controls.

---

trays your subject as too good to be true, ask a couple of questions that are likely to bring out the person's more human side. Some examples:

- If you could rewrite your life story up to the present moment, what part would you delete?
- If someone gave you a lot of money and the only stipulation was that you had to spend it on yourself, what would you buy?
- What's your greatest regret?

Same Photo Subject, Different Camera Angles

One of the major differences between a "portrait" article and a warts-and-all "photograph" kind of story is the number of interviews that the writer conducts. Imagine watching a full-length motion picture that was shot from one angle with one camera that never zoomed in for close-ups or panned the room to show the person in the context of the environment. This would be the ultimate "talking head"—boring, one-dimensional and predictable.

An article based on a single interview with the profiled person can be equally tiresome and superficial. Readers see the individual from only one perspective—his own. Even if the person is candid, witty and wonderfully quotable, he can't make up for the absence of other points of view. The article may be good, but probably won't be *as* good as it could be if you included insights from other sources.

By conducting **support interviews** with a variety of people who know your subject, you move your camera back and forth and up and down. In short, you capture your subject from different angles. How many support interviews are enough? That depends on your time constraints, the availability of sources, the projected word count of your article and the number of personality traits you hope to explore. Beware: It's possible to talk with too many sources and end up with a collection of disjointed comments. Also avoid support sources that give only "cheerleader quotes" such as "she's a wonderful person" without any insight into your subject's character or personality. The key is to choose your interviewees carefully and strive for quality rather than quantity. If an interview subject fails to bring something fresh to the profile, you shouldn't feel any obligation to include the comments.

When identifying support interviews, go back to the idea of the roving camera. You'll probably want at least one close-up. The person's spouse or some other member of the family can best provide this angle. If you want a "view from the top," set up an interview with the person's boss. If you want to focus on the person's hobbies or interests, talk with her tennis partner, roommate or best friend.

Support interviews usually don't require a lot of time, and you sometimes can conduct them on the telephone or, in a pinch, by trading e-mails. (For the most part, we don't recommend electronic interviews.) This doesn't mean support interviews aren't important or don't deserve careful planning. You don't want responses that are generic affirmations or the cheerleader quotes mentioned earlier. ("She's a nice person." "He's very generous." "Everyone likes her." "He has a great sense of humor.") The only way to get past such one-size-fits-all comments is with tightly focused questions that invite anecdotal answers. ("Recall for me the moment when you realized this was the man you would like to marry." "Describe your impression when he arrived at your office for the job interview.")

Some veteran profile writers like to conduct their support interviews first, then schedule their shadowing experience, and, last of all, sit down for their in-depth, one-on-one sessions with their primary subjects. This makes sense and can save time. Conversations with secondary sources often uncover routine information that might have eaten up valuable minutes if you had to gather it during your in-depth interview. ("How long have you been married?" "How old are your children?" "Where did you get your undergraduate degree?")

More important, secondary sources and the shadowing experience often result in great questions that you otherwise might not have considered. A best friend might tell you a funny story that you can recount and get a reaction from your primary interviewee. A wife might tick off several awards that her husband won, whereas the husband would be too modest to mention them without your prodding. You can play one person's comments against another's and end up with a humorous he-said/she-said kind of anecdote.

Developing the Photograph

As an example, let's say you are writing a profile of a prominent man in your community. Before you sit down for your in-depth interview with him, you spend some time talking with his wife of many years. As part of your conversation you ask her to recall their first date. She supplies a colorful anecdote, complete with lots of details. Of course, the story is told from her point of view. A few days later you sit face to face with the husband, and you want to hear his side of the story. The dialogue might go something like this:

Interviewer: "Your wife tells me that your first date was a disaster because you neglected to warn her that you were taking her to a football game . . . in the rain. She says that she spent the first half wrapped in a plastic trash bag and the second half under the bleachers. True story?"

Interviewee: "Yeah; she thought we were going to see a play, but at the last minute a friend gave me tickets to the Bears' season opener. The weather was brutal. But it was a great game, and the Bears won in the fourth quarter."

Resulting article excerpt: Their relationship got off to an icy start when he swapped front-row theater tickets for a couple of passes to a Bears-49ers game. The soft drizzle turned into a Chicago-style downpour and caused her to seek refuge first in a plastic trash bag and then under the bleachers. "We couldn't leave," he explains, adding as justification: "The score was tied, third down and goal to go." The Bears got the win, she got the flu and he got the cold shoulder for two weeks. They now have season tickets . . . to the theater.

Obviously the resulting excerpt required a bit of extra research on the part of you, the interviewer. Since the couple's first date occurred many years ago, both the husband and wife were fuzzy in their recollection of the facts. You compensated for this by asking a lot of follow-up questions and then by visiting the library and finding on microfilm the *Chicago Tribune*'s account of the Bears' season opener. You scribbled down a few notes about the weather and the final play of the game and blended these details with the memories that your interviewees supplied. A great little story emerged.

File for Future Reference

If there is a negative side to collecting strong comments and anecdotes from a variety of sources, it's the fact that you can't include all the material in a single profile article. Most editors don't want a chronological re-hashing of a person's life. Instead, they expect you to weave in just enough background to give context to the interesting and timely focus of your profile. This requires you to sift through your notes and transcripts (if you taped your interviews) and select the information that fits the article's focus and temporarily set aside the material that doesn't make the cut.

But don't throw anything away. Chances are, you'll be able to fold your interviewee's "discarded" comments into any number of future stories.

Here's how it works: Say you research and write a profile article about a student who just completed a summer internship in the White House press office. Although you include some background—she's a junior, majoring in political science and hopes to go to law school after graduation—the focus of your story is on the eight weeks that the student spent in the West Wing. The other material you gathered, such as the way she found out about the internship in the first place, doesn't fit the focus and never makes it to print.

Later, you tackle a how-to article assignment (Chapter 14) that offers tips on how to land dream jobs in a tight economy. Your primary interviewee is the director of the campus career center, who emphasizes that internships attract a lot of attention on résumés. To answer the logical question about how students discover internship opportunities, you pull from your files the comments from the student who beat out the competition and spent a summer in the White House. Whereas she dominated the profile article, she now plays a supporting role in the how-to article and occupies only a paragraph or two. Her contribution is important, though, because she provides an anecdote that illustrates a key point.

The Profile as a Hook

A profile also is a great way to put a "face" on an important issue and cause readers to get involved and care about a topic they might otherwise dismiss. Many magazine and newspaper writers use this tactic in preparing in-depth articles about complex issues. For some journalists who do this, their reward has been the lofty Pulitzer Prize for feature writing. (The full texts of Pulitzer-winning feature articles from 1995 to the present are available online at www.pulitzer.org. They also are compiled in an anthology produced by Iowa State Press.) Some examples:

- Realizing that conservative Midwesterners might find the topic of AIDS uncomfortable in 1987, writer Jacqui Banaszynski focused her three-part series on a likeable, articulate man who was willing to "go public" with his AIDS diagnosis. Banaszynski shadowed him from his Minnesota farm to his various doctor appointments to his eventual deathbed. The journey took months, but in the end, readers of the *St. Paul Pioneer Press* learned about the dreaded disease by walking *through* it with one of its victims. Result: Pulitzer Prize, 1988.
- Many subscribers to *The Wall Street Journal* might not be sympathetic to affirmative action and might be unaware of the struggles that bright students face in attempting to break out of the ghetto. Reporter Ron Suskind spent months shadowing an inner-city teenager who was determined to rise above his environment and attend a top-tier East Coast university and become an engineer. The profile was so effective that readers responded with scholarship funds to benefit the worthy student. Suskind won the 1995 Pulitzer Prize and later turned his research into a best-selling book.

Of course, not all profiles have the potential to change lives, raise money, win Pulitzer Prizes and lead to book contracts. Some articles are merely meant to provide a quick snapshot of a person for the purpose of entertaining or informing readers.

Say "Cheese" — Fast!

The New Yorker invented the term "profile" with its in-depth portraits of 1920s' personalities. When *The New Yorker* celebrated its 75th anniversary, the editor, David Remnick, collected some of the magazine's best profile articles and created a 530-page anthology called *Life Stories*. In his introduction, Remnick admitted that writing a great profile is difficult, and writing a profile suitable for *The New Yorker* sometimes requires months or even years to produce.[1] The problem is, of course, that not every writer—or publication—has the luxury of such open-ended assignments. Also, not every writer—or publication—is interested in producing comprehensive life stories. The result? "We are awash in pieces calling themselves profiles that are about the inner thoughts of some celebrity; more often than not they are based on half-hour interviews and the parameters set down by a vigilant publicist," notes Remnick.[2]

He may be right. But "quick takes" (we call them **snapshots**) are mainstays of some magazines and are very popular with some readers. Why else do magazines such as *People* and *Entertainment Weekly* boast large circulations? Why else are the inside front covers of *USA Weekend* and *Parade* among the best-read pages of those Sunday tabloids?

A snapshot profile can range from a one-paragraph blurb to an article that fills a single page of a publication. The story focuses on an interesting aspect of an interesting person's life. It might be little more than an update or an announcement or a breezy comment about a timely issue. In the case of a celebrity, it might result from a half-hour interview that a "vigilant publicist" has set up and monitored.

But all snapshots don't have to be lightweight efforts with limited journalistic value. A writer can assemble a series of snapshots into an "album" and publish the results as a **round-up article**. As an example, *Marriage Partnership* magazine won a first place award from the Evangelical Press Association in 2003 for a round-up article called "Happily Even After." The writer, Paul Kortepeter, wrote short profiles (about 500 words each) on four married couples who had stayed together and were "happily even after" experiencing a variety of hardships.

Other round-up articles composed of several short profiles might be:

- Five entrepreneurs offer advice on how to start a home-based business.
- Three international students tell about the obstacles they overcame to travel to America to attend college.

- Four female members of Congress explain what it's like to be "Ladies of the House."

Round-up articles can give comprehensive coverage to a topic by including various points of view from people who see the issue through a range of lenses.

The Camera Never Lies

A profile article can take many shapes and forms, and the versatile—and marketable—writer is able to tune into a publication's style and produce the kind of profile that the editors and readers want. As different as portrait, photograph and snapshot profiles are, they should share two characteristics: accuracy and truthfulness.

That said, a writer has flexibility in deciding which quotations to integrate into the story, which characteristics to emphasize, how many details to include and what kind of tone to adopt. Those decisions will determine if the profile emerges as a quick take, a positive glimpse or an in-depth study. Whatever the result, the article should be based on honest reporting because a camera never lies.

Suggested Activities

1. Even if you've already seen the film "Almost Famous," watch it again. This time, tune into the concept of the portrait article vs. the warts-and-all photograph article. How did the young writer use his observations? What did he do right? Wrong?

2. Shadow a person for a day. Meet with her at breakfast and follow her through her workday or class schedule. Leave your tape recorder at home; take numerous notes about how she interacts with people, what she eats, how she drives, the music she listens to, her quirks and habits. From your notes, write a couple of anecdotes to fold into your profile article.

3. Create three profiles from one. First, research and write a profile article that resembles a black and white news photograph. Second, revisit the profile, delete all negative aspects and turn it into a portrait article. Finally, take an excerpt of about 300 tightly focused words and produce a "snapshot" of the person.

4. Subtly change the tone of your profile. If you've referred to your interviewee by her last name throughout the body of your article (Smith), change all references to her first name (Mary). If, when you've quoted your subject, you've used a basic attribution (said Mary), substitute more descriptive verbs (explained Mary, joked Mary). And, while you're reworking the attributions, switch them to present tense (insists Mary, recommends Mary). You can further "warm" your text by adding a few words about Mary's appearance, her body language, her voice and her surroundings. Reread the resulting story and note how the tone is different.

Shoptalk

Round-up article: An article for which a writer solicits several people's points of view on a common topic; often packaged as separate mini-profiles.

Shadowing: A research technique that has the writer accompanying a subject as he goes about his day. The writer observes the subject in a variety of circumstances.

Snapshot: A tightly focused, brief look at a person.

Spin doctors: Writers and public relations people who manipulate information to support their point of view.

Sponsored periodical: An in-house newsletter or magazine that is produced by an organization for its employees, clients, customers or friends. Its goal usually is to promote understanding of the organization and to communicate the organization's goals and views.

Support interview: A supporting source of information; a person who adds a different point of view to a story.

Endnotes

1. David Remnick, *Life Stories* (New York: Random House, 2000), ix.
2. Ibid. xi.

Chapter 13
Real-Life Dramas and Stories

Everyone loves a good story that involves suspense, drama or humor. Publications always look for interesting stories about everyday people and writers who can tell those stories. This chapter teaches you how to recognize, construct and write these real-life stories, which often end up on movie screens. This chapter discusses:

- Characteristics of a good story
- Common plots
- Tips on telling the story

A 96-year-old Fort Wayne, Ind., woman tried skydiving after she visited her son in New York and watched a parachuting team of skydivers. Beatrice Schleinkofer went to a jump school in Gardiner, N.Y., watched a 30-minute instructional video, suited up and climbed into a plane. By the time she hit the ground, she became one of the oldest living skydivers in the United States. First reported in *The Fort Wayne Journal Gazette*, the Associated Press version spread quickly throughout the nation.

Real-life dramas tell true stories about people accomplishing something challenging or dramatic. They answer the basic question: What happened? Real-life dramas answer not by telling about stories; they tell the story. They differ from profiles or biographies in that they focus on specific events in people's lives—not on the people themselves.

Don McKinney, a former editor with *McCall's* and *The Saturday Evening Post*, says these real-life drama stories don't usually make national headlines. "In most cases, they are things that happen to ordinary people in out-of-the-way places and get reported on, if at all, in local newspapers. These are the stories you should be watching for, and when you learn of one . . . then fire off a query. Your chances of a sale are excellent."

McKinney says he published hundreds of these stories during his years at *McCall's*. "Some of these writers were inexperienced in writing for magazines, and their first tries were pretty shaggy. But because they had good stories to tell, we wanted very much to help them succeed. We gave them detailed rewrite instructions, talked to them a number of times about their problems and helped them through several rewrites."[1]

This genre of writing has historical roots in the 1960s when *Esquire, Harper's, The New Yorker* and *Rolling Stone* pioneered "the **New Journalism**." Later called "**literary nonfiction**," its distinguishing characteristic was the use of fiction techniques in nonfiction reporting. Led by Tom Wolfe, Hunter Thompson, Truman Capote, Gay Talese, Joan Didion and others, these writers took stories about people and reported them using the fiction techniques of **narrative, dialogue, description** and **scene-by-scene reporting.**

For example, Tom Wolfe wrote *The Right Stuff*, which chronicled the story of the seven Mercury astronauts who were the first Americans launched into space. Wolfe's story later became a movie by the same name, which won four Academy Awards in 1983. Pulitzer Prize-winning author Tracy Kidder took these story-telling techniques further with his books *Among School Children* and *Among Friends*. His first book chronicled a difficult year in the life of a third-grade schoolteacher, while *Among Friends* told about the year-long tribulations of two men living in a Massachusetts nursing home.

The **plot** of a good story looks like this: You introduce a main character (or characters) with enough admirable qualities to attract the sympathy of readers. You introduce a situation that throws an obstacle or conflict in the person's path. You give your character a possible solution and show him trying to reach that solution. This same type of structure forms the plot for thousands of movies and novels. If you want to learn how to write true-life stories, then watch movies based on real events. Or read novels and carefully study the techniques that the writers use. Most novels have a lot of action, dialogue and character development.

These characteristics help you recognize a good story and guide your questioning when you are interviewing people and building a story. Here are titles of true-life stories from some magazines:

"A haven for Molly: How a baby girl abandoned on a rock at birth found a happy home with a loving family" *(Good Housekeeping)*

"Hamilton takes command: In 1775, Alexander Hamilton's bravery under fire brought him to the attention of Gen. George Washington—and to the threshold of greatness" *(Smithsonian)*

"Dr. Ben Carson: Top surgeon's life-and-death struggle with prostate cancer" *(Ebony)*

"Does anyone know I'm here? For two days she was trapped at the bottom of an abandoned mine shaft" *(Guideposts)*

The real-life drama can have a chronological span ranging from hours to years. Jon Franklin, a two-time Pulitzer Prize-winning feature writer, explains how to write these kinds of stories in his book *Writing for Story*. His book contains the two Pulitzer Prize-winning stories he wrote as a reporter for *The Baltimore Sun*. The first, "Mrs. Kelly's Monster," occurs within a few hours while a doctor operates on Mrs. Kelly to remove a life-threatening brain tumor (see end of this chapter). His other prize-winning feature, "The Ballad of Ole Man Peters," spans more than 50 years as an elementary-school dropout fights to overcome his poverty and lack of education. Eventually, Mr. Peters earns a master's degree, learns five languages and becomes a respected academic librarian.[2]

Characteristics of a Good Story

A good story has four characteristics. First, it has a sympathetic main character or characters. Good stories are about people. Second, it has a plot. That means the main character has to confront and overcome an obstacle or problem. Third, it has a resolution, which means the central character solves the problem. And fourth, it has time and place—it begins and ends at specific times in specific places. Let's look at each of these characteristics.

Main Character

The best stories tell about something that happened to one or two people, not to a group of people. The best stories also focus on sympathetic characters—people who are easy to like because of their admirable qualities. Good writers know how to develop their characters. They ask questions that reveal admirable qualities such as courage, honesty or persistence, then they display these qualities in their stories.

Does that mean you can't write a good story about bad people? Not at all, but it's more difficult. Truman Capote was an author of several novels when he wrote his first nonfiction book *In Cold Blood,* which chronicled the murder of a Kansas farm family by two itinerant drifters. His best-selling book was one of the pioneers of the "New Journalism" and later became a movie. Capote spent hundreds of hours interviewing the two murderers during their five years on death row prior to their executions. His compelling character development in this story revealed their deranged lives and at least gave the reader some sense of why they did what they did.

A good story should also focus on specific events in a person's life. It isn't a profile. *Guideposts* advises prospective contributors: "Don't try to tell an entire life story in a few pages. Focus on one specific happening in a person's life. The emphasis should be on one individual. Bring in as few people as possible so that the reader's interest stays with the dominant character." Stories about one or two people are also easier to report than stories about groups.

Plot

The deepest, oldest conflicts are few and simple: We struggle against nature, we struggle against ourselves, and we struggle against each other. No one enjoys a saccharine-sweet story that is all goodness and light because we know that's not the way life is. On the other hand, no one enjoys a story full of suffering and evil that ends in sadness. We look for realism but also hope for redemption. The conflict between the way things are and the way things ought to be creates the most compelling and powerful stories.

Jon Franklin describes this problem or conflict that the central characters overcome as a "**complication**." Another word is simply "plot." The plot drives the story's action by motivating the central characters. The plot may be a problem, accident, illness, failure or inspirational challenge faced by the central character.

To create a story with literary value, a problem must meet two criteria. First, it must be a basic problem that everyone can relate to. "Basic" in this sense means related to issues that everyone faces: love and hate, life and death, sickness and health, joy and sadness, deprivation and abundance.

"You can write about someone who has a peculiar problem. Not everyone has to have that particular problem, but the reader must identify with the dilemma itself or what it does to the person's family," says New York-based writer Judith Newman.[3]

The second criterion for a good complication is that it must matter enough to the central character that he or she is willing to work hard and fight to overcome it. That means a major problem, not a minor problem.

A broken burner on your stove is a complication. If you have other working burners, or enough money to go out and eat, then it's not a basic problem because it doesn't threaten you with starvation. But suppose you're hiking in the wilderness more than 50 miles from any store, and a bear steals all of your food. That's a basic complication because you're threatened with starvation. You must take significant action to overcome that problem.

The bond between a mother and child is basic to humanity; a complication occurs when that bond is threatened by external forces. One popular movie told about a mother's successful rescue of her daughter from a Middle Eastern country. The mother's divorced husband kidnapped the girl and took her to his native country. The bond between mother and daughter was threatened, and the mother made a dramatic effort to rescue her daughter. The complication was both basic and significant.

Resolution

The problem must have a **resolution**, or it won't fly with readers. That sounds harsh because everyone knows that life presents many sad problems without seeming solutions. That's okay because it's life, but readers of articles and books expect resolutions. A "resolution" doesn't necessarily mean a complete or satisfying solution. It simply means the central character figures out a way to deal with it. Sometimes the resolution means the central character simply accepts an unhappy situation in life and decides to move on to other things.

Time and Place

Think of a good story as one with (a) geography and (b) a clock. "Geography" means it's anchored in real dirt that you can find on a map. The events you describe occur in specific towns, states and countries. The true-life drama tells what the main character did as he or she grew up in Dodgeville, went to college in Dayton and started a career in Duluth.

A "clock" means the story began at a particular time and ended at a particular time. The range of time within a good story can range from a few hours to dozens of years. Maybe our hypothetical hero graduated from Dodgeville High School in 1990 and the University of Dayton in 1994 and was elected mayor of Duluth in 1996.

Common Plots

The following six types of plot themes run the risk of over-simplification because life isn't always this neatly divided. They do, however, characterize the most common types of themes found in stories. All good plots serve to create suspense and make the reader wonder how the story will end. These themes, therefore, begin with a type of problem or complication and end with a type of resolution.

"Failure to Success"

Failure and success are common themes to everyone. The only person who never fails is one who never tries. Failure-to-success stories involve aspects of life as diverse as weight loss, finances, education, careers, romance and marriage.

For example: In "The Art of Rebounding," *Men's Health* profiled Randy Pfund, who achieved his lifetime dream of becoming head coach of a professional basketball team. However, after two dismal losing seasons, he was fired as head coach of the Los Angeles Lakers. After spending time re-assessing his life, he decided to try something different. He went into sports management and became a chief executive for the Miami Heat. In the same article, *Men's Health* profiled four others who achieved success after failure: Deborah Norville, television news anchor; Michael Dukakis, former Massachusetts governor and candidate for president; Dan O'Brien, Olympic athlete; and Barry Minkow, who became pastor of a large San Diego church after founding a company and serving time in prison for business fraud.[4]

"Victim to Survivor"

Victims suffer unfairly due to either the negligence or malevolent intent of others. They are the end result of crimes, ignorance or simple accidents. The best victim/survivor stories have specific causes that you can easily describe. It's easier to write about a girl who survives an abusive father and alcoholic mother than one who survives a "deprived childhood." It's easier to write about a man forced by poverty to quit school in the fifth grade than it is one who grew up with "limited educational opportunities."

In a *Reader's Digest* story, for example, Richard and Penni Domikis watched their house in Fredericksburg, Va., burn down one night. That evening was only the beginning of their suffering, however, because they discovered that their insurance company refused to pay for the full cost of rebuilding. The insurance company claimed that an obscure amendment on their original policy meant it didn't have to pay full replacement costs. The couple fought back and won.[5]

"Danger to Safety"

The most common types of "danger to safety" stories involve people who overcome injuries, illnesses, danger and natural disasters. "Lost in the wilderness" and "accident recovery" stories have provided plots for many articles, books and movies. The best healing and recovery stories come from those that defy predictions because the sufferer has a courageous, determined desire to get well and return to normal life. These stories tell not just what happened but how it happened because of the sufferer's inner resolve and courage.

"Chaos to Meaning"

In "chaos to meaning" stories, change occurs inside the central character more than in his or her outward circumstances. These stories are more difficult to write because you have to describe psychological, emotional or spiritual changes. A "chaos to meaning" story might describe how a man or woman finds new meaning in life after losing a spouse to death or divorce. For example, in "The Tender Mercy of Cheryl Kane" (*Good Housekeeping*), a Boston nurse "lost all zest for life . . . the pain was just excruciating," she said. After her middle-aged husband died, Kane found new meaning in life working in a street outreach program giving medical care to the homeless.[6]

"Saving the World"

These "one person can make a difference" stories have a positive, inspirational quality. In this type of problem and resolution, a motivated citizen confronts a social problem and organizes the resources to bring about a solution.

For example, *Reader's Digest, Clarity* and other magazines told the story of a Los Angeles woman who founded "The Garden," a cemetery for babies who were abandoned by their mothers in Dumpsters and trash bins. Debi Faris lobbied the California legislature to pass a "safe haven" law that allows young mothers to give up their babies for adoption without fear of retribution. We reprint a version of this story in Chapter 17.

Another example: *The New Yorker* told the remarkable story of Zell Kravinsky, who grew up as the son of a poor Russian immigrant. After starting out as an inner-city school teacher, he began investing in real estate and eventually earned millions of dollars. After he gave away almost his entire $45 million real estate fortune to charity, he felt he needed to do still more for humanity. So he donated a kidney to a complete stranger—something only 134 other Americans had ever done.[7]

"Love Conquers All"

These stories follow a separation-reunion theme and also have a positive, upbeat tone. They tell the story of the separation and reunion of lovers, siblings, parents and children or even long-lost friends. Dozens of stories have been published about adopted children who located their biological parents after a long search. Many newspapers and magazines have published features telling about couples who were high school sweethearts and, after graduation, married someone else. Many years later, their marriages ended in death or divorce. Then the sweethearts found each other, often with the help of the Internet, and rekindled their romance and married.

Tips on Telling the Stories
Build Suspense

Predictability kills a good story. The problem that you introduce must make the reader wonder how the story will turn out. That's why good mystery novels are bestsellers. People love to get hooked in the **tension** of a "page turner" and will read past midnight to see how it turns out. The plots described earlier naturally introduce an element of unpredictability. For example:

Failure plot: Will he succeed?
Victim plot: Will she survive?

Ten Tips on Telling Stories

1. Interview the central character several times and do supporting interviews with several friends or family members. A one-interview or one-source story never succeeds.
2. People create a story, not places or things. Spend a lot of time developing interview questions that will bring out not only the action, but your subject's values, beliefs and emotions.
3. When you interview your sources, ask them to tell you what they thought and felt at the time, not just what they said and did.
4. Look for the problem, conflict or tension that will provoke readers' curiosity and keep them involved with the story.
5. Record dialogue and quotations accurately by using a tape recorder. Buy one if you don't have one. You will always need it as a writer.
6. Create complex, multi-dimensional characters. Reveal the faults and weaknesses of your heroes and the admirable qualities of your villains. No one is all saint or all sinner.
7. Find the meaning or "take-away" value for readers in your story. What is the point of the piece? Is there a moral engine that drives the story? Make it more than simply a factual chronology.
8. Record little details about the person and the physical surroundings you are writing about. However, use only those details that reveal character and move the story along. Don't include this description just for the sake of exercising your literary talents.
9. Spend time with the people you are writing about where they live and work. Hang around. Don't just depend on interviews in a neutral place. Capture the mood and ambience of their lives.
10. Set your story in its wider context. For example, if a person suffers from a rare disease, then do some research to provide details and context. Include facts, statistics, issues or history about the larger issue that your story involves.

Danger plot: Will he escape?
Chaos plot: Will she discover meaning?

Meg Grant is the West Coast editor at *Reader's Digest* who has edited some of its "Drama in Real Life" stories that appear in every issue. She says, "These stories have to be told in a dramatic way in the same way a fiction writer would. The piece has to be crafted to be suspenseful and not give it all away in the first couple of paragraphs. You have to take the reader on this journey."[8]

Chronicle the Events

As a writer, your job is to lead the reader through the actions the central character has taken to confront and resolve the problem. These events can be physical or psychological; psychological events are more difficult to describe than physical events. Meg Grant edited a *Reader's Digest* story about a kayaker who was lost in the ocean for three days. She says, "There was some question about whether there would be enough sustained action, because basically he sat on a kayak for three days. There wasn't a whole lot that happened. But there was the mental action, the hallucinations, that really carried the piece."

She adds, "Sometimes you have these things happen too fast, and you can't make that work either. You can have a helicopter crash and everything happens in an instant. That wouldn't work as a dramatic narrative because you have to have some time that elapses and some different things that happen."[9]

An important part of that story is the plot point. It's the moment when the central character recognizes what he has to do to solve the problem that he faces. In the story about the insurance company that wouldn't pay for rebuilding the couple's house, Richard and Penni Domikis recognized they needed to take legal action when the company refused to budge. After Debi Faris learned that the county cremated and dumped abandoned babies in a communal grave, she realized that she needed to raise money and find land to create a cemetery for them.

Develop Character

Character development is what novelists do best; most journalists need some practice. To develop character, you must create empathy in the reader for the characters you are writing about. Character development results from several interviews preceded by good preparation. You must not only get your subject to describe what happened; you must ask questions that will bring out her motivating values and beliefs. You must ask her not only what she said and did, but what she thought and felt as these events happened.

Character also is developed through effective and frequent use of dialogue. Dialogue and quotations are not the same. Dialogue is a conversation between two or more people. Monologue, which originates from one person, is what writers normally call "getting quotes." Good quotes are better than no quotes, but conversation between two people really brings a story to life. Conversation also brings out the character of the people whose story you are telling.

Meg Grant says that *Reader's Digest* editors are trying to emphasize more character development in these real-life dramas: "Sometimes the action in these stories received more emphasis than the character development. Part of what we're trying to do now is put the character back in and make the character important. The mental and emotional journey is part of the story." When a freelance writer proposes one of these stories, "We need to know that the writer can focus on one or two characters, get in their heads and sort of go through what they went through psychologically," she says.[10]

Create the Ending

Happy endings are more fun to read than sad endings. Can a true-life story have a sad ending? Many human stories do, and we could all tell a few of our own. The more relevant question is whether readers accept an unhappy ending. Can you publish a story that has an unhappy ending? You can, but it's tricky and you have to handle it skillfully.

Think about yourself. When are you willing to watch a movie with an unhappy ending? Some sad movies end with a sense of closure and resolution, but others simply end. You leave the theater feeling like something was missing.

Readers accept an unhappy ending if it leaves them with a sense of closure, resolution and meaning. The central character learns from his mistakes and decides to move on. The parent accepts the death of a child killed by a drunken driver and finds new meaning in lobbying for stricter drunk-driving laws. The victim of an accident accepts her disability and discovers a new talent that allows her to earn a living.

Just as there is no one right lead, there is no one right ending. If it is a sad ending, the reader knows it could end no other way. Find some image, quote or anecdote that ties together the theme of the story and brings it to an emotionally satisfying ending. The ending should leave the reader feeling satisfied, inspired or moved.

Finally, you can't write a great story until you find a great story. No amount of careful reconstruction and literary polish will make a mundane story fascinating. Watching and listening to everyday conversations is one way to find them. Reading newspapers for short stories you can build from is another way. Beatrice Schleinkofer's story about her sky-diving expedition first appeared as a 500-word newspaper article. An ambitious freelance writer could do several interviews with her and her friends and write a 2,000-word piece about what motivates a 96-year-old woman to try something that most adults wouldn't even think about doing.

Or just do something new and adventurous. When an Indiana student was assigned to write a story like this, she ventured out one Saturday morning, took skydiving lessons and made her first jump that afternoon. She had her story and earned an "A."

Suggested Activities

1. Spend an hour in a public place watching and listening to people. Take notes and record incidents you observe and conversations you hear. Write a 100-to-300-word anecdote based on your observations.

2. Discuss some popular movies based on true stories and which types of plots discussed in this chapter they display.

3. Find examples of real-life stories from newspapers and magazines. Write one-sentence summaries of their plots.

Shoptalk

Complication: The central problem encountered by the central character in a story. The process of solving or overcoming the complication forms the plot for the story.

Description: The depiction of physical details of a character's appearance, dress or environment when the use of these details help move the story forward.

Dialogue: The description of conversation between two people that occurs at a specific time and place. It differs from quotes that simply involve the reporting of later reflections and observations from one person.

Literary nonfiction: The term that eventually replaced "New Journalism." Both refer to the use of fiction techniques in nonfiction reporting.

New Journalism: A writing genre that developed during the 1960s, later called "literary nonfiction." Its distinguishing characteristic is the use of fiction techniques—especially narrative, dialogue, description and scene-by-scene reporting—in nonfiction reporting.

Plot: The problem or complication in a story that the central character(s) must solve. A good plot also creates tension and helps keep the reader interested and involved.

Real-life drama: A true story that describes how a central character encounters a complication that she fights and overcomes.

Resolution: The outcome of the central character's effort to solve the complication, which may involve a happy or sad ending.

Scene-by-scene reporting: A description of the unfolding scenes of a narrative as it moves from one event to another.

Tension: The introduction of an unsolved problem at the beginning of a story that writers use to attract and sustain readers' attention.

Endnotes

1. Don McKinney, *Magazine Writing That Sells* (Cincinnati: Writer's Digest Books, 1993), 104.

2. Jon Franklin, *Writing for Story* (New York: Penguin Books, 1986)

3. Telephone interview, Dec. 11, 2003.

4. Bruce Schoenfeld, "The Art of Rebounding," *Men's Health* (January-February 2003), 114-119.

5. M. Robicheau, "Raked Over the Coals," *Reader's Digest* (November 2002), 124-129.

6. Elizabeth Gehrman, "The Tender Mercy of Cheryl Kane," *Good Housekeeping* (January 2004), 79-83.

7. Ian Parker, "The Gift," *The New Yorker* (Aug. 2, 2004), 54-63.

8. Telephone interview, Nov. 29, 2003.

9. Ibid.

10. Ibid.

Sample Story

A Pulitzer Prize-Winning Feature Story

This story won the inaugural Pulitzer Prize in feature writing in 1979. Jon Franklin, who wrote it for The Baltimore Sun, sat in the observation room while Dr. Thomas Ducker performed life-or-death surgery on Edna Kelly. Note how the story contains all the characteristics discussed in this chapter: suspense, character development, dialogue and a chronological scene-by-scene development that occurs within the span of a few hours. The suspense builds as the outcome remains uncertain until the very end.

For more examples, we recommend www.pulitzer.org, which contains online versions of all Pulitzer Prize-winning stories since 1995. For the best examples of real-life drama stories, look at winners in the "Feature Writing" category.

Mrs. Kelly's Monster
by Jon Franklin

Reprinted with permission of the author and The Tribune Company.

In the cold hours of a winter morning Dr. Thomas Barbee Ducker, chief brain surgeon at the University of Maryland Hospital, rises before dawn. His wife serves him waffles but no coffee. Coffee makes his hands shake.

In downtown Baltimore, on the 12th floor of University Hospital, Edna Kelly's husband tells her goodbye. For 57 years Mrs. Kelly shared her skull with the monster: No more. Today she is frightened but determined.

It is 6:30 a.m.

I'm not afraid to die," she said as this day approached. "I've lost part of my eyesight. I've gone through all the hemorrhages. A couple of years ago I lost my sense of smell, my taste. I started having seizures. I smell a strange odor and then I start strangling. It started affecting my legs, and I'm partially paralyzed.

"Three years ago a doctor told me all I had to look forward to was blindness, paralysis and a remote chance of death. Now I have aneurysms; this monster is causing that. I'm scared to death . . . but there isn't a day that goes by that I'm not in pain, and I'm tired of it. I can't bear the pain. I wouldn't want to live like this much longer."

As Dr. Ducker leaves for work, Mrs. Ducker hands him a paper bag containing a peanut butter sandwich, a banana and two Fig Newtons.

Downtown, in Mrs. Kelly's brain, a sedative takes effect.

Mrs. Kelly was born with a tangled knot of abnormal blood vessels in the back of her brain. The malformation began small, but in time the vessels ballooned inside the confines of the skull, crowding the healthy brain tissue.

Finally, in 1942, the malformation announced its presence when one of the abnormal arteries, stretched beyond capacity, burst. Mrs. Kelly grabbed her head and collapsed. After that the agony never stopped.

Mrs. Kelly, at the time of her first intracranial bleed, was carrying her second child. Despite the pain, she raised her children and cared for her husband.

She began calling it "the monster."

Now, at 7:15 a.m. in operating room eleven, a technician checks the brain surgery microscope and the circulating nurse lays out bandages and instruments. Mrs. Kelly lies still on a stainless steel table.

A small sensor has been threaded through her veins and now hangs in the antechamber of her heart. The anesthesiologist connects the sensor to a 7-foot-high bank of electronic instruments. Oscilloscope waveforms begin to build and break.

Dials swing. Lights flash. With each heartbeat a loudspeaker produces an audible popping sound. The steady pop, pop, popping isn't loud, but it dominates the operating room.

Dr. Ducker enters the O.R. and pauses before the X-ray films that hang on a lighted panel. He carried those brain images to Europe, Canada and Florida in search of advice, and he knows them by heart. Still, he studies them again, eyes focused on the two fragile aneurysms that swell above the major arteries. Either may burst on contact.

The one directly behind Mrs. Kelly's eyes is the most likely to burst, but also the easiest to reach. That's first. The surgeon-in-training who will assist Dr. Ducker places Mrs. Kelly's head in a clamp and shaves her hair. Dr. Ducker checks to make certain the three steel pins of the vise have pierced the skin and press directly against Mrs. Kelly's skull. "We can't have a millimeter slip," he says.

Mrs. Kelly, except for a six-inch crescent of scalp, is draped with green sheets. A rubber-gloved palm goes out and Doris Schwabland, the scrub nurse, lays a scalpel in it. Hemostats snap over the arteries of the scalp. Blood spatters onto Dr. Ducker's sterile paper booties.

It is 8:25 a.m. The heartbeat goes pop, pop, pop, 70 beats a minute, steady.

Today Dr. Ducker intends to remove the two aneurysms, which comprise the most immediate threat to Mrs. Kelly's life. Later, he will move directly on the monster.

It's a risky operation, designed to take him to the hazardous frontiers of neurosurgery. Several experts told him he shouldn't do it at all, that he should let Mrs. Kelly die. But the consensus was that he had no choice. The choice was Mrs. Kelly's.

"There's one chance out of three that we'll end up with a hell of a mess or a dead patient," Dr. Ducker says. "I reviewed it in my own heart and with other people, and I thought about the patient. You weigh what happens if you do it against what happens if you don't do it. I convinced myself it should be done."

Mrs. Kelly said yes. Now Dr. Ducker pulls back Mrs. Kelly's scalp to reveal the dull ivory of living bone. The chatter of the half-inch drill fills the room, drowning the rhythmic pop, pop, pop of the heart monitor. It is 9 o'clock when Dr. Ducker hands the two-by-four-inch triangle of skull to the scrub nurse.

The tough, rubbery covering of the brain is cut free, revealing the soft gray convolutions of the forebrain.

"There it is," says the circulating nurse in a hushed voice. "That's what keeps you working."

It is 9:20. Eventually Dr. Ducker steps back, holding his gloved hands high to avoid contamination. While others move the microscope into place over the glistening brain, the neurosurgeon communes once more with the X-ray films. The heart beats strong, 70 beats a minute, 70 beats a minute. "We're going to have a hard time today," the surgeon says to the X-rays.

Dr. Ducker presses his face against the microscope. His hands go out for an electrified, tweezer-like instrument. The assistant moves in close, taking his position above the secondary eyepieces.

Dr. Ducker's view is shared by a video camera. Across the room a color television crackles, displaying a highly magnified landscape of the brain. The polished tips of the tweezers move into view.

It is Dr. Ducker's intent to place tiny, spring-loaded alligator clips across the base of each aneurysm. But first he must navigate a tortured path from his incision, above Mrs. Kelly's right eye, to the deeply buried Circle of Willis.

The journey will be immense. Under magnification, the landscape of the mind expands to the size of a room. Dr. Ducker's tiny, blunt-tipped instrument travels in millimeter leaps.

His strategy is to push between the forebrain, where conscious thought occurs, and the thumb-like projection of the brain, called the temporal lobe, that extends beneath the temples.

Carefully, Dr. Ducker pulls these two structures apart to form a deep channel. The journey begins at the bottom of this crevasse. The time is 9:36 a.m.

The gray convolutions of the brain, wet with secretions, sparkle beneath the powerful operating theater spotlights. The microscopic landscape heaves and subsides in time to the pop, pop, pop of the heart monitor.

Gently, gently, the blunt probe teases apart the minute structures of gray matter, spreading a tiny tunnel, millimeter by gentle millimeter, into the glistening gray. "We're having trouble just getting in," Dr. Ducker tells the operating room team.

As the neurosurgeon works, he refers to Mrs. Kelly's monster as "the AVM," or arterio-venous malformation.

Normally, he says, arteries force high-pressure blood into muscle or organ tissue. After the living cells suck out the oxygen and nourishment the blood drains into low-pressure veins, which carry it back to the heart and lungs.

But in the back of Mrs. Kelly's brain one set of arteries pumps directly into veins, bypassing the tissue. The unnatural junction was not designed for such a rapid flow of blood, and in 57 years it slowly swelled to the size of a fist. Periodically it leaked drops of blood and torrents of agony. Now the structures of the brain are welded together by scar tissue and, to make his tunnel, Dr. Ducker must tease them apart again. But the brain is delicate.

The screen of the television monitor fills with red.

Dr. Ducker responds quickly, snatching the broken end of the tiny artery with the tweezers. There is an electrical bzzzzzt as he burns the bleeder closed. Progress stops while the blood is suctioned out.

"It's nothing to worry about," he says. "It's not much, but when you're looking at one square centimeter, two ounces is a damned lake."

Carefully, gently, Dr. Ducker continues to make his way into the brain. Far down the tiny tunnel the white trunk of the optic nerve can be seen. It is 9:54.

Slowly, using the optic nerve as a guidepost, Dr. Ducker probes deeper and deeper into the gray. The heart monitor continues to pop, pop, pop, 70 beats a minute, 70 beats a minute.

The neurosurgeon guides the tweezers directly to the pulsing carotid artery, one of the three main blood channels into the brain. The carotid twists and dances to the electronic pop, pop, popping. Gently, ever gently, nudging aside the scarred brain tissue, Dr. Ducker moves along the carotid toward the Circle of Willis, near the floor of the skull. This loop of vessels is the staging area from which blood is distributed throughout the brain. Three major arteries feed it from below, one in the rear and the two carotids in the front.

The first aneurysm lies ahead, still buried in grey matter, where the carotid meets the Circle. The second aneurysm is deeper yet in the brain, where the hindmost artery rises along the spine and joins the circle.

Eyes pressed against the microscope, Dr. Ducker makes his tedious way along the carotid.

"She's so scarred I can't identify anything," he complains through the mask.

It is 10:01 a.m. The heart monitor pop, pop, pops with reassuring regularity.

The probing tweezers are gentle, firm, deliberate, probing, probing, probing, slower than the hands of the clock. Repeatedly, vessels bleed and Dr. Ducker cauterizes them. The blood loss is mounting, and now the anesthesiologist hangs a transfusion bag above Mrs. Kelly's shrouded form.

Ten minutes pass. Twenty. Blood flows, the tweezers buzz, the suction hose hisses. The tunnel is small, almost filled by the shank of the instrument.

The aneurysm finally appears at the end of the tunnel, throbbing, visibly thin, a lumpy, overstretched bag, the color of rich cream, swelling out from the once-strong arterial wall, a tire about to blow out, a balloon ready to burst, a timebomb the size of a pea.

The aneurysm isn't the monster itself, only the work of the monster, which, growing malevolently, has disrupted the pressures and weakened arterial walls throughout the brain. But the monster itself, the X-rays say, lies far away.

The probe nudges the aneurysm, hesitantly, gently.

"Sometimes you touch one," a nurse says, "and blooey, the wolf's at the door."

Patiently, Dr. Ducker separates the aneurysm from the surrounding brain tissue. The tension is electric. No surgeon would dare go after the monster itself until this swelling killer is defused.

Now.

A nurse hands Dr. Ducker a long, delicate pair of pliers. A little stainless steel clip, its jaws open wide, is positioned on the pliers' end. Presently the magnified clip moves into the field of view, light glinting from its polished surface.

It is 10:40.

For eleven minutes Dr. Ducker repeatedly attempts to work the clip over the neck of the balloon, but the device is too small. He calls for one with longer jaws. Soon that clip moves into the microscopic tunnel. With infinite slowness, Dr. Ducker maneuvers it over the neck of the aneurysm.

Then, in an instant, the jaws close and the balloon collapses.

"That's clipped," Dr. Ducker calls out. Smile wrinkles appear above his mask. The heart monitor goes pop, pop, pop, steady. It is 10:58.

Dr. Ducker now begins following the Circle of Willis back into the brain, toward the second, and more difficult, aneurysm that swells at the very rear of the Circle, tight against the most sensitive and primitive structure in the head, the brainstem. The brainstem controls vital processes, including breathing and heartbeat.

The going becomes steadily more difficult and bloody. Millimeter, millimeter after treacherous millimeter the tweezers burrow a tunnel through Mrs. Kelly's mind. Blood flows, the tweezers buzz, the suction slurps. Push and probe. Cauterize. Suction. Push and probe. More blood. Then the tweezers lie quiet.

"I don't recognize anything," the surgeon says. He pushes further and quickly finds a landmark.

Then, exhausted, Dr. Ducker disengages himself, backs away, sits down on a stool and stares straight ahead for a long moment. The brainstem is close, close.

"This is a frightening place to be," whispers the doctor. In the background the heart monitor goes pop, pop, pop, 70 beats a minute, steady. The smell of ozone and burnt flesh hangs thick in the air. It is 11:05 a.m., the day of the monster.

The operating room door opens and Dr. Michael Salcman, the assistant chief neurosurgeon, enters. He confers with Dr. Ducker, who then returns to the microscope. Dr. Salcman moves to the front of the television monitor.

As he watches Dr. Ducker work, Dr. Salcman compares an aneurysm to a bump on a tire. The weakened wall of the artery balloons outward under the relentless pressure of the heartbeat and, eventually, it bursts. That's death.

So the fragile aneurysms must be removed before Dr. Ducker can tackle the AVM itself. Dr. Salcman crosses his arms and fixes his eyes on the television screen, preparing himself to relieve Dr. Ducker if he tires. One aneurysm down, one to go.

The second, however, is the toughest. It pulses dangerously deep, hard against the bulb of nerves that sits atop the spinal cord.

"Technically, the brainstem," says Dr. Salcman. "I call it the 'pilot light.' That's because if it goes out . . . that's it."

On the television screen the tweezer instrument presses on, following the artery toward the brainstem. Gently, gently, gently, gently it pushes aside the gray coils. For a moment the optic nerve appears in the background, then vanishes.

The going is even slower now. Dr. Ducker is reaching all the way into the center of the brain and his instruments are the length of chopsticks. The danger mounts because, here, many of the vessels feed the pilot light.

The heartbeat goes pop, pop, pop, 70 beats a minute.

The instrument moves across a topography of torture, scars everywhere, remnants of pain past, of agonies Mrs. Kelly would rather die than further endure. Dr.

Ducker is lost again. Dr. Salcman joins him at the microscope, peering through the assistant's eyepieces. They debate the options in low tones and technical terms. A decision is made and again the polished tweezers probe along the vessel.

Back on course, Dr. Ducker works his tunnel ever deeper, gentle, gentle, gentle as the touch of sterile cotton. Finally the gray matter parts.

The neurosurgeon freezes.

Dead ahead the field is crossed by many huge, distended, ropelike veins.

The neurosurgeon stares intently at the veins, surprised, chagrined, betrayed by the X-rays.

The monster, by microscopic standards, lies far away, above and back, in the rear of the head. Dr. Ducker was to face the monster itself on another day, not now. Not here.

But clearly these tangled veins, absent on the X-ray films but very real in Mrs. Kelly's brain, are tentacles of the monster.

Gingerly, the tweezers attempt to push around them.

Pop, pop, pop . . pop . . . pop . . . . pop . . . . pop.

"It's slowing!" warns the anesthesiologist, alarmed.

The tweezers pull away like fingers touching fire.

. . . pop . . . pop . . pop . pop, pop, pop.

"It's coming back" says the anesthesiologist.

The vessels control blood flow to the brain stem, the pilot light.

Dr. Ducker tries to go around them a different way.

Pop, pop, pop . pop . . pop . . . pop . . . .

And withdraws.

Dr. Salcman stands before the television monitor, arms crossed, frowning.

"She can't take much of that," the anesthesiologist says. "The heart will go into arrhythmia and that'll lead to a . . . call it a heart attack." Dr. Ducker tries a still different route, pulling clear of the area and returning at a new angle. Eventually, at the end of a long, throbbing tunnel of brain tissue, the sought-after aneurysm appears.

Pop, pop, pop . pop . . pop . . . pop . . . .

The instruments retract.

"Damn," says the neurosurgeon. "I can only work here for a few minutes without the bottom falling out."

The clock says 12:29.

Already the gray tissue swells visibly from the repeated attempts to burrow past the tentacles.

Again the tweezers move forward in a different approach and the aneurysm reappears. Dr. Ducker tries to reach it by inserting the aneurysm clip through a long, narrow tunnel. But the pliers that hold the clip obscure the view.

Pop, pop . pop . . pop . . . pop . . . .

The pliers retract.

"We're on it and we know where we are," complains the neurosurgeon, frustration adding a metallic edge to his voice. "But we're going to have an awful time getting a clip in there. We're so close, but . . . ."

A resident who has been assisting Dr. Ducker collapses on a stool. He stares straight ahead, eyes unfocused, glazed.

"Michael, scrub," Dr. Ducker says to Dr. Salcman. "See what you can do. I'm too cramped."

While the circulating nurse massages Dr. Ducker's shoulders, Dr. Salcman attempts to reach the aneurysm with the clip.

Pop, pop, pop . pop . . pop . . .pop . . . .

The clip withdraws.

"That should be the aneurysm right there," says Dr. Ducker, taking his place at the microscope again. "Why the hell can't we get to it? We've tried, ten times."

At 12:53, another approach.

Pop, pop, pop . pop . . pop . . . pop . . . .

Again.

It is 1:06. And again, and again, and again.

Pop . . . pop . . . pop, pop, pop . . . pop . . . pop-pop-pop . . .

The anesthesiologist's hands move rapidly across a panel of switches. A nurse catches her breath and holds it.

"Damn, damn, damn."

Dr. Ducker backs away from the microscope, his gloved hands held before him. For a full minute, he's silent.

"There's an old dictum in medicine," he finally says. "If you can't help, don't do any harm. Let nature take its course. We may have already hurt her. We've slowed down her heart. Too many times." The words carry defeat, exhaustion, anger.

Dr. Ducker stands again before the X-rays. His eyes focus on the rear aneurysm, the second one, the one that thwarted him. He examines the film for signs, unseen before, of the monster's descending tentacles. He finds no such indications.

Pop, pop, pop, goes the monitor, steady now, 70 beats a minute.

"Mother nature," a resident growls, "is a mother."

The retreat begins. Under Dr. Salcman's command, the team prepares to wire the chunk of skull back into place and close the incision.

It ends quickly, without ceremony. Dr. Ducker's gloves snap sharply as a nurse pulls them off. It is 1:30.

Dr. Ducker walks, alone, down the hall, brown paper bag in his hand. In the lounge he sits on the edge of a hard orange couch and unwraps the peanut butter sandwich. His eyes focus on the opposite wall.

Back in the operating room the anesthesiologist shines a light into each of Mrs. Kelly's eyes. The right pupil, the one under the incision, is dilated and does not respond to the probing beam. It is a grim omen.

If Mrs. Kelly recovers, says Dr. Ducker, he'll go ahead and try to deal with the monster itself, despite the remaining aneurysm. He'll try to block the arteries to it, maybe even take it out. That would be a tough operation, he says without enthusiasm.

"And it's providing that she's in good shape after this."

If she survives. If. If.

"I'm not afraid to die," Mrs. Kelly had said. "I'm scared to death . . . but . . . I can't bear the pain. I wouldn't want to live like this much longer."

Her brain was too scarred. The operation, tolerable in a younger person, was too much. Already, where the monster's tentacles hang before the brainstem, the tissue swells, pinching off the source of oxygen.

Mrs. Kelly is dying.

The clock on the wall, near where Dr. Ducker sits, says 1:40.

"It's hard to tell what to do. We've been thinking about it for six weeks. But, you know, there are certain things . . . that's just as far as you can go. I just don't know . . . ."

He lays the sandwich, the banana and the Fig Newtons on the table before him, neatly, the way the scrub nurse laid out the instruments.

"It was triple jeopardy," he says finally, staring at his peanut butter sandwich the same way he stared at the X-rays. "It was triple jeopardy."

It is 1:43, and it's over.

Dr. Ducker bites, grimly, into the sandwich.

The monster won.

Chapter 14

How to Write How-to Articles

At the heart of most how-to articles are steps that, when followed, produce either tangible or intangible results for readers. How-to articles are relatively short, very specific and usually consist of four parts. Among the highlights of this chapter are:

- The unspoken messages of service articles
- Four steps to writing a how-to story
- Tangible vs. intangible goals of how-to articles
- Crossroads of great ideas

Imagine that you're walking through an airport to catch a flight. You pause briefly at a newsstand to pick out a couple of magazines to pass the time between naps. How do you choose among this month's issues of *People, Vanity Fair* or *Elle*? What causes you to reach for *Fitness* rather than *Self*? Your flight is boarding; you only have a few seconds to make your decision, so you can't dawdle over the tables of contents. If you're like most magazine buyers, you make your selection based on two factors.

First, the face featured on the cover tells you that a profile article is inside the issue. (See Chapter 12, Profiles.) If the person—usually an A-list celebrity—interests you, chances are you'll buy the magazine to learn more about the personality behind the photo.

Cover lines are the second determining factor. We discussed these four-to six-word blurbs in Chapter 3, but now it's time to consider the psychology behind them. One editor we know describes cover lines as little "marquees"—usually arranged on either or both sides of the celebrity's cover photograph—that promote key articles inside. Editors write their cover lines carefully because they know the impact that the blurbs have on **single-copy sales**.

Among the most successful cover lines are those that promote how-to articles. Many a newsstand browser will buy a publication because a how-to article, touted on the magazine's cover, has succeeded in its mission to grab the attention of shoppers.

Unspoken Message: "Buy Me!"

How-to articles fall into the general category of **service articles** because they promise readers some kind of benefit or service. Some service articles merely provide readers with useful information but don't necessarily prescribe how-to steps. The unspoken message of a how-to article is: "If you buy this magazine, read this article and follow these steps you'll be better, smarter, happier, thinner, richer" or some other desirable characteristic. How-to articles are mainstays of home remodeling and decorating magazines, but they're equally appropriate for publications that focus on fitness, business, women, travel, gardening or investments. Editors like them because they invite readers to get involved and experiment with the advice the authors share. Here's a sampling of the range of how-to articles you're likely to see promoted on the covers of magazines:

"How To Ease Tension With Yoga"
"How To Craft A Winning Résumé"
"How To Spot A Lie"
"How To Fly High At Low Cost"
"How To Create a Low-Maintenance Garden"
"How To Outsmart The Stock Market"

For variety, an editor can take these same articles and give them titles that imply but do not include the "how to" words. The intention is the same, but now the articles are labeled: "Easing Tension With Yoga," "Crafting A Winning Résumé," "Spotting A Lie," "Flying High At Low Cost," "Creating a Low-Maintenance Garden" and "Outsmarting The Stock Market." The "how to" is understood even when it isn't articulated.

The more specific the how-to title is, the more irresistible it is to the reader. An article that promises to tell golfers "How To Shave 5 Strokes Off Your Game This Winter" is more powerful than merely "How To Play Better Golf." An article that outlines "Three Steps To Beating The Blues" is more engaging than "How To Overcome Depression." A travel article, "Planning A Getaway Weekend Under $250," generates more interest than "How To Plan A Getaway Weekend." Whatever the words, the underlying promise is that this article is going to give readers information they can use and reap quick, positive results.

Four Steps to the How-to Article

The most effective how-to article is very specific, relatively short—1,200 to 1,500 words—and usually contains four parts, the last of which is optional. Here's the formula that many writers follow:

- Introduction
- Transition
- Steps/tips
- Wrap up (optional)

Because the goal of a how-to article is to instruct or educate readers, the author wants to get to the point as quickly as possible. The introduction is often the only place that the writer can exhibit creativity; even so, the opening paragraph should be short and tightly written. The "job" of the introduction is to clearly set up the rest of the article. Let's look at two examples of effective introductions.

Ask a Question

For a January issue of *CompuServe Magazine*, a how-to article about tension and stress began this way:

> Prediction: This year—if it's anything like last—more than 65 percent of all visits to family doctors will be for stress-related problems. What are some quick techniques for relieving pressure on and off the job? Allan Stevens, manager of the Health and Fitness Forum, suggests four easy stressbusters that can reduce tension and boost energy.[1]

The topic of stress is an old one, but the author of the article, Holly Miller, makes the article timely by opening with a New Year's prediction (remember, this is a January issue) and a surprising statistic (fresh research is a key to all how-to articles). Since the article was packaged as a sidebar to a major story with a title that suggested readers should "Make Wellness Your First New Year's Resolution," it could occupy only one page in the magazine. The limited space required the writer to make the **transition** from the introduction to the four steps/tips very quickly. She used a question ("What are some quick techniques for relieving pressure on and off the job?") to set up the heart of the sidebar article. Each of the four steps was given a boldface subheading and then explained in a paragraph or two.

Create a Scene

A scenario is another good way to introduce a how-to article. An introduction that describes a brief moment that readers can relate to is particularly effective if they've been in a similar situation. For example, say you are writing an article titled "How To Make A Speech . . . And Survive!" Chances are, readers who have suffered wobbly knees and near-panic attacks when standing in front of an audience will want to learn how to ease their nervousness. The writer further establishes common ground with readers with this introduction:

> Your heart was pounding as you took a final gulp of ice water and blotted your mouth with the napkin. Breathe deeply, you told yourself. Inhale . . . one, two, three . . . exhale . . . one, two, three. Why had you ever accepted the invitation to speak at the mother-daughter banquet?
>
> The waiter cleared the last dish from the head table, and the emcee began her introduction. There was no turning back. You were on.[2]

Having grabbed the reader's attention with the scenario, the writer next creates a transition sentence or paragraph and introduces the expert source of information. This person might assure readers that they can survive the ordeal of making a speech if they follow five (or whatever number you choose) easy steps. These steps, often packaged in a bullet format, offer specific strategies to help readers through their next public-speaking obligation. The bullets, containing words of advice from one or more experts whom you've interviewed, might look like this:

- **Slow down:** Sometimes nervousness causes you to speak too fast. Professor John Smith suggests that when you rehearse your speech you should keep an eye on the clock. "Try to talk at a rate of about 120 words per minute," he recommends.
- **Dress code:** Strive for a look that is slightly more formal than your audience, says fashion coordinator Mary Brown. A navy blue suit and crisp white shirt will help you feel like the cool professional that

you are. As an added benefit, the jacket will provide a dark background that will hide the inevitable clip-on microphone.

The advice you offer must come from recognizable experts. Even if you, as the author of the article, have had some experience in public speaking, you probably do not have credentials that will impress your readers. In the bulleted pieces of advice above, the sources have a blend of professional training and field experience. Note, too, each piece of advice is supported by a quote or an illustration.

And In Closing . . .

The final element of a how-to article is the optional conclusion. If you have a strong wrap-up comment from one of your expert sources, this is where to use it. Otherwise, you can merely end the article with the last step or tip. Remember: It was the advice, not your clever introduction or closing paragraph, that attracted the reader to your article in the first place.

Deliver the Goods

A how-to article must deliver what it promises. If a title and cover line promise an article that explains how to relieve pressure on the job or how to survive a public speaking ordeal, the article inside should offer fresh ideas from reliable experts. This requires the writer to identify and interview credible sources of information who are willing to share their knowledge.

You damage your credibility by luring readers into an article with a provocative title and then rehashing information that is common knowledge. This was the case several years ago when a women's magazine offered this cover line on a December issue: "How to Look Like You've Lost 10 Pounds Overnight." Readers who bought the magazine were dismayed by the article's tired suggestions: Wear something black and remember to stand up straight.

Good service articles should contain such creative tips that readers cut them out, tack them on bulletin boards, tuck them under magnets on their refrigerator doors and stuff them into their wallets and purses.

Tangible vs. Intangible How-to Articles

Most how-to articles fall into either the **tangible** or the **intangible** category. The tangible variety offers steps that, if followed, will lead to the creation of an object or an event. The results are visible. Three examples of this type of service article are:

- "How To Plan The Perfect Wedding"
- "How To Launch A Home-Based Business"
- "How To Build A Backyard Barbecue"

Keys to writing a successful tangible how-to article are to keep the directions simple and illustrate them with examples and anecdotes. Too many steps can overwhelm and confuse readers. One way to avoid a complex topic is to narrow the focus. One example is "How To Plan A Garden Wedding Under $500." This variation of the broader article—"How To Plan The Perfect Wedding"—limits the focus by season (summer), location (garden) and budget ($500).

Intangible how-to articles often are described as "self-help" articles and reap results that may not be visible. Instead, they may involve personal changes. Three examples of this popular category are:

- "How To Be More Content In Your Job"
- "How To Control Your Jealousy"
- "How To Cope With Failure"

The types of expert sources vary widely, depending on which type of how-to article you write. For the tangible service article you will want to talk with people with first-hand experience and a great deal of expertise in the topic—a wedding planner, a small-business owner, a home-improvement specialist who has built dozens of backyard barbecues. Note: Just because your best friend planned her own wedding does not qualify her as a quotable expert. She may make a good anecdote or an example, but she does not have the credentials necessary to serve as your expert source.

For an intangible how-to article you typically will interview a person with impressive academic degrees and formal training in the topic—a counselor or a psychologist. Too often, articles by beginning writers, especially how-to articles and informational pieces, display what we call the "authority problem." This means the person writes in his or her own voice and doesn't give examples, illustrations, or quote experts or authorities about the subject of the article. The reader may distrust the information and react by thinking, "Who says so?"

We recall a writer who once wrote about how to use proper nutrition and vitamins in solving common medical problems. Since she had no training in medicine or nutrition, we questioned her authority in giving advice on the issue. In another case, a young man wrote about how to buy a sports car for under $20,000. He rattled off a list of names of used automobiles available for purchase under $20,000. Again, he quoted no one and gave no examples of people who had bought the cars he was recommending.

How-to Articles as Sidebars

Editors often want **article packages**. These generally include a main story plus related sidebars, graphics and other illustrations. Taken together, a package can be more visually attractive than a single article because it involves several elements that break up a text-heavy page. The package also benefits readers because it offers variety and choice. A reader can read any or all of the elements on the page. How-to articles often make good sidebar accompaniments to long articles. Here are some examples:

Main Article	How-to Sidebar
Five Off-Season Honeymoon Cruises	How To Pack For A Week At Sea
Road Rage Heats Up	How To Keep Your Cool
Training Tips For Your First Marathon	How To Choose The Right Shoes

When packaged as a sidebar, a how-to article should not exceed one-fourth the length of the main story. It shouldn't repeat any information or quote the same sources as the article that it accompanies. It complements the main story and is placed in close proximity to the major feature. Many readers choose to read sidebars before they decide whether to read the longer story. Because of their short length, sidebars seem less intimidating and require less of a commitment by the readers.

Where to Look for How-to Ideas

Because how-to articles are in demand at most magazines and newspapers, writers interested in earning bylines and building portfolios should master the format. Where are the best ideas for how-to articles? A writer's personal experience is the most obvious place to begin the search for topics. For example, we know an animal activist who created a series of how-to articles aimed at pet owners, pitched the articles to the features editor of her community's daily newspaper and was rewarded with a weekly column. Even with her extensive knowledge of animals, this writer probably couldn't sustain a column for several months (or years) if she depended only on her personal experience. She supplements her knowledge by frequently interviewing veterinarians, trainers and other experts who provide a stream of fresh insights and information.

Most beginning writers are not acknowledged experts in anything—yet—but their personal experiences and interests may provide them with a launch point. As a student, you probably have some knowledge about how to choose a college major, how to cope with homesickness and how to avoid the "freshman 15." Your experience or the experiences of your friends might provide you with a colorful introduction or anecdotes. The tips and steps will come from credible sources such as a career counselor, psychology professor, physical education instructor or nutritionist.

Another way to discover viable how-to topics is to think in terms of crossroads. People typically face many crossroads in their lives—points where they must choose to follow one course of action or another. They look for help in making the right decisions at these crossroads, and help can come in the form of how-to articles. Here are several examples:

Crossroad	How-to Article
Graduation	How to Master the Job Interview
Serious relationship	How to Know if You're Compatible for Life
Buying a home	How to Avoid Hidden Closing Costs
Retirement	How to Know When to Go
Family illness	How to Choose the Right Nursing Home

Because today's magazines are so specialized, you can tune into a publication's demographics and surmise the decisions—minor and major—that its readers are likely to face. For instance, *Child* magazine is obviously aimed at families with young children. In its promotional letter to prospective subscribers, it promises articles that will show parents how to choose kids' books, pick the best preschool, solve sleep problems and decorate a nursery. On the other end of the age spectrum, *More* magazine, geared to women over the age of 40, appeals to prospective subscribers by promising articles that will help readers learn how to "unscramble your nest egg," rejuvenate vitality with natural products and survive an adult child who moves back home.

An obvious place to look for how-to article ideas is within the back issues of the publications that you plan to approach. Many magazines have perennial how-to topics, and they are always looking for fresh angles and new sources. For example, *Prevention* magazine runs some variation of a "how to lose weight" article in almost every issue. *Runner's World* frequently revisits the topic of how to choose running shoes. *Consumer Reports* tells readers how to purchase some kind of computer hardware several times a year.

Another place to look for strong how-to article ideas is in broadcast and print media that typically report new research and surprising statistics. A retirement bulletin, for example, revealed that in the next 18 years, an American will turn 50 every 18 seconds and that more than 22 million Americans are in their 50s. The smart writer takes those bits of information and asks: What kinds of help will these people need to cope with all the changes they will face in the upcoming years? What crossroads will they encounter? What how-to articles will they be interested in reading? The answers should keep writers supplied with enough ideas to explore for a long, long time.

Suggested Activities

1. Brainstorm and try to come up with:

- Five ideas for how-to articles related to the Christmas-New Year's holiday season.
- Five ideas you could develop into how-to sidebars to accompany an in-depth feature on cosmetic surgery.
- Five ideas for how-to articles that fall under the intangible/self-help category.
- Five ideas for how-to articles that would be appropriate for a publication geared to young married couples.
- Five ideas for how-to articles that *you* would like to read.

2. Choose one "crossroad" that people in their 40s may face. Come up with three how-to articles related to the crossroad.

3. Revisit the list of article ideas that resulted from the brainstorming exercise above. Who would be an expert source of information for each of the ideas?

4. From the list of ideas that you've created, select one that appeals to you and write a compelling introduction to it.

Shoptalk

Article package: Separate but related elements that cover a topic in a comprehensive way. In addition to the main story, these elements might include sidebars, databoxes, graphics and illustrations.

Intangible how-to article: Self-help article that often leads to internal changes rather than the creation of some object that you can see and touch. For example, "How To Feel More Content."

Service article: Article that "serves" or benefits readers in a variety of ways; one type of service article is the how-to feature that teaches readers how to do or accomplish something.

Single-copy sales: The opposite of subscription sales, these refer to newsstand sales of a publication.

Tangible how-to article: An article that leads to the creation of something that can be seen and touched. For example, "How To Build A Sundeck For Under $300."

Transition: Words that serve as a "bridge" or a segue to move an article from one point to the next.

Endnotes

1. Holly G. Miller, "Tense? Me, Tense?" *CompuServe Magazine* (January 1991), 16.

2. Dennis E. Hensley and Holly G. Miller, *Write on Target* (Boston: The Writer, Inc., 1995), 71.

Chapter 15
The Calendar-Content Connection

Articles linked to the season, an anniversary or a special observance make publications timely and relevant. Because editors plan their content well in advance, writers must fast forward the calendar to look for ideas. In this chapter you'll learn how to:

- Create a seasonal link
- Move past ho-hum holiday stories
- Give new life to tired topics
- Find calendar connections on the Internet

Christmas comes in July for most writers and editors at monthly magazines. With **lead times** that vary from four to six months, publication staffs generally work at least a season or two ahead of the calendar. This means they're planning back-to-school issues in March, looking for spring gardening features in November and considering Christmas fiction submissions in July. Because monthly and quarterly magazines can't compete with the Internet, television, radio, daily newspapers and weekly magazines in reporting **breaking news**, staff members at these publications work hard to offer material that is relevant and timely.

In addition to a handful of highly anticipated annual features—*Sports Illustrated*'s famed swimsuit edition has become a spring tradition since its launch in 1964—calendar-related material includes articles that are linked to seasonal events and activities (June weddings, October tailgate parties), stories that mark anniversaries (Sept. 11 terrorist attacks) and features that call attention to special observances (Father's Day gift ideas). The smart writer looks to the calendar for timely article topics and offers these ideas to publications several months in advance.

To tune into the creative ways that editors tie content to the calendar, simply review the covers of several magazines published in the same month. Note the seasonal articles promoted on the covers and listed in the tables of contents. For example, a July issue of *House Beautiful* offered "Summer Splendor: Cool Rooms to Relax In."[1] At the same time, *New York* gave its readers "32 Strategies for a Cool, Calm Carefree Season;"[2] *Shape* tracked "Summer's Hot Beauty Trends,"[3] and *Organic Style* explained how to "Get That Vacation Glow."[4]

Calendar-linked articles can deal with serious and lightweight topics. A spring issue of *Scholastic Instructor*, a magazine geared to teachers, suggested "Poolside Picks: Top Professional Titles"[5] for subscribers who anticipated using their vacation time to catch up on educational resources. Because the first issue of any year is a logical time to help people make their annual resolutions, in January 2004 *Smart Money* urged readers to "Set Your Course Now For The Year Ahead." April is an appropriate month to offer articles about investments and money management because readers are preparing their income tax returns.

Creating a Seasonal Link

Occasionally writers manipulate articles to make them seem seasonal. A visit to a southern spa once resulted in a feature story for a November issue of *The Saturday Evening Post*. It began with the question: "Time for a winter tune up? Florida's newest spa will strip you of stress, wrap you in luxury and send you home fit for the holidays." Had the writer offered the same article for publication in a May issue of the magazine, she might have changed the introduction to: "Time to shape up for swimsuit weather? Florida's newest spa will strip you of stress, wrap you in luxury and send you home fit for long afternoons at the beach."[6]

A creative writer with a good topic can tweak a feature story to make it seem appropriate for any season. An article about home security—"How To Burglar-Proof Your Home"—might point out that intruders often take note of houses left vacant during the summer vacation season. A different spin on this same topic might remind readers that winter weather keeps neighbors inside where they're oblivious to the sights and sounds of nearby break-ins. Since the topic is an evergreen—of perennial interest to readers—it takes on an element of importance with the insertion of a few sentences that link it to the season.

Some months lend themselves to easy content-calendar connections. Other months, like February and March, seem to challenge writers and prompt them to stretch to come up with timely ideas. Two competing magazines—*Parents* and *Parenting*—once featured similar cover lines for their February issues. The title of one article was "Be My Valentine: Sweet Ways To Make Your Kids Feel Special;"[7] the title of the competition's article was "I Love You: Little Ways To Make Your Child Feel Special."[8] Apparently the editors were on the same wavelength.

Several years ago, editors at the now-defunct *Aspire* magazine, a Christian publication aimed at female readers, produced a special issue for February dedicated to "The Pleasures and Perils of Romance." Articles tracked "Marriage Miracles" (couples who "saved" their troubled unions), explained "Why Men Dread Valentine's Day" and offered tips to women who form "Dangerous Liaisons" with the wrong men. The magazine's cover underscored the passionate nature of that month's content. The dominant color was bright red.[9]

Forget "The First Thanksgiving"

If the calendar is a good place to begin the hunt for timely article ideas, it's only a starting point. You have to look beyond the obvious and avoid predictable topics that sound like retreads from your sixth-grade spiral notebook of essays. No editor is interested in your take on "The First Thanksgiving," your musings about "What Christmas Means To Me" or your recollections of "How I Spent My Summer Vacation." One of our writing colleagues warns her students against "I-strain," her label for the dangers of writing from a first-person point of view.

An easy way to move beyond predictable article ideas is to brainstorm with a calendar in front of you. For January, move past the general topic of New Year's resolutions and think about specific changes that you've heard people say that they want to make in their lives. January gives people the feeling of a fresh start, a clean slate, a new beginning. Perhaps this is the year they hope to get out of debt, go back to school, lose weight, start exercising, kick a bad habit or strengthen a key relationship. Each resolution can lead to a how-to feature. (See Chapter 14.) For example, readers who resolve to get out of debt and be more fiscally responsible this year might want to read an informative article titled "How

To Cut Your Credit Card Debt In Half." Its timing seems right on target in January.

Other ideas: For the month of May, consider spin-off topics loosely linked to Mother's Day. Interview three or four successful people from different walks of life who credit their adult success to their mothers' influence when they were children. Include lots of anecdotes as you tell their individual stories in a round-up article called "Model Moms." Or, talk with a handful of well-known people and ask them to recall the best advice their mothers ever gave them. Sometimes by working through press secretaries and public relations representatives, you can solicit comments from celebrities, politicians and other public figures who welcome the opportunity for positive media exposure.

For a June publication, a student writer might ask a handful of professors, college administrators and prominent alumni to offer parting words of wisdom to the senior class that is about to graduate. The writer might follow up with this question: "What do you know now that you wish you had known when you walked across the stage and picked up your diploma so many years ago?" (Beware: Some interviewees, when asked such open-ended questions, can't resist delivering lofty sermons in response.)

New Life for Old Topics

An old topic can gain new life when it is tied to an observance or an anniversary. Many writers have probed the serious issue of teen pregnancy, but Mother's Day provides an appropriate time to revisit the topic. The resulting article—call it "Moms Too Soon" or "Premature Moms"—might update readers on current teen-pregnancy statistics and new efforts to discourage the trend of kids having kids. The Mother's Day connection also might prompt an article about professional women who delay motherhood until they've successfully launched their careers. The topic isn't new, but the calendar connection makes it seem worthy of another look.

Historic anniversaries provide endless opportunities for writers. When the United States observed the 60th commemoration of D-Day, the story made the cover of *Time*. Much more than merely reminding readers of the date and recapping the event, *Time* asked the question, "D-Day: Why It Matters 60 Years Later."[10] A second story featured the recollections of 10 veterans who witnessed the Normandy landings firsthand.

The anniversaries of landmark Supreme Court cases give writers good reasons to revisit hot topics. Brown vs. the Board of Education of Topeka, Kan., which led to public school desegregation, was decided in May

1954. Fast forward 50 years and many magazines took a look at education in America and questioned if schools are offering equal opportunity to all students. Another important case, Roe vs. Wade, legalized abortion in the United States. The court handed down its decision in 1973 and writers have revisited the controversial issue on subsequent anniversaries.

The key to a successful anniversary article is making the topic pertinent to the present. Whereas writers should weave enough history into a feature story to educate readers on the event's significance, they should avoid merely retelling what historians have already documented in textbooks. Among the most interesting calendar-related stories are those that bring to the forefront anniversaries that are unknown to most people. Let's look at three diverse examples.

Historic event: In 1956, Josephine Bay became the first female business executive to lead a company that was a member of the New York Stock Exchange.

Anniversary article idea: Fifty years later (2006), what kind of progress have women made in corporate America? How real is the glass ceiling? How many female CEOs now lead companies large enough to be traded on the New York Stock Exchange? This timely article wouldn't dwell on Josephine Bay, but would quickly explain who she was and use her as a "bridge" to the present.

Historic event: In 1962, a controversial bestseller, *Silent Spring* by Rachel Carson, warned the world that the balance of nature was at risk if people didn't stop using insecticides and chemical pollutants. The author, ridiculed by critics, is considered today to be the founder of the modern environmental movement.

Anniversary article idea: Forty years after Rachel Carson's death in 1964, how seriously have we taken her warning? What's the status of the environmental movement? How environmentally conscious are America's families, campuses and communities? What laws have legislators passed to clean up the air and water? Since Rachel Carson and *Silent Spring* are still well known—a 40th anniversary commemorative edition of the classic book was released in 2002—the writer of this article doesn't have to go into great detail about Carson. A sidebar might recap some of the key points set forth in the book.

Historic event: The luxury steamship Titanic, on its maiden voyage in April 1912, sank after hitting an iceberg. More than 1,500 people died.

Anniversary article idea: In spite of numerous books, films and documentaries that have told and retold the story of the ill-fated ship, people are still fascinated by it almost 100 years later. As the centennial approaches, what kinds of commemorations are planned? What Titanic memorabilia are available on eBay? What are people willing to pay for keepsakes? With all of the tragedies that have claimed many more lives, why does the Titanic story endure?

If you're familiar with the History Channel on television, you may be aware of its Web site at www.history.com. This is a great place to identify approaching anniversaries of historic events. The Web site's menu has a link to "This Day in History." By typing in a date, you will be alerted to major events that occurred on that day. Let your creativity take over and see what kinds of ideas you come up with. Example: On April 30, 1927, the first federal prison for women opened its doors (and cells). More like a fashionable boarding school than a jail, the facility taught its inmates to can vegetables and fruit and offered them singing lessons. In 2007, on the 80th anniversary of the prison's opening, a timely article might compare prison life for women, then and now. The story would be of interest in light of the increased number of women currently serving sentences for everything from white-collar crimes to murder.

Capitalizing on History

Sometimes editors create anniversary issues that directly or indirectly celebrate the publications that they edit. These often generate extra advertising revenue and attract record newsstand sales. *Rolling Stone* produced a special issue in June 2004 that celebrated the 50th anniversary of rock and featured "50 Moments That Changed The History Of Rock & Roll."[11] In September 2003, *Esquire* marked "70 Years Of *Esquire* Style."[12] In 1988, *Today's Christian Woman* commemorated its 10th year of publication by inviting several writers to recall key turning points that had occurred in their lives since the magazine's founding. Another article in the same issue highlighted celebrity interviews that the magazine's editors had conducted over the preceding decade.[13]

Typically magazines use five-year markers to call anniversaries to the attention of their readers. A 10th, 15th, 20th or 25th anniversary is more appropriate than a 17th, 23rd or 51st anniversary. Of course, some calendar-related events are so extraordinary that magazines begin the celebration well in advance. This was the case when the millennium approached. Starting in April 1998, *Time* issued a series of editions that cited the most influential people of the past 100 years. The project, according to managing editor Walter Isaacson, was "more popular than we dared dream."[14] For its last magazine of the century, *Time* announced its choice of "Person of the Century"—Albert Einstein.[15]

To show how a writer can pursue an unusual angle on a story, let's look at a millennium-related feature that was published in *Indianapolis Monthly* as part of what the magazine touted on its cover as its "Special Millennium Issue" (December 1999). Among a range of articles linked to the calendar was "Living History," which had a clever gimmick at its core. The editor assigned Holly Miller to locate and interview three Indianapolis residents who shared one common characteristic: All three had lived in three centuries. How is that possible? These senior citizens were born late in the 1800s, had lived through the 1900s, and when they woke up on Jan. 1, 2000, they entered their third century. The resulting article is a round-up feature because it solicits comments from different people on a central topic. The article is also a series of mini-profiles as well as a calendar-related story.

As you read "Living History," ask yourself these questions:

- What difficulties might the writer have encountered in interviewing these people?
- What kind of research, besides the three interviews, adds depth to the story?
- How do the boldface subheadings help the writer make transitions from one interview to the next?
- How does the ending bring the story full circle to the beginning?

Sample Story
Living History

Reprinted from Indianapolis Monthly, *December 1999.*

Living History
By Holly G. Miller

> *While some people read about the past*
> *in textbooks, others saw it with their own eyes.*

Their partying days are over. An exchange of kisses at midnight is unlikely, and compiling a list of resolutions seems presumptuous. On Jan. 1, at midnight, an exclusive group of Hoosiers will move quietly into the next century: their third. Born in the 1800s, they've lived through the 1900s and soon will wake up to the year 2000. Not that the Millennium means much to people who have defied the actuary tables by decades, watched the passing of 19 presidents from Cleveland to Clinton, and experienced the coming and going of a hundred New Year's Eves.

From retirement homes, continuing care centers and assisted living communities around the city, they remember the past in amazing detail and aren't shy about sharing their views on politics, sex and scandal. Just mention Bill Clinton's name, and expect the unexpected. "What he did wasn't right," concedes Frata Sarig, 105, who served as executive secretary to Reginald Sullivan, a Democrat mayor of Indianapolis in the early 1940s. Then, as an afterthought, she adds, "But he sure is good-looking."

They're at their best when recalling vivid moments that aren't connected to any major historical event. They don't remember much about Prohibition, D-Day or women's suffrage, but they can describe the interior of their first Chevy and recall their family's first telephone and the ring—"one short, three longs," says Frata—that distinguished their calls from those of their neighbors. "Of course, everybody listened in on the party line."

The War Hero

"I remember the day I got my card from the draft office and figured, 'What the hell, I might as well enlist,'" recalls Gustave Streeter, reminiscing from a huge green lounge chair—an unlit cigar between his fingers and an erasable tablet and marker within arm's reach. His hearing and eyesight are failing, and visitors who want to tap into his vast memory bank have to print their questions on the tablet in oversized black letters. It's worth the effort. He's a bona fide war hero, and proof of his bravery is pinned to his shirt under his Perry Como cardigan. It's a handsome green and white medal, the *Croix de Guerre*, awarded by the French government in 1999 to commemorate his service during World War I. He was a gunner, took part in seven campaigns in France and Germany, was hobbled by shrapnel in both legs, treated himself from his first-aid kit and kept going. "I was a pharmacist," he explains. "I knew if I reported my injuries they'd send me to a hospital. I wanted to stay and fight."

Streeter stayed, and in one bloody exchange was responsible for saving the lives of several U.S. Marines. He later wrote about his war experiences in a collection of reminiscences published by the Little Sisters of the Poor and aimed at the next generation. "I can't remember many (fellow soldiers') names," he wrote, "but frequently during these twilight years of my life, I can see them pass in review, their heads high, their bodies erect and their expressions noble."

He lives at St. Augustine Home now, his room decorated with pictures from the Great War and mementos from his most recent birthday, his 103rd. There are framed greetings from Bill, Hillary and the senior Bushes, a stack of cards and a helium-filled balloon with the message, "Aged to Perfection." Trading his independence for institutional life was difficult a couple of years ago, especially since current house rules prevent him from enjoying two long-standing pleasures of his past: a cigar in the afternoon and a Rob Roy before dinner. Shortly after he moved into the Catholic retirement center, Streeter confided to one of the nuns that he sure missed the ritual of an evening cocktail. "That night I came back to my room and sitting right here by the bed was a gold-rimmed, stemmed glass with a Rob Roy in it," he says with some surprise. "I don't know where it came from, and it only happened once."

A miracle.

The Doctor's Wife

"You'll think I'm a little goofy," confides Beaty Segar, 100, "but every night when I go to bed, I sing the same three songs: 'Hello, Dolly,' 'Singin' in the Rain' and 'Tea for Two.' Of course I usually go to sleep before I get to the third one."

Music has been a part of her life since her early years in Chicago, when she and her sister sang for the troops who were home on leave from World War I. She moved to Indiana in 1922, the bride of Dr. Louis Segar, the state's first full-time pediatrician, and together they were active in community theater and "went to the symphony from the day it opened." Dr. Segar, an IU graduate, had interned at Boston's Children's Hospital, where he traded rotations with other young doctors, taking on extra pediatric assignments so he could get additional experience. "He came back to Indianapolis, opened an office and sat there day after day," says Beaty. "Nobody came in. At one point he told his father he was going to quit medicine. Then, finally, he got a call to consult on a case of scarlet fever." He was good, word got around, and his long, successful career was launched.

As newlyweds, the Segars lived on North Alabama Street, and each afternoon Beaty would walk to her husband's downtown office so she could accompany him on his house calls. "We rode all over the state," she says. If a call came late at night, Beaty would slip a robe over her nightgown and travel with him. "He was a 24-hour-a-day doctor, and he carried his black satchel with him everywhere."

Sometimes he prescribed a dose of common sense rather than a shot of medication. "One child refused to talk," recalls Beaty. "His parents knew he could speak, but they couldn't convince him to do it. Finally, my husband put the boy in the hospital with instructions to leave him alone and not to feed him. After one day the kid said to the nurse, 'Damn it, I'm hungry!'" He was cured.

She's been a widow for 35 years now, and describes her health as good "from the neck up." When problems with her eyesight threatened to curb her insatiable appetite for reading she discovered books on tape. She just finished a biography of FDR and has moved on to an in-depth look at Truman. "I'm probably better educated now than I have been in a hundred years," she says. Reading about the Depression has put into perspective the lean years when her husband's patients often couldn't pay for the medical services he delivered. No one withheld treatment, and no one filed a lawsuit. Beaty remembers the butcher settling a bill with a pound of ground chuck, which she promptly stretched into a meatloaf. She recalls the Shapiro family, of delicatessen fame, helping out by sending over dinner. "They gave us enough food for a week."

If she misses anything about days gone by, it's the sense of friendliness that permeated the neighborhoods. "We grew up without fences," she says. "Kids played in each other's backyards. Our doors were open, and so were our refrigerators. Today things seem more divided. My daughter, who lives out of state, just told me about being in a grocery store and talking to a little boy. His mother rushed up, grabbed the child and said, 'I told you not to talk to strangers!' Things like that hurt."

The Career Girl

Frata Sarig drove her little Chevy until she had a fender bender at age 98. No one was hurt, but she reluctantly hung up her keys because "I felt from then on, no matter what the trouble was, the insurance people would say it was my fault." Now, at age 105, she still recalls the wonderful sense of independence when, years ago, she drove solo from one coast to the other. "I would stop for gas, and people would ask me where I was going. I always fibbed about it because I didn't want anyone to know I was alone and traveling so far. I didn't want them to follow me."

Sarig had already had two careers when she and her husband moved to Indiana more than 65 years ago. She had taught in a one-room schoolhouse in Iowa and had worked in a Kansas City biological laboratory. Once settled in Indianapolis, she joined city government and eventually served on the mayor's staff as executive secretary. Later she sold real estate, retiring at age 75. "A home back then cost anywhere from $12,000 to $35,000," Sarig says. She sold her share of them, "made quite a bit" and invested well. Good thing, she notes, because "I never expected to live this long."

As progressive as she was in her professional life, so was she ahead of her time when it came to her health. She never drank alcohol or used tobacco—"my grandmother, dear soul, smoked a clay pipe"—and she underwent hormone replacement therapy before it was fashionable. Sarig stopped taking hormones at age 70, and later, when a niece asked her why, she answered, "I guess I took the Bible literally. I didn't think I would live beyond three score and 10 years." That was 35 years ago.

Cheers

All three centenarians agree that tomorrow isn't quite as mysterious when you've already seen 100 years of yesterdays. Beaty Segar's love for words once prompted her to consider writing a book about the people she's known, but the project seemed daunting, and she settled for poems instead. She recites from memory the lines she composed to mark her 100th birthday in July. Its closing words say: "I have cherished every year. You see me standing here. Believe it or not, it's really me, and I have lived a century."

She took poetic license with the line "you see me standing here." These days she travels by wheelchair, although that hasn't slowed her pace. "I don't think anybody ever lives too long," she says, "not if they have something to offer." Segar dismisses the foibles of age as inevitable, and refuses to dwell on them. "Everybody has aches and pains," she says. Failing eyesight? "I know my lunch is in front of me, but if I put in my fork I'm not sure what I'll come up with." Hearing loss? "Yesterday I was talking with a woman and I said, 'It's a beautiful day.' She answered, 'I'm so glad you like it. I haven't worn it for a while.'"

Like birthdays, ringing in another year—even another century—"doesn't mean much at this stage of life," admits Sarig. For persons who have seen a hundred years, any celebration is likely to be quiet and private. A chorus of "Hello, Dolly" would be nice, followed by a memory of tapping the accelerator of a little Chevy and toasting the journey with something cold. Make it a Rob Roy.

Suggested Activities

1. Choose a favorite monthly magazine and review all 12 issues from one year. Jot down the calendar-related cover lines that you see.

2. Come up with three feature article ideas with a connection to the winter season. Come up with three ideas linked to September. Come up with three ideas related to the Fourth of July. Come up with three ideas tied to the 100th anniversary of the founding of the NAACP.

3. With the help of an almanac or other reference book, identify at least two historic events that will mark either 25- or 50-year anniversaries in the next 18 months. How might you give a current spin to the anniversary? Whom would you interview? What kind of research would you conduct?

Shoptalk

Breaking news: Events that are in the process of unfolding and that the media are reporting to their audiences.

Lead time: The number of days, weeks or months required by a publication's staff to produce an issue.

Endnotes

1. *House Beautiful* (July 2004), cover.

2. *New York* (28 June-5 July 2004), cover.

3. *Shape* (July 2004), cover.

4. *Organic Style* (July/August 2004), cover.

5. *Scholastic Instructor* (May/June 2004), cover.

6. Holly G. Miller, "Southern Comforts," *The Saturday Evening Post* (November/December 2001), 62-63.

7. *Parents* (February 2004), cover.

8. *Parenting* (February 2004), cover.

9. *Aspire* (February 1996), cover.

10. *Time* (May 31, 2004), cover.

11. *Rolling Stone* (June 24, 2004), cover.

12. *Esquire* (September 2003), cover.

13. *Today's Christian Woman* (July/August 1988), cover.

14. Walter Isaacson, "Why Picking These Titans Was Fun," *Time* (7 Dec. 1998) 6.

15. *Time* (31 Dec. 1999), cover.

Chapter 16
Trends, Conflicts and Controversies

News features report on trends, conflicts and controversies in many areas of human interest, not simply in current events. Investigative journalism falls in this category. Investigative stories explore complex issues from a range of viewpoints. This chapter will help you recognize, research and write these types of stories by studying these key points:

- Identifying common characteristics
- Choosing the best angle
- Doing the reporting
- Knowing when to quote

One example of an investigative story, "Kids at Risk: The Alarming Truth About Safety Seats,"[1] focused on the many parents who do the right thing by using safety seats but put their small children in greater danger. The *Reader's Digest* article addressed the more than 30,000 injuries and 200 deaths that occur every year to small children riding in child safety seats. Safety experts have concluded that more than 90 percent of these seats are not properly installed by parents. This widely reprinted article had a significant influence on new safety legislation passed by several states.

Features such as "Kids at Risk" report on **trends**, **conflicts**, **controversies** and other developments by relying on multiple viewpoints and expert sources. They help readers understand their world by explaining what, why and how things happen. They report on issues in any field of human interest, recreation or endeavor. And, most important, they explain how these developments affect readers.

Common Characteristics

The following common characteristics will help you recognize, research and write news features:

- Their main purpose is to inform and educate readers, not entertain.
- They can discuss any topic. Every field—business, health and safety, entertainment, sports, science, politics, psychology and religion—has its trends and controversies.
- Some groups of people may be helped by the developments you write about, while others may be harmed.
- Your research must report the viewpoints and experiences from many people and multiple sources. These stories neither focus on a single person nor can they rely on a single interview.
- They have an action angle because people disagree; people's lives are changed; or a phenomenon is increasing or decreasing, getting bigger or smaller or changing in some fashion.
- Because of unfolding developments, they can quickly become outdated. You must continually look for fresh angles and approaches to these topics.

These feature stories generally fall into two categories: conflicts/controversies and trends. The difference between **conflicts** and **controversies** is one of degree: Conflict stories report on something people disagree about. Controversy stories report on something people argue or fight about. **Investigative reporting** stories often result in controversy. It's important to avoid hard distinctions between these types of stories whose boundaries may overlap. But here are some tips on recognizing and writing each one.

Conflicts or Controversies

Conflicts result from disagreement on issues by affected parties, such as labor and management, customers and owners, or faculty and administration. Serious conflicts turn into public arguments (or controversies) between opposing parties. Some trends turn into controversies because people disagree about their causes, cures or both. The debate may range from mild and polite to colorful and vehement. Newspaper feature editors may want balanced stories with comprehensive, equal coverage of opposing points of view. Magazine editors may permit writers to argue a point of view depending on the magazine's tradition.

Following are two examples in which magazines (*National Review* and *The Nation*) wrote stories from their own point of view favoring one side or another:

National Review: "PETA vs. KFC: A Dirty War Against the Colonel" criticizes tactics used in a campaign by People for the Ethical Treatment of Animals (PETA). PETA charged KFC with treating chickens inhumanely.[2]

The Nation: "Fields of Poison: While Farm Workers are Sickened by Pesticides, Industry Writes the Rules" examines numerous health dangers faced by farm workers who use pesticides. It charges that the farm industry pressured the government against adopting protective regulations.[3]

As we mentioned in Chapter 4, *Congressional Quarterly Researcher* (*CQ Researcher*) is a good place to find great ideas and background for articles on conflicts and controversies. It provides a balanced overview of issues the public is debating, such as national security, civil liberties, the gambling industry, media ownership, cyber security, gay marriage, homeland security, water shortages, race in America, prescription drug prices, the SUV debate and medical malpractice.

You can find a local angle on any one of these national issues. You could write a story on a proposed local casino and how it relates to the national trend of growth in legalized gambling. Find local authorities to comment on the subject and depict how the issue will affect the community. You can also take a national issue and develop an angle for a niche audience who reads a special interest magazine. For example, you could write an article for a denominational magazine explaining how its religious leaders are responding to the growth of legalized gambling.

Again, it's important to stress that the conflict and controversy you write about need not be a public issue or be political in nature. Every special interest and niche magazine has its own set of issues and controversies.

Trends

A trend is a social or economic phenomenon with quantifiable dimensions such as growth or decline, acceleration or slowing or increase or decrease. Some trends may be dangerous or controversial while others are positive or even humorous. In "Why U.S. workers are losing the tug of war over toilet paper," *The Wall Street Journal* reports on the "controlled delivery" trend in company and public restrooms. They save on paper costs by making dispensers tricky to use. It quotes a building services manager who defends the practice, and includes statistics related to the most popular complaints about public restrooms.[4]

Trends with harmful consequences turn into controversies as people debate solutions to the problems. For example, *Jane* reported on "Women who rape: A scary trend you don't hear about: female sex offenders."[5] This story reported on the increasing number of female sex offenders. In "Why some brothers only date whites and 'others'," *Ebony* quoted experts who said the rise in interracial dating and marriage can be partly attributed to the cross-racial, hip-hop culture.[6]

"Those trend stories can start with the anecdote or the big picture. Trend stories can come from statistics and can come from having a friend who is having some problem," says Ted Spiker, a journalism professor and former senior editor at *Men's Health*. Spiker says anecdotes bring a story to life, but the statistics add credibility. "If you don't have a number there, you haven't proven to me there's a trend," he says.[7]

One place to get ideas and background information for trend stories is the monthly magazine *American Demographics*, which most large libraries carry. Its main purpose is to report on social, demographic and economic trends in America. Is obesity really a trend? An *American Demographics* cover story reported that the percentage of obese children under 12 increased from 4 percent in 1971 to 15 percent in 2000.[8]

In another issue, *American Demographics* did a story on a U.S. Census Bureau report showing that the percentage of mothers who have infant children and who are in the workforce fell for the first time since 1976, dropping from a record-high 59 percent to 55 percent in 2000.[9]

However, Gail Belsky, a former editor at Time Inc. and *Working Mother*, says trend stories originate in everyday life before they show up in statistics. "When I was the executive editor of *Working Mother*," she says, "the census had just come out that showed for the first time in 24 years that the number of women who returned to work after having a baby went down."

Yet, she says, she already knew about it. She had seen younger colleagues and friends debating returning to work, and a few who actually quit. Then, a colleague of hers who was on maternity leave asked her to lunch. "She said she did not know a single friend who had returned to work after having a baby. To me, that speaks volumes. That is the trend, far more than waiting for the census bureau to spit out a number. You see that kind of anecdotal information once you start looking around and seeing what's going on."

Belsky continued, "You see it once, you think hmmm. You see it twice and you know there must be a third one. You know if you do a little walking and talking and scratching it up, you're going to come up with more."[10]

Choosing the Best Angle

Every trend and controversy probably offers dozens of angles you can pursue. You can look at the people who are for it, the people against it or the people who don't care. If it's a trend, you can look at the people it hurts or the people it helps. Some people remain unaffected, but have definite reactions to the trend. To choose the best angle, start by analyzing the trend or controversy from these three perspectives:

- **Central development:** Something begins to happen. For example, American electronics companies begin exporting jobs and factories to countries with cheaper labor.
- **Effects on some:** As the development advances, it affects people, places or institutions in specific ways. Electronics workers may lose jobs, but consumers get cheaper televisions, DVD players and stereo equipment. Developing countries get new jobs and a higher standard of living.
- **Reactions from others:** As the effects take place, impacted groups try to slow, stop, take advantage of or hasten this development. Labor groups may pressure Congress for import restrictions. The shipping industry, which benefits from the trend, lobbies for eliminating tariff restrictions.

Each of these three phases of development, however, involves different directions for the writer. For each one you can look at *magnitude* (how much, how many, how often), *location* (which regions or countries are most affected), *diversity* (which groups of people are affected) or *intensity* (to what degree or extent they're affected).[11]

These four perspectives on three central developments give you at least a dozen angles from which to pursue the story:

Central development:	Magnitude (how many?)
	Location (where?)
	Diversity (to whom?)
	Intensity (to what extent?)
Effects on some:	Magnitude (how many?)
	Location (where?)
	Diversity (to whom?)
	Intensity (to what extent?)
Reactions from others:	Magnitude (how many?)
	Location (where?)
	Diversity (to whom?)
	Intensity (to what extent?)

In summary, every issue or trend has at least a dozen directions in which you can go. The direction you take depends on several factors:

- The nature of the audience for which you are writing
- What's already been written about it
- Which questions remain unanswered
- Which experts and affected persons you have access to
- Any other primary source information you can uncover

If you can find new sources of information and answer unresolved questions, then you're on your way toward a great story.

Doing the Reporting

Feature stories on trends and conflicts can't depend on a single source. Hal Karp, a contributing editor to *Reader's Digest* and *Parents* magazine, says, "What people don't understand—feature writing is even more about reporting than hard news reporting because you have so much more depth. They take a lot of time and require a lot of sources." These trend and conflict stories require reporting from five different sources.

People who are the actors. The **actors** in the events are principal sources—the people involved at street level in the nitty-gritty of the action. This is the mother who lost a child in an auto accident or the police officer who filed the accident report.

People who are experts. The **experts** earn a living from finding, fixing or dispensing information. They may be doctors, lawyers, researchers, academics or even auto mechanics.

People who are observers. The **observers** are witnesses. Sometimes they see events first-hand and sometimes they write articles about them. They appear on TV talk shows. They are not as interesting as the actors or as informed as the experts, but often add insight and context.

Facts come from both interviews and background research. They add background, context and depth. They can tell you where, when, why or how these types of events occur.

Numbers convey the magnitude, enormity or frequency of any phenomenon. Too many numbers in too rapid succession bore readers. Numbers show you did your homework, but use them carefully.

A solid story may require dozens of hours in the library followed by dozens of interviews. It depends on background research for context and interviews for color. Too much secondary research without interviews makes a story dull. Likewise, interviews alone with too little background research makes a story irrelevant or outdated.

Hal Karp says the first step is to read everything published on your topic. "The most important thing I can do is locate what's already out there. I have to do as much research as possible, which is incredibly time consuming. I ask myself, 'Who's looked at this topic?' and 'What science is behind it?' I will really dig into the research and find all the primary materials."

Karp says that good features require a combination of anecdotes and hard factual evidence. "You have to have both. Anecdotes bring it to life and make readers see themselves in the topic. You can read statistics all day long about how many kids die in car crashes, but you may not think about it much until you read about a mother who lost her kid in a crash. It's really important to have both."

Advocacy groups are a good source of referrals, according to Karp. Any type of social problem or issue probably has an association or advocacy group representing it. "A lot of the time those people are going to be my best finders," he says. "They're interested in getting the word out because that's their job. They want to help journalists."[12]

When to Quote

Stories can contain too few or too many quotes. Stories with too few quotes run the risk of boring readers or overwhelming them with too many facts. Stories with too many quotes can make them work harder to interpret what's being said. Most readers prefer a healthy balance of interpretive reporting by the writer with colorful and insightful quotes from sources.

Karp says, "I use quotes kind of like exclamation marks as the final point—the point that really drives it home. I also use quotes to balance an article. People like reading articles that are some quotes and some paraphrases. Sometimes you quote because you just need to break it up."[13]

In general, paraphrase facts and numbers in your own words. Use direct quotes from the actors, experts or observers in these three cases: (1) when you have an expert source and the quote adds weight and credibility that it wouldn't hold if it came in the writer's own words, (2) when the quote is colorful and adds a touch of humor or irony to the issue and (3) when it expresses a key point in a particularly trenchant or concise way.

Finally, good pacing depends on the logical movement of ideas throughout the article. You can improve the pace of these stories by ensuring that each paragraph or section thematically progresses from one to the next in a logical fashion. Both sentences and paragraphs should follow one another in logical sequence. And each paragraph must contain a significant idea about your main theme. Each paragraph also must contain a unique idea that adds, contrasts or in some manner develops the theme.

Controversies and trends begin behind the scenes before they turn into news stories or statistics. These stories often begin with a hunch based on personal observations and conversations. Following that hunch into interviews and some research can give you a real "scoop" if you're the first to report a new trend or controversy. For curiosity-filled writers, it's one of the most exciting and interesting types of stories to write.

Sample Story

A Trend Story on Home Automation

This story discusses the growing number of "smart houses" that use new technology for wireless networks and home automation. The reporting included background research to discover the latest trends in technology followed by interviews with technology experts.

For more examples, we again recommend www.pulitzer.org, which contains online versions of all Pulitzer Prize-winning stories since 1995. For the best examples of trend and conflict stories, look at winners in the "Explanatory Journalism" category.

Do You Need a "Smart" House?
By David E. Sumner

Reprinted from Angie's List, *September 2003*

Home automation allows you to listen to music, surf the Internet, share computer files, or watch television from any room in the house using a centralized audio, video or computer source. It will even turn on the irrigation if it hasn't rained in a few days or call you on the phone if an unwanted intruder steps into your yard.

Nathan Olmscheid, who owns a "smart" home near Minneapolis, said, "The neatest thing is that my computer will wake me up, turn on the lights and even turn the radio on to the favorite station that I listen to in the bathroom while I am taking a shower."

Olmscheid built a new home and wired it for home automation including ceiling speakers with volume controls, multi-line phone system, complete network, TV/video distribution, and remote controls. "My sprinkler system will be tied into the computer system as well. When completely finished I will be able to control all my lights, garage doors, appliances, and media equipment," he said. Mr.

Olmscheid recommends and uses "homeseer" software (www.homeseer.com) for his system.

With today's technology, you can control almost anything that uses electricity with a remote control unit, telephone, or computer. Making your house "smarter" is like decorating it. You can go all out and install all of the bells and whistles at once. Or you can build it up little by little as time and budget allow. Many projects and new gadgets cost less than $100, while all the "bells and whistles" can cost thousands.

"People-less" robotic lawn mowers use sensors to avoid traveling beyond an underground wire surrounding the yard's perimeters. "We have had a robo-mower since 2001 and, as an 'end-user' wife, I love it," said Beth Gould of Kokomo, Ind. "The hardest part is laying the ground wiring and that's just because of the physical labor," she added.

The most inexpensive form of remote technology is X-10—a communications "language" that allows compatible X-10 products to link to each other via the existing 110-volt electrical wiring. It also allows you to begin with a starter system and expand later. An X-10 controller plugged into a bedroom outlet can control the lights or appliances in any other room of the house with an X-10 receiver outlet.

For example, Smarthome (www.smarthome.com) sells an X-10 home lighting automation starter kit for about $225. Smarthome.com also offers an online virtual "tour" of an automated home. The tour allows you to go from room to room and see how various electronic components are used in each room. Links give you detailed product descriptions and costs.

In general, you can use X-10 and other home-automation equipment in one of two ways:

- perform actions in one part of the house while you're in another part of the house
- automate actions either on a predetermined schedule or upon activation by sensors (such as light or motion detectors)

When you move beyond X-10 technology, two more choices are necessary: connection system (hardwired vs. wireless) and interface system (X-10 controller, computer, telephone keypad or voice).

---

10 Cool Things You Can Do with Home Automation

1. Use an electronic feeder and "cat toilet" so you won't have to find someone to take care of your cats while you are away for up to four days. (There is nothing invented yet to pet the cats.)
2. Monitor any room in your home with a Web cam from anywhere in the world via the Internet.
3. Use a telephone to call home and give voice commands to control anything in your home (except children).

4. Turn your sprinklers on when there's an intruder in the yard between 9:00 p.m. and 7:00 a.m. or any other time you program.

5. Observe and talk to people who knock on your door before you invite them in.

6. Lie in your hammock while you watch a robotic lawn mower cut your lawn.

7. Use a motion detector to call you at the office when your children arrive home from school.

8. Download (legal) music from the Internet, save it and play it in any room in your house or on outside speakers.

9. Watch your cable or satellite TV programs from a portable TV in any room.

10. Install a voice-activated lie detector on your telephone system to tell you when your caller isn't telling the truth. Just kidding—that hasn't been invented yet!

Hardwired vs. Wireless

Hardwired systems are more reliable and less prone to outside interference, but cost more and are difficult to retrofit into an existing home. If you are building a new home or remodeling, consider hiring an installer to put in a structured wiring system. That includes a drop ceiling installed in the basement and a PVC pipe with wiring running from the basement to the attic. This will permit a simpler connection of devices on any floor.

Wireless networks are increasingly popular and affordable, however. The main benefit of wireless systems is ease of installation: you don't need to tear down drywall or drill holes in your wall. You can also take them with you if you move. Wireless networks can be slower than wired networks, however, and may require multiple transmitters or access points to maximize speeds.

Interface systems

The interface system is the central unit that allows you to control the various electronic devices in the home.

X-10 controller. The simplest interface system is the X-10 controller unit. You can also use a remote control unit (similar to the one you use for the television or DVD player) to activate the X-10 controller. Professional users believe that X-10 has its limitations.

"X10, coming from a professional standpoint, is not reliable. It can't be customized as easy; it has to go through electrical signals and there's always room for interference there. But from a cost standpoint, it's great," said Gerrit Demik, a home and office automation installer for ITA in Cincinnati. His company uses

AMX, a proprietary software (www.amx.com) designed for the central control panel of an automated home or office.

Mr. Demik recently helped install an automated board room for Pfizer, Inc. "It's AMX controlled. It has a DVD/VCR, an amplifier with speakers, a ceiling projector and electric screen, and a switcher. It all goes back into a touch panel. They can press the Pfizer logo, which will bring a screen up, and they can switch to any of four laptop ports."

Keyboard. Using a graphical interface, you can use your computer keyboard and mouse to program timed events for your home automation system. AMX and other advanced systems use a keyboard or touch control panel. If you have your own Web site, available software will enable you to control any part of your system from anywhere that you have access to the Internet.

Telephone. By using your computer's modem, you can dial into your home computer from remote locations and use touch-tone key commands to activate various parts of the home automation system.

Voice. Voice-recognition systems such as HAL2000 (www.automatedliving. com) and HomeVoice (www.appliedfuture.com) enable you to use a telephone connection or even a microphone connected to your PC to speak commands to trigger remote commands. These systems can also answer back to provide confirmation of the commands.

Toy or Necessity?

When all is said and done, do you really need an automated home? Industry officials admit that sales of home automation technology have not taken off as rapidly as hoped. Why spend good money to turn off living room lights from the bedroom when all you have to do is walk in and flip a switch? Good question, especially if your bank account doesn't have six or seven digits.

The two most practical and popular forms of home automation are security systems and local area networks (LAN) for computers. A wireless LAN, for example, will allow you to tap into the Internet on your laptop from anywhere in the house or even in the backyard. It allows parents and children in different rooms to use the Internet simultaneously without interfering with telephone service. Different users can exchange files and use the same printer and software without installing it on every computer.

"Basically my tablet PC acts as a universal remote control for my entire house," said Mr. Olmscheid. "I can sit in my bed to access a DVD player downstairs and then play it on a television that's in the bedroom. So you only have to have one DVD player, but you can use it in various rooms in the house," said Mr. Olmscheid. He also uses a wireless Internet service provider that beams his Internet access from a tower that is eight miles away. He said wireless Internet access, such as that provided by Stonebridge Wireless (www.sbwireness.net), is especially convenient in rural areas that don't have cable or high-speed DSL lines.

Home security systems have become increasingly sophisticated, effective and affordable. Sensors can detect opened doors, windows, broken windows, human (or pet) motion, and even pressure caused by someone walking on your floors or driveway. Sensor activators can do almost anything you want them to: call you, call the police, record video and sound, turn on the radio, or activate sirens and flashing lights. If you haven't investigated the latest home security technology, then it's worth another look.

If you're interested in learning more, Olmscheid recommended, "Talk to someone who has an automated home so you can see what types of things are available and get a demonstration of what you're interested in doing. Find out whether you can do it yourself or whether you will need a professional installer."

He added, "The most exciting thing about owning an automated home is that I'm always thinking of new things to do. Almost anything you can think of or imagine, you can find a way to do. The technology is there. The possibilities are endless."

Suggested Activities

1. Choose a recent trend or controversial issue and develop three angles based on the approaches discussed in this chapter: (a) central development, (b) effects on some and (c) reactions from others.

2. Choose one issue discussed in *CQ Researcher* and write a 500-word summary on the key facts and opinions related to this topic. Use this as a starting point for developing your own story.

3. Read a trend story from *American Demographics*. Write a one-page report summarizing that trend and suggest an angle to take for an original feature article on that trend.

Shoptalk

Actors: Story sources directly involved with the event or issue that a story describes. Actors may be victims, perpetuators or participants in some other way.

Conflict: Disagreement on issues or events by affected parties, such as labor and management, customers and owners or faculty and administration.

Controversy: The difference between conflict and controversy is one of degree: Serious conflicts turn into public arguments (controversies) between opposing parties.

Experts: Story sources publicly recognized as knowledgeable in a field of endeavor. Experts may be, for example, professional practitioners, academic experts or government researchers.

Investigative reporting: Producing stories that report deceit, fraud or dishonesty on the part of corporate, government or other public officials. After publication, they usually result in public controversy.

News feature: A broadly used term that includes investigative reporting and articles about trends, conflicts and other issues that are not "hard news."

Observers: Story sources who witness events or have some knowledge about them as a result of their profession or hobby. For example, newspaper columnists and editors of trade magazines are observers of the various issues they report on.

Trend: A social or economic phenomenon with a quantifiable dimension such as growth or decline, acceleration or slowing or increase or decrease.

Endnotes

1. Hal Karp, "Kids at Risk: The Alarming Truth About Safety Seats," *Reader's Digest,"* March 1999.

2. Jay Nordlinger, "PETA vs. KFC.: A Dirty War Against the Colonel," *National Review* (Dec. 22, 2003), 27-29.

3. Rebecca Claren, "Fields of Poison: While Farm Workers are Sickened by Pesticides, Industry Writes the Rules," *The Nation* (Dec. 29, 2003), 23-25.

4. Jared Sandberg, "Why U.S. workers are losing the tug of war over toilet paper," *The Wall Street Journal* (Sept. 10, 2003), B1.

5. "Women who rape: a scary trend you don't hear about: female sex offenders," *Jane* (February 2003).

6. Zondra Hughes, "Why some brothers date only whites and 'others'," *Ebony*, (January 2003), 70-72.

7. Interview, Toronto, Ontario, Aug. 5, 2004.

8. Louise Witt, "Why we're losing the war against obesity," *American Demographics* (December 2003-January 2004), 26-31.

9. Rifka Rosenwein, "The Baby Sabbatical," *American Demographics* (February 2002), 36-39.

10. Telephone interview, Nov. 15, 2003.

11. Credit goes to William Blundell in *The Art and Craft of Feature Writing* (New York: Penguin Books, 1986) as the original source of these concepts.

12. Telephone interview, Aug. 2, 2004.

13. Ibid.

Chapter 17
Writing to Inspire

Writers who want to produce articles related to faith should avoid predictable hot-button topics, a judgmental tone and religious jargon that mystifies readers. Learning to appeal to a reader's spiritual side requires skill and sensitivity. This chapter shows you how to:

- Become familiar with hundreds of inspirational publications
- Write in degrees
- Avoid common writing "sins"
- Recognize the line between spiritual and religious

Writer-editor Terry Whalin cringes when he remembers a manuscript that an author once sent him via e-mail with this note attached: "God told me to write this. You need to publish it." Without intending to alienate Whalin, the writer had committed two serious mistakes. First, he had assumed that Whalin had time to open the file containing the unsolicited article, format its many pages, print them and read them. Second, by crediting God with the submission, he had laid a heavy burden on the seasoned editor. The not-so-subtle message was: How could Whalin possibly risk rejecting a submission sent from heaven by way of the Internet?

"Because they see their writing as a ministry, many inspirational writers don't understand that they have to exhibit the same level of professionalism as **secular writers**," explains Whalin, a former associate editor at *Decision* and the author of 55 inspirational books. "Religious publications have higher standards than they used to have, and the challenge for every writer is to study a magazine, understand its purpose and figure out what its editors want."[1]

The Business of Publishing

In his online writers' magazine, *Right Writing News*, Whalin emphasizes that religious publishing is a business and "at the end of the day, editors have to make a profit if they are to stay in business." Although not all inspirational publications are commercial enterprises—many are sponsored by church denominations and other faith-based organizations—their editors expect the same excellent writing as editors whose publications compete on the newsstand. Their goal is to turn out first-class products that please subscribers and, in some cases, attract advertising dollars.

It isn't easy. Many inspirational magazines—*Moody, Aspire, Clarity, Virtue* and *Eternity* among them—have ceased publication for reasons usually related to red ink on the bottom line. Even financially secure publications generally have smaller circulations and fewer advertising pages than their secular counterparts. Still, the inspirational magazine industry is healthy. As proof:

- The Evangelical Press Association includes in its membership more than 250 periodicals with a combined circulation exceeding 20 million.
- The Associated Church Press encompasses nearly 200 publications, Web sites, news services and individual members.
- The American Jewish Press Association represents more than 150 newspapers, magazines, journalists and affiliated organizations.
- The Catholic Press Association is an organization of 190 newspapers and magazines with about 12 million readers.

These professional organizations maintain lively Web sites, some of which offer links to member publications' Web sites. Writers can visit the individual publication's Web sites to sample the writing style, study the writers' guidelines and learn the names of key editors.

Often a single church denomination has many opportunities for writers because it supports a range of magazines aimed at readers of different ages. As an example, the Assemblies of God operates its own Gospel Publishing House that produces one weekly, five monthly, two bimonthly, 15 quarterly, three semi-annual and eight annual publications each year. Factor in its various Sunday school curriculum items and the press prints 14 to 16 tons of gospel literature every day.

Although hundreds of inspirational magazines exist, writers of spiritual material aren't limited to selling their stories to publications that label themselves "inspirational," "spiritual" or "religious." Many newspapers devote a page or an entire section in their Saturday editions to feature stories linked to faith. Editors at secular magazines often are open to inspirational topics if the articles are well written, not preachy in tone and don't offend readers of different faiths. Some publications even encourage the submission of **crossover material** that deals with spiritual issues but is written with a light hand and aimed at all readers regardless of their beliefs. The same general categories of articles that are in demand at secular publications are of interest at inspirational magazines. Among them are:

- Calendar-related features, particularly those that offer new angles on religious holidays and traditions. For example: A travel article about Eureka Springs, Ark., where each Easter the entire town puts on its version of the passion play.
- Profiles of people who are involved in community service or ministry. For instance, a profile of a college football coach who takes his team on a mission trip to a third world nation each spring break.
- How-to articles that help readers who are struggling with spiritual issues. Some examples: "How to Forgive and Move On," "How to Witness to a Co-worker," "How to Raise Mission-minded Kids."
- Essays that explore life-changing personal experiences, such as "My Battle With Clinical Depression."
- Stories that delve into hot topics that range from ethics in the workplace to stem-cell research. For example: "Women Speak Out On a Wife's 'Duty' to Submit to Her Husband."

At a time when Judeo-Christian values are a popular topic for politicians of all persuasions, they're certainly fair game for the media. The key to an article's success is the writer's ability to adjust the intensity of the spiritual content to suit the comfort level of readers.

Learning to Write in Degrees

If you've ever prepared a bath for a young child, you understand the importance of getting the water temperature just right. Typically one hand adjusts the faucets while the other hand makes sweeping motions under the tap. You are at the controls, and you are constantly testing to make sure the water is not too hot for the sensitive bather.

Inspirational writers go through a similar exercise. They, too, are at the controls and must take care not to deliver a message that is uncomfortably "hot" for their sensitive readers. They regulate the flow of the words and intensity of the message. If the story becomes too emotional, too dogmatic, too manipulative or too religious, their readers are likely to object—loudly. The magazine that publishes such an article can expect angry letters complaining that the publication is preaching to them. "If I want a sermon, I'll go to church!" is a familiar line.

Smart writers place publications on an imaginary continuum. At one end of the continuum are publications that would never run an inspirational article regardless of how "cool" the message. On the other end of the continuum are magazines aimed at the most devoutly religious readers. The challenge is to study the glut of magazines between the two extremes and discern their likely positions on the continuum. Some publications might consider stories that are morally uplifting (tepid); others might include material that falls into the "lite-inspiration" category (lukewarm); still others might be willing to publish downright spiritual articles (hot). A skilled writer can take the same topic and write it differently depending on the magazine's place on the continuum.

As an example, a writer once interviewed a TV anchorwoman in the Midwest and sold one version of the profile article to an inspirational women's magazine and another version to a secular city magazine. In the article aimed at religious readers, the writer traced the anchorwoman's "faith journey" and explained how she had had a "spiritual reawakening" and now was including brief inspirational stories as part of the evening newscast. The version published by the city magazine took a less emotional approach and explained the anchorwoman's efforts to balance bad news with good news and occasionally "mention God in a sound bite." The city magazine also chose to include comments from critics who objected to what they perceived as her overly "sunny material." Although the topic of both articles was identical (the anchorwoman's picture ended up on the cover of both publications), the language and tone were different. The profile in the inspirational magazine was much like the "portrait" article that we described in Chapter 12. Its content was 100 percent positive. The city magazine's profile resembled the warts-and-all "photograph" article also explained in Chapter 12.

Seven Deadly Writing Sins

Whether your goal is to sell inspirational articles to inspirational or secular publications, you need to beware of certain minefields in both markets. In keeping with this chapter's topic, we'll call these the seven deadly sins of prospective inspirational writers.

Tired topics. When it comes to looking for appropriate article ideas, too many inspirational writers can't think beyond predictable hot-button topics. These include abortion, prayer in public schools, gay marriage, the death penalty, sexual abstinence for singles and dozens of other subjects that deserve a rest. Yes, these issues are important, and that's precisely why they have been the subjects of endless speeches, sermons, editorials, articles and books. Our best advice: Don't add to the overload. Instead, review the topics that are on everyone's mind and ask yourself if there is a spiritual dimension that you might explore.

False assumptions. To their credit, many inspirational writers can quote the Bible by chapter and verse. But they make a mistake if they assume that their readers are equally knowledgeable. So often inspirational writers include in their articles shorthand references to scripture that mean nothing to people who didn't grow up in a church. Especially if you are trying to write a crossover article for a secular publication, you cannot alienate readers with words like, "As we know from the story of Mary and Martha . . . ." What story? Mary who? Martha who?

Bad language. Some inspirational publications put restrictions on some words. Paul W. Smith, a senior editor for Gospel Publishing House, explains that "words such as 'golly' are viewed as euphemisms for the word 'God'"[2] and are not appropriate for the publications he oversees. On the other hand, editors at secular magazines have little patience for manuscripts that contain what they sometimes call "evangicalese." These might include references to people being "saved," having a "burning bush experience" or exhibiting the "wisdom of Solomon." Such language confuses readers who aren't fluent in religious jargon.

Style is another concern. Some publications, inspirational and secular, are specific about how they handle references to the deity. For example, after the first mention of God, should a writer capitalize He and Him? And how about words like heaven, scripture and Bible?

Lop-sided arguments. The writer who explores just one side of an issue, without acknowledging that another side exists, is being unfair to readers. Many articles that qualify as "inspirational" take a distinct point of view. They advocate or support certain behaviors and beliefs. That's acceptable, but it doesn't mean that an inspirational writer should preach to readers, manipulate information to support an argument or fail to mention the other sides of an issue. Accuracy, balance and objectivity are equally important whether you are writing to inform, writing to inspire or writing to do both.

Sources without clout. Whom you choose to interview for an article sometimes depends on the readers you're trying to reach. We know a writer who earned a byline in a Christian magazine for an article about how to communicate with teenagers. Her expert source was a Christian "personality" who had written several books aimed at Christian parents and was a frequent guest on Christian talk radio. The doctor's name was familiar to people who consumed Christian media, and his advice had clout within that audience. Interestingly, he was virtually unknown in the secular world. This meant that if the writer wanted to rewrite the same article for a secular publication, she would need to find an expert whose credentials would impress secular readers. The Christian world and the secular world often are worlds apart.

Out of touch with reality. Along the same lines, inspirational writers who want to reach secular readers need to know the world they want to change. This means becoming familiar with pop culture, keeping up with trends, consuming newspapers and best-selling books, knowing which films people are flocking to see and which TV shows draw the largest audiences. Writers who don't approve of what's happening in society, and therefore retreat from it, often have difficulty connecting with contemporary readers. They can't use examples with mass appeal; they can't drop names that everyone recognizes.

Bad writing. The skills that translate into success for a secular writer serve the inspirational writer equally well. Just because a writer professes to support the beliefs of a certain publication doesn't mean the writer's bad articles automatically will be published. As Terry Whalin noted at the beginning of this chapter, all writers need to exhibit the same level of professionalism. The expectations for inspirational writers actually may be higher rather than lower. In addition to the standard skills—recognizing interesting topics, conducting good interviews, organizing complex materials, telling good stories—inspirational writers have to understand and respond to the special requirements and sensitivities of inspirational publications.

Walking the Fine Line

America has been called a melting pot because of the ethnic, cultural and religious diversity of its citizens. Although the majority of Americans identify themselves as Christians, other faiths are present and growing. For this reason, some magazines try hard to be inspirational without being overtly Christian. This presents challenges for writers who have to walk a fine line. They want to appeal to readers' spiritual side but not their religious side. They want to write in a way that is meaningful to all, offensive to none. At the same time they don't want to water down their inspirational message to the point that their articles are bland.

The article that we include in this chapter, "The Least Of These," was written by Holly Miller and published in a magazine geared to women of all faiths. In fact, the phrase on the magazine's cover explains that the publication is for "the thinking, believing woman." As you review the article, ask yourself these questions:

- Recalling the continuum of magazines, from overtly secular to overtly religious, how "hot" is the inspirational content of this article? Where does it belong on the continuum?
- Whereas the article mentions God several times, is it aimed at a particular faith or denomination? Would it be equally acceptable to Christian, Jewish and Muslim readers?
- What does the author hope the readers of this article will do with the information it contains?
- If the author wanted to recycle this article for a secular magazine, how would she need to change it?
- How does the author turn this local story into a national story?

Sample Story
The Least Of These

Versions of this story, written by other authors, have been published in numerous secular magazines and newspapers. This version appeared in Clarity, *June-July 2000.*

The Least Of These
by Holly G. Miller

Debi Faris had one eye on dinner and the other on the 5 o'clock news the night she heard the story that changed her life. Someone had abandoned a baby several miles from her hometown of Yucaipa, Calif., and the televised account of the tragedy left her immobile, too horrified to walk across the kitchen floor to silence the report's graphic details. She could do nothing but stand there and absorb the painful description of a newborn boy who had been stuffed into a duffel bag and tossed from the window of a car speeding down a freeway. The story ended with the assurance that police were looking for the parents, and viewers should stay tuned. Not that Debi had a choice. "I couldn't move," she says. "I kept thinking, 'How can this be? How have we become a society that throws away its children as if they are nothing?'"

Four days later, the story still haunted her. Somehow she had to find out what happens to a child's body that no one claims. Is the baby given a name? Does he have some kind of funeral? Does anyone say a prayer over his grave? She thought about contacting the police, the Los Angeles County coroner, somebody, but she didn't know what to say or how to explain her growing obsession with the little boy. "I didn't know why this particular child was touching me so deeply," she says. "I didn't know why I couldn't get on with my life. Finally, I asked God what he wanted me to do, and I felt him saying, 'Debi, pick up the phone and make the call for me.'"

An Act of Love

The information she gathered did little to relieve her anguish. The investigator in the coroner's office was kind, but the procedure that she described seemed routine and uncaring. The bodies of abandoned babies—and the county tallied as many as 15 a year—were assigned numbers, were eventually cremated, and the ashes were stored until enough had accumulated to justify the opening of a common grave. Debi thought about the newborn, the duffel bag, the speeding car and the freeway. "I just can't have that for this child," she said.

With the blessing of her husband, Mark, and their three children, she asked that the authorities release the baby to her for burial. She secured permission, and in her conversations with Gilda—the coroner's investigator who was fast becoming her friend—she learned of another unidentified newborn awaiting cremation. Could she care for him, too? she asked Gilda.

While she waited for the answer, her search for two burial places took her to Desert Lawn Cemetery in Calimesa, where an attendant pointed out an available plot in one area and another in a different section. "Somehow I knew we would be caring for more babies than these two," says Debi, "and I wanted a special place where they could all be together." She asked if there was a larger open area, and soon settled on what has become "a cemetery within a cemetery"—a peaceful portion of Desert Lawn that she calls the Garden of Angels. Her premonition proved right; more babies were in her future.

"Gilda called me one morning and said that the two little boys were ready for release and that I could come pick them up. Then she hesitated and told me that they also had the body of a little girl, about age 2, who had washed up on the beach in Malibu some time ago. She said, 'We know she belongs to somebody. She's been on this earth close to two years; who wouldn't miss her?'"

The coroner had been given the order to cremate the child's body. Gilda asked, "Debi, would you be willing to take care of her, too?" Overwhelmed, Debi told Gilda she needed time to think, but she never doubted her response.

"I knew when I hung up the phone that we would be taking three caskets to the cemetery, but first I needed time alone with God. I remember praying, 'I don't think I can do this, God. I don't think I have the courage.' I stayed quiet for a while until I sensed that what we were doing was right. It was an act of love, and at that moment I made a commitment to offer it to any child who needed it."

A Gift from God

Of the 41 babies she has helped bury since that August in 1996, Debi has given names to five of them herself. (She has enlisted help from others to name the other babies.) The gesture is symbolic rather than official since the law prevents a stranger from naming a baby. The first three, Mathew, Nathan and Dora, were easy to bestow. Each name means "a gift from God," and she believes all children are just that. Then there was 5-year-old Jeremiah, "seeker of truth"—whom the coroner had labeled "John Doe" during the months his body was stored at the morgue while police officers struggled to piece together clues to his identity, his death and the whereabouts of his parents. Most recently Debi named an abandoned newborn for the maintenance worker who found him among the refuse piled high in the bed of his trash truck. Tiny "Joel" had been alive when his mother discarded him, but had bled to death because she did not clamp his umbilical cord before putting him into a beachside Dumpster.

As a way of offering healing to the police officers who investigate the deaths of abandoned children, Debi invites them to name the babies and participate in the services that honor the children. "They're the ones who have to remove the babies from the trash cans, the Dumpsters and the roadways," she says. "I thought it might help for them to be part of something loving that was planned for these children." The police often accept her offer, arriving at the cemetery in full dress uniform and carrying stuffed animals to tuck into the small caskets. "Sometimes they even bring their pastors with them, or they buy the blankets to wrap around the children, or they read poems and release doves as part of the services," says Debi.

The Bigger Picture

Word of Debi's ministry has spread, and volunteers have rallied to help with details that range from making pillows to tuck under the babies' heads to tending the flowers that decorate the Garden of Angels. She has recruited a group of pastors to conduct the services, and her dad makes the white crosses that serve as markers. Local students plan fundraisers to help with expenses, and Debi's 14-year-old daughter, Jessica, sometimes accompanies her mom to the morgue to accept the small bundles that are wrapped in plastic. "At first I was leery because I wanted to protect Jessica from seeing such things, but she's very mature and has asked to go," says Debi. "Preparing the babies (for burial) is the hardest thing I do. I think it's an honor to put my arms around these children, love them and pray for them."

Until recently she handled all of the arrangements from a spare room in her home. Thanks to an anonymous gift she has moved this year to an office in the center of Yucaipa, where she spends more and more time overseeing efforts to lobby government in favor of a "safe abandonment" law. She hopes California soon will follow the lead of Texas in giving reluctant parents—who are often panicked teenage girls—an alternative to the reckless acts that end in death for their newborns. Under a safe abandonment law (which several other states are also in the process of developing), a mother could bring her unwanted baby to a safe place, such as a hospital emergency room or a police station, with the assurance that she won't be prosecuted. The legislation is controversial because opponents believe it allows parents to duck their responsibility and casually dispose of a child whose arrival is inconvenient.

Even more controversial is the notion of baby banks, where a mother can "deposit" her newborn into an incubator-like receptacle equipped with sensors that summon caregivers on call. The idea isn't new—Hamburg, Germany, currently is phasing in a pilot program. A group of churches is working to bring the idea, which they've dubbed "Safe Arms," to Southern California.

The Silence Within

By lobbying for legislation and investigating programs like Safe Arms, Debi hopes to reduce—better yet, eliminate—the need for her Garden of Angels cemetery. Until then, she tends the garden and honors its babies by telling their stories to service clubs, church groups and middle-school students. "It will always be our mission to try and keep children from coming to the Garden of Angels," she tells her audiences. "Until then, by sharing the stories of the children who rest there, we have become their voices."

People who hear the stories often are moved to come to the garden and see for themselves. First-time visitors usually compliment Debi on the lakeside setting with its well-tended flower beds and the tidy white markers decorated with pink and blue hearts, all bearing names. Sounds from the nearby freeway serve as a daily reminder of a baby's death four years ago that caused her to pause and listen to God. "When I see people rushing to get from Point A to Point B, I remember how important it is not to miss what is between one place and another," she says. "I think about the importance of stopping and listening to the urgings of our hearts."

Suggested Activities

1. Review an article that you have written in the past and determine how, without completely rewriting the story, you could add a slightly inspirational dimension.

2. Beginning with the well-known news magazines (*Time, Newsweek, U.S. News & World Report*), analyze several secular publications and identify articles that contain any references to faith or religion. Are the articles promoted in cover lines? Do the writers cover religion objectively, or do you detect attempts to influence readers?

3. Visit the Web site of the **Amy Foundation** (www.amyfound.org) and click to the page that contains the winning entries from the foundation's annual writing contest. Remembering that these cash awards go to inspirational articles published in secular newspapers and magazines, read the first-place winner. How "hot" is the religious content? Who might it alienate? Is it worthy of its $10,000 award? How drastically would the writer have to change the article to delete all inspirational content?

Shoptalk

Amy Foundation: Founded in 1976, it sponsors an annual writing contest that awards $34,000 in prize money. Among criteria for entries: The articles have to contain a verse from the Bible and have to have been published in the secular mass media.

Crossover article: Inspirational article geared to a secular audience.

Secular publication: Magazine or journal containing reading material that is not religious or spiritual. A **secular writer** is one who contributes to secular publications.

Endnotes

1. Interview, July 16, 2004.
2. Interview, April 14, 2004.

Chapter 18

Writing for the Business-to-Business Media

Everyone from accountants to zoologists reads publications that help them do their jobs better. The business-to-business media include thousands of magazines, newsletters and Web sites for every conceivable job and profession. This chapter offers the following tips on how to write for these publications:

- Identifying the readers
- Finding a magazine
- Finding the right idea
- Writing annual reports
- Identifying career opportunities

You've probably never heard of these magazines: *American Window Cleaner, Balloons and Parties, Box Office, Coal People, Hard Hat News, Onion World, Portable Restroom Operator* or *Wines and Vines*. All of these publications look for articles from freelance writers. Most people who want to write for magazines don't dream of someday writing for *Pet Product News* or *The Beverage Journal*. Bylines in *Rolling Stone, Maxim* or *Cosmopolitan* more likely top their wish lists than *Automotive News*. Yet opportunities for careers and freelance sales are greater at these lesser-known periodicals that serve the nation's workforce.

"Writers who have discovered trade journals have found a market that offers the chance to publish regularly in subject areas they find interesting, editors who are typically more accessible than their commercial counterparts and pay rates that rival those of big-name magazines," says Writer's Market,[1] a reference book aimed at freelance writers.

Identifying the Readers

The term **business-to-business media** describes companies that produce magazines, Web sites and trade shows for people in specific jobs, careers and professions. They are businesses that serve businesses by providing professional information to help their readers improve their job performance, increase profits or improve customer service. They also cover trends, mergers, hiring news and other business news within their industries. **Trade journals** or **trade magazines** are more casual but frequently use terms describing the print media produced by these companies.

"Our readers are reading for business information, for news they can use, for the latest trends and developments that will help their business. Our biggest foe is time pressure," says Aric Press, editor-in-chief of *The American Lawyer*.[2]

Writers' guidelines for *Electronic Musician* state: "We like to provide readers with solutions to the various problems encountered in the process of composing, producing, recording and mastering music using electronics." Guidelines for *Thoroughbred Times* explain: "Articles must help owners and breeders understand racing to help them realize a profit." *Vacation Industry Review* wants articles about "anything that will help our readers plan, build, sell and run a quality timeshare or vacation-ownership property."[3]

Just as **convergence** is affecting newspapers, television and radio stations, it's also occurring in the business-to-business media. In addition to print magazines, many of these companies now produce trade shows and constantly updated Web sites. The industry association, American Business Media, represents 230 companies that produce 1,750 print publications, 2,000 Web sites and 850 trade shows each year. Many publishers use **controlled circulation**, which means free subscriptions to targeted readers with key management or decision-making responsibilities. Their advertisers are eager to reach this audience.

The average executive who reads business to business (or b-to-b) magazines spends 2.2 hours per month reading 4.6 titles monthly, according to a recent study by Yankelovich Research for American Business Media. The same study found that almost 70 percent of executive or professional-level subscribers read three or more titles per month.

In appearance, most of these magazines look just like any consumer magazine. Their frequent use of glossy covers, exciting graphics and compelling four-color photography means that all of the production techniques are the same. Content includes news stories and analysis, profiles, trends and issues, how-to articles, book and product reviews and even humor. For example, *Successful Farming* published a story about the author's visit to the National Liars Hall of Fame in Dannebrog, Neb.[4] The same story easily could have been written for many different types of magazines and audiences. We know another writer who sold identical profile articles about radio commentator Paul Harvey first to *The Saturday Evening Post* and then to a business journal serving the carpet industry. The reason for the second sale? One of Harvey's sponsors was a carpet manufacturer. Ironically, the carpet journal paid the author a higher fee than the general interest magazine.

While most consumer magazines have Web sites that replicate their print content, b-to-b companies are more likely to update their content daily or weekly. Whitney Sielaff, publisher and editorial director for *National Jeweler*, says his magazine was historically known as a news magazine in the jewelry business. "The Internet forced us to change it to a news-analysis magazine. We had to back that up with a hard news site that provides constantly updated news to our readers." The extension into various forms of content delivery means, "We are not just writers for a magazine; we are content providers," says Sielaff.[5]

The most mistaken notion about trade magazines is that you have to be an expert or practitioner in the field to write for one of its magazines. Almost all trade journal editors and publishers say they have had better success hiring journalists and training them in the specialty than they have had hiring experts and training them in journalism. Experts more likely write with technical jargon that even readers of a particular specialized magazine might not understand.

Sielaff says when he hires writers or editors for *National Jeweler*, he looks primarily for a journalism degree and newswriting experience. "I want someone who knows how to turn around copy and meet deadlines. I want someone who can copy edit, who knows AP Style and knows how to use a dictionary. I want people who are curious, interested and willing to learn."

Rob Spiegel, a senior editor at *Electronic News*, says b-to-b editors "always choose writing abilities over technical education. They are not interested in engineers who are not trained and adept at reporting."[6]

Another mistaken notion is assuming trade publications want only positive, gushy pieces about products or companies. Writers often have to walk the fine line between being an advocate for an industry and being objective about its products. Some of the best investigative journalism is done by b-to-b reporters who report on defective products, unethical business practices or serious problems affecting their industries. For example, a cover story on "The Workers' Compensation Crisis" in *Entrepreneur* magazine reported how work-related injuries cost U.S. businesses nearly $1 billion per week.[7]

All you really need to write for a trade magazine is an interest in the field and access to some of its practitioners. While highly technical magazines may require some expertise of their writers, others deal with everyday products and services sold in almost any town. Does one of your relatives own a successful carpet-cleaning business? Then send a query to *Cleaning Business*, which looks for "interviews with top professionals" on how they manage their business. Do you know about a great Mexican restaurant in your town? Then look up *El Restaurante Mexicano* in *Writer's Market*. Editor-owner Kathleen Furore, who is based in the Chicago area, says she looks for stories about "unique Mexican restaurants and about business issues that affect Mexican restaurant owners." She adds, "No specific knowledge of food or restaurants is needed; the key qualification is to be a good reporter who knows how to slant a story toward the Mexican restaurant operator."[8]

Rob Spiegel at *Electronic News* says, "The market is robust and even in hard times these publications need freelancers. Yet they receive few queries or inquiries from freelancers."[9]

Finding a Magazine

Unlike consumer magazines, which anyone can subscribe to or purchase, business press magazines are not readily available to consumers. Newsstands don't carry them; they're available by subscription only. The best online source for information is American Business Media's Web site: www.americanbusinessmedia.com. You can click on "membership directory" to browse through an alphabetical listing of 230 companies, links to their Web sites and names and addresses of the magazines that they publish. Or you can search for specific magazines by category or geography. The sidebar on the next page contains information on a dozen of the largest companies that publish between 30 and 300 magazines each.

The best print source is the venerable *Writer's Market,* which contains listings for more than 1,500 trade publications in 60 categories. For the

The Business-to-Business Media: Contact Information

American Business Media
Founded in 1906, this 230-member association of business media companies represents 1,750 print publications, 2,000 Web sites and 850 trade shows and special events.

www.americanbusinessmedia.com
675 Third Avenue
New York, NY 10017-5704
Tel: (212) 661-6360
info@abmail.com

The following list represents 12 of the largest business media companies that publish the most magazines and periodicals. Most of them have numerous regional and international publishing offices outside of their corporate headquarters (listed below).

Advanstar, Inc. (100 publications)
www.advanstar.com
7500 Old Oak Blvd.
Cleveland, OH 44130-3369
Tel: (440) 243-8100

CMP Media LLC (41 publications)
www.cmp.com
600 Community Drive
Manhassett, NY 11030-3847
Tel: (516) 562-5000

Crain Communications, Inc. (30 publications)
www.crain.com
1155 Gratiot Ave.
Detroit, MI 48207-2997
Tel: (313) 446-6000

IDG Publishing (300 publications)
International Data Group
www.idg.com
One Exeter Plaza, 15th Floor
Boston, MA 02116-2851
Tel: (617) 534-1200

The McGraw-Hill Companies (31 publications)
www.mcgraw-hill.com
1221 Avenue of the Americas
New York, NY 10020
Tel: (212) 512-2000

PennWell Corporation (39 publications)
www.pennwell.com
1421 South Sheridan Road
Tulsa, OK 74112
Tel: (918) 835-3161

Penton Media, Inc. (58 publications)
www.penton.com
Penton Media Building
1300 E. 9th Street
Cleveland, OH 44114-1501
Tel: (216) 696-7000

Primedia Business Magazines (60 publications)
www.primediabusiness.com
9800 Metcalf Ave.
Overland Park, KS 66212-2216
Tel: (913) 341-1300

Reed Business Information (162 publications)
www.reedbusiness.com
360 Park Avenue South
New York, NY 10010
Tel: (646) 746-6400

Thomson Media (72 publications)
www.thomsonmedia.com
One State Street Plaza, 27th Floor
New York, NY 10004
Tel: (212) 803-8200

Vance Publishing Corp. (26 publications)
www.vancepublishing.com
400 Knightsbridge Parkway
Lincolnshire, IL 60069-3628
Tel: (847) 634-2600

VNU Business Media (52 publications)
www.vnubusinessmedia.com
770 Broadway
New York, NY 10003-9595
Tel: (646) 654-5000

---

same price (about $30), you can purchase a year's access to writersmar-ket.com, which contains guidelines with frequently updated information on these same 1,500 publications.

Another way is to ask people who work in that field what magazines they read. Dave Lawless, a Panera Bread store manager, says, "The one magazine I've stuck with most of my life is *Nation's Restaurant News*. It has new product news, service trends, health issues and just a lot of practical information to help me run a restaurant." Mike McKinley, an assistant fire chief in Indiana, says he regularly reads the online magazine firehouse.com, which also publishes *Firehouse Magazine*. He says he's especially interested in reading news about firefighter accidents and injuries so he can learn how to prevent them from occurring to his crew.[10]

Chances are you have favorite restaurants, retail stores or service providers who are especially good at what they do. Maybe you have noticed something unique or outstanding at their places of business. Strike up a conversation with the manager, and it probably won't take long to learn what accounts for the difference. Ask about the manager's favorite trade magazines, and you may be ready to contact one of their editors.

Finding the Right Idea

The types of articles most frequently published in b-to-b magazines are:

Profiles of Successful Businesses

This is the most typically written feature by non-experts. Jamel Moledina, editor-in-chief of *Game Developer*, says, "For profiles of a successful business, I ask for quantifiable data. One purpose of doing such a piece is to provide a "how-to" to others looking for specific practices."[11] Rick Levine, editor of *Made to Measure* says, "We look for features about large and small companies whose employees wear uniforms—restaurants, hotels, hospitals, public safety and so forth."[12]

Profiles of Successful Owners or Professionals

These articles focus on successful owners and what makes them successful. Michael Griffin, an editor at *Alternative Energy Retailer*, says, "A freelancer can best break into our publication with features about retailers. These profile stories focus on one aspect of business management or sales and marketing techniques that make this dealer or retailer stand out in some way. Stick to details about what has made this person a success."[13] *Chief of Police* magazine editor Jim Gordon says, "Writers should contact law enforcement officers right in their own areas and we would be delighted. We want to recognize good commanding officers who are involved with the community."[14]

New Products and Book Reviews

Most products reviewed in trade publications are not consumer products, but b-to-b products purchased by one company from another. These products help businesses improve their manufacturing techniques, customer service or employee management. B-to-b publications also look for reviews of new books covering practices, trends and issues in their industries.

Management Tips, Strategies and Trends

These articles report on what's happening in the field or what successful people do. For example, Kim Williamson, editor-in-chief of *Boxoffice*, says, "We are a general news magazine about the motion picture and theater industry and are looking for stories about trends, developments, problems or opportunities facing the industry."[15]

As another example, *Successful Farming* published a story called "It's About Time," which described the time-management techniques used to manage a herd of 35 beef cows. Don Lowenstein, a part-time Missouri farmer, used computer analysis to determine the time required to complete each herd management task. His yearly labor totaled about 100 hours, resulting in a net profit of $6,000 or about $60 per hour. "I've kind of got the cow herd on autopilot. I'm either the world's laziest farmer or the most efficient," he told *Successful Farming*.[16]

Pet Product News guidelines advise prospective writers to "Talk to pet store owners and see what they need to know to be better business people in general and how they deal with everything from balancing the books and free trade agreements to animal rights activists."[17] Guidelines for *Qualified Remodeler* say, "We focus on business management issues faced by remodeling contractors—just about any matter addressing small business operation."[18]

Writing Annual Reports

Writers often plead ignorance when it comes to economics. They think they could never write an organization's annual report because they aren't fluent in the mysterious jargon that "explains" a company's profits and losses. They think they surely would need a degree in business to have a hand in producing a publication that contains endless pages of numbers, pie charts and bar graphs.

Think again. The trend in annual reports is toward including human-interest stories that put a "face" on an organization. The financial information—provided by accountants, not by feature writers—remains at the core of the book, but feature material tells about the people behind the numbers. For example:

- The 2003 annual report issued by Bristol-Myers Squibb Co. contained an article about a coast-to-coast cycling event called the Tour of Hope. The cyclists were cancer survivors; their spokesperson was Lance Armstrong, himself a cancer survivor and multiple winner of the Tour de France. The company's involvement as the event's sponsor and as the maker of cancer-fighting drugs was included only in a low-key way. The message of the story was that a cancer diagnosis isn't a death sentence, and a team of cyclists had pedaled from Los Angeles to Washington, D.C., to prove it.
- An article in the 2003 IBM annual report explained the plight of Spanish-speaking Internet users. Because English is the dominant language of most Web sites, many Latinos couldn't access important information. In response, IBM created and donated translation software to nonprofit organizations that serve Hispanic Americans. The emphasis of the story wasn't on IBM but on the problem and its solution.

- When the Field Museum in Chicago wanted to bring priceless fragments of the Dead Sea Scrolls to its galleries, it requested financial support from Lilly Endowment in Indianapolis. The endowment made a $300,000 grant and later published a story about the scrolls in its 2000 annual report. The article barely mentioned the endowment's generous gift but stressed the historic significance of the antiquities and how area schoolchildren benefited from exposure to the items.

An organization's annual report has similarities to a high school or college yearbook. It chronicles the events, successes and failures of the previous 12 months. The federal government requires publicly held companies—those with stockholders—to issue honest and accurate statements of their financial conditions. What a company provides in addition to the financial data is up to the company. Many organizations, even those not required by law to produce annual reports, issue some kind of year-end book as a way to reach out to their customers, clients, patrons and constituents. Like editors of college yearbooks, annual report editors usually choose a theme and then create feature material to support it. Often they hire freelance writers to bring a fresh perspective to the organization's stories. The result isn't objective journalism but advocacy journalism. An annual report doesn't constantly pat its sponsoring organization on the back, but it does maintain a positive point of view. If a story has a negative aspect, that aspect is acknowledged, explained and put into context.

Identifying Career Opportunities

The major reason b-to-b media offer good career choices is that they publish twice as many magazines as the consumer press. Experts estimate the number of consumer magazines at between 2,000 and 2,500, whereas trade magazines number more than 4,000. While most consumer magazines are published in New York City, business press publishers are scattered around the country in cities such as Atlanta, Cleveland, Chicago, Denver, Detroit, Houston, Kansas City, Seattle and Washington, D.C. And although New York City is a wonderful place to build a magazine career, many people simply don't want to live there.

If you're looking for a job, the best place to conduct a geographic search is the *Gale Directory of Publications*, which most large libraries carry. This four-volume annual directory contains an alphabetical state and city listing of all radio and television stations, magazines and newspapers in every U.S. city.

Sielaff of *National Jeweler* has spent his 15-year career in the business-to-business media. He sees three advantages to a b-to-b career over a consumer magazine career: more opportunities to write, more influence on your audience and more interaction with an educated professional audience.

First, he says, "If you really want to write, you can get that done easier in this field. The Web offers some good opportunities as well." Second, "You're catering to a higher level of educated audience. Most of those you're writing for are heads of companies or business owners and smart entrepreneurs. If you're writing for a newspaper, chances are you're out there talking to people on the street." And third, he says, "You can really have an effect. You are helping people improve in what they do on a daily basis. You can become an integral part of their work."[19]

Suggested Activities

1. Browse through your city's yellow pages. Find five different types of businesses and call their owners or managers. Ask which trade magazines they read and what types of articles they find most helpful.

2. Find profiles of five successful businesses, managers or professionals in business-to-business magazines. Use americanbusinessmedia.com or your library to locate these magazines. Discuss the angle that each profile takes and what specific type of useful information it offers to readers.

3. Identify five business-to-business magazines in *Writer's Market* that you think you would like to write for. Telephone or e-mail one of the editors and ask what type of articles you would have the best chance of publishing from where you live.

Shoptalk

Business-to-business media: A term describing companies that produce magazines, tabloid newspapers, newsletters, Web sites and trade shows serving people who work in specific jobs, careers and professions. Their main purpose is to provide information that serves the professional needs of their readers and users.

Controlled circulation: Free subscriptions offered by trade publishers to targeted readers with key management or decision-making responsibilities in their companies or organizations. Some publishing companies offer free subscriptions to these targeted readers and paid subscriptions to others.

Convergence: The trend toward one company owning a variety of media outlets and having their writers and editors produce content for all of these outlets. They may include newspapers, magazines, newsletters, Web sites and television and radio stations.

Trade magazines: The print publications produced by companies that comprise the business-to-business media, who may also produce tabloid newspapers, newsletters, Web sites, conferences and trade shows that serve their industries.

Endnotes

1. Kathryn S. Brogan, editor, *Writer's Market 2004* (Cincinnati: F&W Publishing, 2004), 768.

2. Aric Press to author, Aug. 23, 2004.

3. *Writers Market 2004* (Cincinnati: F&W Publishing, 2004).

4. Roger Welsch, "Musings From the Mud Porch," *Successful Farming* (April 2004), 65.

5. Telephone interview, Aug. 2, 2004.

6. Rob Spiegel, "Writing For Trade and Business Publications," *2004 Writer's Market Online* (Cincinnati: F&W Publishing, 2004), 60; see also Robert Lee Brewer, "What trade editors want to see," in writersmarket.com (accessed November 27 2002).

7. Joshua Kurlantzick, "The Workers' Compensation Crisis: Can It Be Fixed?" *Entrepreneur* (January 2004), 57.

8. Kathleen Furore to author, July 9, 2004.

9. Rob Spiegel, "Writing for Trade and Business Publications," *2004 Writer's Market Online* (Cincinnati: F&W Publishing, 2004), 60.

10. Both quotes came from personal interviews, July 2004.

11. Jamel Moledina to author, July 19, 2004.

12. *Writers Market 2004* (Cincinnati: F&W Publishing, 2004), 798.

13. Ibid., 809.

14. Jim Gordon to author, July 14, 2004.

15. Kim Williamson to author, July 13.

16. Gene Johnston, "It's About Time," *Successful Farming* (April 2004), 44.

17. *Writers' Market 2004* (Cincinnati: F&W Publishing, 2004), 867.

18. Ibid., 786.

19. Telephone interview, Aug. 2, 2004.

Chapter 19

Writing for the Internet

Good writing is good writing regardless of the medium, so writing for the Internet means following all of the advice in the previous chapters. Yet, writing for online publications and Web sites poses unique challenges. This chapter explains and discusses:

- Why Internet writing is different
- Eight tips for Internet writing
- Where to get published
- Electronic rights

The Internet offers many opportunities for beginning writers. This electronic market is expanding and will continue to grow as more people use the Internet and wireless access expands. It's easier to get an article accepted on a Web site or Internet-only publication than in print. Internet editors are more accessible than print editors and usually respond quickly to e-mail questions and queries. While the pay is less, many editors purchase first electronic rights, which allows you to continue to look for print publishers for the same material.

What's the difference between an Internet market and an online market? **Internet markets** consist of publishers whose material is available on traditional Web sites. **Online markets** include Internet markets as well as private **intranets**—not accessible to the public—and CD publishers. Since these types of publishers are limited, this chapter focuses on the widely expanding Internet market.

Internet markets provide diverse opportunities for sales. Some of the markets that pay freelance writers include:

- Internet-only magazines (sometimes called **"zines"** or "E-zines")
- News sites
- E-mail newsletters
- Specialized content (such as travel and health) sites
- Trade magazines and association sites

The success of all Web sites depends on one thing—their ability to make users return. There's one way to do that—offer original content and update it regularly. Consequently, writing for the Internet requires top-notch research skills. Online readers are highly literate and probably know what's in current newspapers and magazines. So when they come to the Internet, they expect fresh information.

Why Internet Writing is Different

The average person is more likely to read a 2,500-word article in a print publication than on a computer screen. Anything appearing on a computer screen is more difficult to read for at least six reasons. These six reasons apply to any type of online publishing or reading:

- Readers must concentrate harder on screen text because the text has less resolution. Laser printer text has 600 dots per inch and a full-color magazine photo may have 2,400 dots per inch. Computer screens, however, only have 72 to 96 dots per inch.
- Screen text reading is slower. One study found that most people read screen text 25 percent slower than print text. They likely spend less time reading an Internet article than reading a book or magazine. And they often comprehend and recall less.
- Screen text lacks the context of print material. You can't view as much on a screen as you can on a magazine or newspaper page. Therefore, online text often lacks the visual cues of magazines (side-bars, subtitles, captions, photos, etc.) that help reveal the text's meaning. When you pick up a magazine, you usually look first at its cover and contents page. When you turn to an article, you glance at the photos and other graphics. Internet users, however, can jump straight to an article from an outside link without ever seeing the home page or other contextual material.
- Screen text lacks the permanence of print material. It's "here" right now but gone in a click—sometimes an accidental click. When you read a magazine article, you can flip back to the previous page to re-

fresh your memory. Internet text requires more time and effort to move back, forward and around. Readers get more easily distracted and may not return after clicking a link to another article or Web site.

- Screen text restricts the mobility of its users. You can put a book in your pocket or roll up a newspaper or magazine and carry it under your arm. Unless it's a wireless laptop, reading a screen requires users to sit in a particular position in a particular chair. They can't read while sitting back or stretching out on a couch in the same way they can with print material.
- Reading screen text feels like work—not fun—for many people because it's what they do at their jobs all day. These people turn to the Internet for work-related reasons, not for entertainment.

These obstacles make writing for the Internet and other online venues more difficult than it appears. You can't write in the same style you do for print publications. Magazines and newspapers can't "dump" their print material onto a Web site and expect users to read, enjoy and use it in the same way. Any article in any magazine is more likely to be read by subscribers than the same article appearing on a Web site where thousands of surfers click in and click out daily.

Eight Tips for Internet Writing

These principles of Internet writing are based on the premise that busy readers zoom in and out of Web sites quickly. "When you're writing for the Web, you have to be hyper-aware of our audience's lack of patience. Think of our text in terms of short bites," says an editor of an online magazine.[1] Another adds, "Online writing needs to be snappy and exciting because it's harder to read on computer screens, and I think much harder to retain the information . . . . Use provocative leads, short paragraphs and lots of subheads to break up the text and make it easier on the eyes."[2] Therefore, we offer you these practical suggestions to make electronic writing more compelling and likely to keep readers' eyes on the screen.

Begin With the Most Important Information

Internet articles are more likely to be read when the most important information comes first, whereas print magazine readers are more likely to remain with a writer's logical presentation in a long piece. Internet writers, therefore, may have to use the traditional "inverted pyramid" structure of newspaper writing.

Not only should the most important idea introduce an article, Internet writers should also begin every paragraph with the main point. "Research on reading printed text shows that people generally understand and remember paragraphs best when the paragraphs start out with the main point. When people skim through text on a page, they are most likely to read the first sentence of every paragraph," say Jonathan and Lisa Price in *Hot Text: Web Writing That Works.*[3]

Write Simple and Write Short

Writing short and simple is a time-tested principle of print journalism, but the Internet requires you to economize even more for its impatient readers. Writing short and simple doesn't mean you have to avoid profound ideas or complex information. It simply means you have to work harder to present profound ideas and complex information in a shorter amount of space. Here are three suggestions to help you do that.

Use Fewer Words

Economical writing packs more ideas into fewer words. For example, suppose an editor assigns the same story to two writers about how a local hospital staff makes bioethical decisions involving life and death. Suppose that story involves 20 facts. Writer "A" comes back with a 1,000-word story, while Writer "B" returns with a 2,000-word story. Therefore, Writer "A" has used 50 words per fact whereas writer "B" used 100 words per fact. Like a hybrid car with higher gas mileage, writer "A" is a more efficient writer.

Use Short Sentences and Paragraphs

Create simple declarative sentences. The period is your best friend. Use it frequently to avoid compound and complex sentences. In general, limit paragraphs to three to five sentences.

Use Everyday, Concrete Language

Imagine that every reader has a split-second to comprehend every word you use. If it doesn't register in the brain in that split second, then it's lost. Consequently, choose nouns that describe everyday objects and events and verbs that display specific actions.

Make It Punchy and Personal

You have more freedom to put voice and style in Internet writing. Make it quick and punchy with a little "attitude." Too many publications publish cold, faceless prose. Let the reader feel emotion behind your writing. *Hot Text: Web Writing That Works* says that writing for Internet magazines requires the writer's personal involvement: "Some of the best writing in Webzines steams with emotion and attitude. Why? To get the readers' attention."[4] The book's authors suggest playing with metaphors, puns and irony; being conversational; ranting occasionally; and intentionally provoking discussion. Finally, encourage response by giving readers your e-mail address. Get to know your readers in a way that print publishing won't allow.

Create Subheadings

Internet writers structure and organize their material into chunks of easily highlighted information. Remember that Internet readers often browse through the subheadings of an article before deciding to read it.

Use Bulleted and Numbered Lists

Internet readers look for quick bites and chunks of information. Bulleted and numbered lists provide several advantages:

- They quickly capture the reader's scanning eye
- They highlight important information
- They summarize main points
- They provide contrast and emphasis

Lists do another favor for the reader. In essence, the writer edits the material for the reader and says, "If you've only got a minute, here are the most important things you need to know."

Think Links

Links are two-edged swords. Too many can distract readers and tempt them to leave your page. The right kinds, however, add credibility to your material by linking to examples and substantiating evidence. They can include tutorials or "how-to" Web sites, case studies and examples, reports or background information. You can place links in a separate sidebar or within the text itself. If you include links within your text, put them at the end of the sentence or paragraph.

Emphasize Key Words

Some Internet search engines return results based on how frequently **key words** and phrases appear in a document. Others, such as Google, rank results according to how often key phrases are linked with other Web sites with similar content. You can also emphasize key words by linking to other Web sites with similar content as the key words.

Emphasize Useful Information

Readers are more likely to come to the Internet for specific information than entertainment or amusement. It's just not as much fun to read a page-turning novel on the screen as on a couch. Therefore, you'll find a higher predominance of service journalism on the Internet than in print. Consumers want to know where to go on vacation, what kind of tires to put on their cars, which medicine to use or where the good restaurants are.

Where to Get Published

Because of rapidly changing Web sites, we're reluctant to recommend specific Internet publications that accept or pay for freelance articles. Any that we recommend today may be gone before you read this. However, we do recommend some Web sites that specialize in offering resources and information for online writers.

Writer's Market Online and writersmarket.com both come from F&W Publishing, which also publishes the monthly magazine *Writer's Digest*. A writersmarket.com subscription costs $30 but provides constantly updated writers' guidelines and information on key markets. We talk more about these Internet resources in Chapter 20.

Hundreds of Web sites specialize in information and resources for print and Internet writers. Those that offer specific information on paying markets charge a fee. However, here are some of the best that are up to date at the time of this book's publication:

- www.journalists.org is maintained by the Online News Association. The organization was founded in 1999 by working members of the online press. ONA is open to journalists from around the world who produce news on the Internet and other digital platforms and to others with an interest in online news.

- www.marketsforwriters.com is published by Anthony and Paul Tedesco, authors of *Online Markets for Writers*. While it doesn't offer free market information, you can purchase an e-text copy of their newest book full of guidelines for paying markets.
- www.webwritingthatworks.com is published by Jonathan and Lisa Price, authors of *Hot Text: Web Writing That Works*. It doesn't offer a lot of market information, but it does provide numerous articles and tip sheets for online writers. You can also purchase a copy of their book.
- www.writing-world.com is published by Moira Allen, author of *Writing.com* and *2,000 Online Markets for Writers*. This site offers free resources and how-to articles for writers. Although it doesn't have free market information, you can purchase an inexpensive e-text copy of her book *2,000 Online Markets for Writers*.

Know Your Electronic Rights

Electronic rights have become a battlefield between writers and publishers. In the 2001 decision "Tasini vs. *New York Times*," the U.S. Supreme Court ruled that newspapers and magazines had to obtain the writer's permission before selling their freelance contributions to electronic databases such as LexisNexis. The court also ruled that "first rights" meant first rights for one medium only (such as print or Internet), but not both unless specifically agreed upon.

That sounds like good news for writers, but it also means that more magazines demand "all rights" from freelance writers so they can publish the articles in any medium. We know of one writer who sold an article and then saw it posted on the magazine's Web site. She went back to the editor and demanded more payment. Unfortunately, she had sold all rights without realizing it. So if you plan to sell to an online-only magazine, make sure you're specific about selling "electronic rights" or "first electronic rights," so you have the freedom to seek a print publisher.

Once an article appears on a Web site, regardless of whether the writer sold specific "electronic rights," the author might have difficulty selling it elsewhere. That's because many print publishers regard anything published on the Internet—including personal Web sites—as previously published material.

The electronic market shows no signs of slowing down. Handheld computers now allow wireless access to the Internet—even in automobiles—where a wi-fi network exists. Hundreds of restaurants and coffee shops offer wireless access to their customers. For example, much of the Internet research for this book was completed using wireless access. Despite growing pains, the electronic market is expanding and will continue to grow as more people use the Internet and wireless access increases.

Suggested Activities

1. Write a 750-word how-to article using the tips in this chapter.

2. Use terms such as "Internet markets for writers" or "online writers' markets" in search engines such as www.askjeeves.com, www.google.com or www.yahoo.com. Develop a list of the five Web sites for writers that you think are most useful, practical and free.

3. Use the Yahoo magazine directory to locate writers' guidelines from five magazines. Remember that not all magazines offer guidelines on their Web sites, and you may have to search through at least 10 sites to find them.

Shoptalk

Internet markets: Web sites that pay freelance writers to produce content. These sites may be sponsored by publications, companies, associations or nonprofit organizations.

Intranet: Electronic distribution of articles and information within a company or private organization. Intranets are not accessible by the public.

Key words: Words and phrases that emphasize the main theme of an article. Key words should be used frequently enough to allow search engines to rank them highly in Web searches.

Online markets: Paying markets for writers that include Internet markets as well as e-mail newsletters, private intranets and CD publishers.

Zines: Sometimes called "E-zines" or "Webzines," these special interest publications are published only on the Internet.

Endnotes

1. Quoted in Anthony Tedesco and Paul Tedesco, *Online Markets for Writers* (New York: Henry Holt, 2000), 43.

2. Ibid., 48.

3. Jonathan and Lisa Price, *Hot Text: Web Writing That Works* (Indianapolis: New Riders, 2002), 199.

4. Ibid.

Part IV
Selling Feature Articles

Chapter 20
Marketing Your Words

Books, Web sites and numerous other tools are available to help freelance feature writers sell their articles. Among the best strategies for tuning into a periodical's needs is analyzing the contents of the publication and determining its target audience. This chapter offers:

- An overview of marketing resources
- Techniques for understanding readers' preferences
- Ways to pick up on editorial "clues"
- Keys to a publication's personality

A good way for feature writers to build their reputations, expand their portfolios and attract the attention of editors is to accumulate published **clips** early in their careers. Rather than explain to an editor what you think you can do, it's better to show an editor what you've already done. Clips prove your writing ability.

Up to now, this book has concentrated on teaching the skills needed to create interesting and informative feature articles. Now we're shifting the emphasis and discussing how to market the words that you write. Specifically, how do feature writers sell articles to publications on a freelance basis? Newcomers to the profession tell us this is an important question to answer for at least four reasons.

- Freelance bylines sometimes lead to full-time jobs. Certainly a benefit of being published is the ability to tuck a **tear sheet** into the envelope that contains your résumé. Clips set you apart from those who don't have them.

- If you work in public relations, part of your job may involve writing and placing articles about your client or employer. A media relations specialist needs to know how to approach editors and convince them that a feature idea is newsworthy.
- Staff members of local newspapers occasionally write articles that may interest readers beyond their immediate circulation area. The idea of earning a byline in a national publication is appealing, but these writers need help in knowing where to look and how to identify likely markets for their stories.
- Often people who have worked full-time for media organizations decide for a variety of reasons to leave their salaried jobs and try their hands at freelancing. They want to know how to make the transition from one side of the editor's desk to the other.

Tuning into Available Help

Hundreds of resources are available to freelance writers hoping to break into national print. In fact, an entire industry has emerged to serve people who want to sell their words to newspapers and magazines. Products include reference books that list the names and addresses of publications; monthly and bimonthly writers' magazines that offer tips on how and where to sell freelance articles; writers' workshops that schedule marketing sessions led by editors; newsletters that keep subscribers up to date on changes in the publishing industry; and writing-related Web sites that sponsor chat rooms where writers swap tips about potential markets.

We can't begin to cover all the places where you can go to tap into marketing advice. The number of products expands and contracts daily as Web sites and newsletters come and go. All we can do is to introduce you to a few major print and electronic resources and let you take it from there. We also can suggest several ways that you can evaluate a publication on your own to determine if it is a good place to send your queries, proposals and manuscripts.

A logical launch point for any discussion of marketing is writersmarket.com, a searchable database that includes information on some 2,300 magazines. The roots of this online resource wind back to 1921 when the first edition of *Writer's Market* hit the bookstores. Still published annually, the 1,100-page *Writer's Market*—like its electronic counterpart—provides the names and addresses of publications and indicates the editors to whom you should send your query letters. Both the print and online products let you know if a magazine accepts e-mail submissions, how long you are likely to wait for a response from an editor, whether a publication expects photos to accompany the words and what the pay scale is.

As an example, if you look up *Seventeen* magazine, you find that freelancers write about 20 percent of the publication's content. That's encouraging. More good news: Writers who are fortunate enough to sell articles to this publication are paid about $1 a word, and their articles have a potential audience of 2.4 million readers. If you think you have a story idea suitable for *Seventeen*, you need to know the kind of proposal that the editors prefer to see. The guidelines specify that the staff wants each query letter to include an outline of the proposed article, a possible lead paragraph and clips of the writer's previously published work.

The value of the electronic version of *Writer's Market*, of course, is its capacity to stay current. From month to month, the overseers of writersmarket.com are likely to make hundreds of changes to their listings. Editors are a mobile bunch; they frequently change jobs, titles and responsibilities. The editorial needs of publications also shift. It's possible that information gleaned from any printed market guide is out of date by the time you read it. You don't want to pitch an idea to an editor who no longer works at a magazine. Worse yet, you don't want to send a proposal to a magazine that has ceased publication.

The simplest way to make sure you're pitching the right article to the right editor is by making a telephone call to the magazine. Call the number listed in *Writer's Market* and explain to the receptionist, "I'm writing an article about X topic and would like to know which editor I should send it to." At smaller magazines you may even get to talk to the editor who can give you advice and suggestions.

Similar to *Writer's Market* is *The Writer's Handbook*, which offers marketing information on some 1,700 magazines in 50 categories. Both books are available in the reference areas of most libraries and in major bookstores. Both books also are affiliated with monthly writing magazines. The parent company of *Writer's Market* publishes *Writer's Digest* magazine, and the company that publishes *The Writer's Handbook* produces *The Writer* magazine. A third writers' magazine is the bimonthly publication *Writers' Journal*. All three magazines include marketing information in every issue. They usually cluster potential markets by categories. One month they might focus on publications geared to teens; the next month they might choose to highlight men's muscle magazines. Each listing gives an editor's name and tells what he or she wants to see.

For people interested in writing for religious or inspirational publica-

tions, the 20-year-old *Christian Writers' Market Guide,* updated and released each January, offers contact information for more than 650 print
periodicals and 100 online magazines. Sally Stuart is the author of the
guide and overseer of the Web site at www.stuartmarket.com. She also updates marketing information in her monthly column in *The Christian
Communicator* magazine and discusses marketing trends and techniques
in its sister publication, the bimonthly *Advanced Christian Writer.*[1] These
resources are particularly helpful because many writers are unaware of the
number of inspirational publications that exist. Most of the magazines
have small staffs, are not sold on newsstands and are available only by
subscription or as giveaways by churches. Stuart's Web site includes links
to many of the magazines listed in her guide. This enables potential contributors to follow the links that lead to specific marketing advice from the
publications' staffs.

Collecting Writers' Guidelines

The writers' guidelines that magazines distribute directly to writers re-
questing them may help more than anything else. These guidelines, available at no charge, describe the kinds of materials the editors are interested
in seeing, the preferred length of articles and typical payment that contributors can expect. Some editors go into great detail and offer separate
guidelines for different types of submissions—travel article guidelines,
fiction guidelines, photography guidelines, etc. Writers sometimes can
find guidelines posted on the publications' Web sites. Of course you also
can receive writers' guidelines through the mail. If you request guidelines
via snail mail, remember to include a self-addressed, stamped envelope.

Some publications also are willing to share their future editorial calendars with writers. This is especially true of magazines that select themes
for their issues and actively solicit articles that support the themes. For example, a bimonthly national women's magazine once announced on its
Web site that the theme for its upcoming January-February issue would be
"career women, including at-home careers." The same publication
planned to examine health-related topics in its March-April issue and
wanted feature articles about mentoring and parenting for its May-June
issue. Recalling that most magazine staffs work on a lead time of four to
six months (see Chapter 15), the smart freelance writer studies the editorial calendar and then pitches an idea about a home-based business in July
for the January issue, proposes a wellness story in September for the
March issue and offers a parenting article in November for the May issue.

Even if a publication doesn't adopt specific themes, its staff is likely to plan at least part of the magazine's content a year in advance. This ensures that the menu of articles is well balanced and in tune with readers' interests. For example, *The Midwest Traveler* magazine, which covers Missouri and certain parts of Illinois, Indiana and Kansas, produces a printed version of its editorial calendar that lists the major stories for each of its bimonthly issues as well as the **closing dates** for the issues. A recent editorial calendar announced articles that focused on each of the geographic regions that the magazine serves. These stories were carefully spaced from issue to issue and took the form of round-up articles ("Midwestern Candy Kitchens" for January-February, "Perfect Picnic Sites in Missouri" for May-June) and calendar-related stories ("Collegiate Football Tours" for September-October and "Decorating Midwest Historic Sites for the Holidays" for November-December).

Editorial calendars serve as tools for a publication's advertising staff. The calendars give potential advertisers an idea of the content of each issue of the magazine. Based in part on that information, an advertiser decides whether or not to buy space. For example, if a travel magazine plans to publish a round-up article on remote skimobile trails in Upper Michigan for its December issue, a manufacturer of skimobiles might want to purchase space in that issue. Although editors usually assign major stories to regularly contributing writers well in advance of circulating their editorial calendars, the shorter articles often are up for grabs. Writers who receive a calendar can quickly put together query letters. If a publication accepts telephone queries, they might call an editor in the hope of "claiming" stories for themselves.

Analyzing Markets—On Your Own

Besides visiting Web sites, accessing guidelines and tracking down editorial calendars, a writer can learn a lot about a magazine by analyzing back issues. When done carefully, this analysis alerts the writer to the kinds of articles that editors are likely to buy. It also can indicate whether or not the publication welcomes freelance submissions from newcomers.

Part of a writer's challenge is to figure out the **demographics** of the publication's readers, pick up on new directions that the editors are pursuing and determine if the magazine is mostly staff written. As you conduct your analysis, take note of how often a publication revisits a topic and if it recently has covered the topic you want to propose. All this information, plus the tips you glean from reference books, Web sites, guidelines and

How to "Nationalize" a Story

Many writers fail to sell their work to national publications because the articles that they submit are too local in scope. For example, a story about a college basketball team that devotes several hours a week to tutoring underprivileged kids may earn rave reviews from readers of the school's newspaper. Offer the same article to a national magazine and you can expect a rejection. Why? The story is of limited interest because it involves just one campus.

Don't be discouraged. Often a writer can "nationalize" an article by doing a limited amount of additional research. Let's continue with the example of the basketball team and see how nationalization works.

- **Determine if it is a trend.** Perhaps what is happening on the local campus is also happening at other schools. Send e-mails to athletic directors at a sampling of universities across the country and ask if they encourage athletes to do community service. If a sizable number of the ADs answers "yes," you've documented a national trend. Your story's readership has just expanded.
- **Do the math.** Based on your e-mail survey, create some statistics that verify the trend. Your assertion that a trend exists will acquire credibility when you write, "Of the 20 schools surveyed, more than half support programs to involve athletes in volunteer activities."
- **Look for quotable sources.** When you write a local story, you interview local sources. When you write a national story, you solicit comments far beyond your circulation area. Go back to your survey and identify one or two out-of-state athletic directors whose observations will have clout with national readers. Conduct brief interviews. An additional quote from a NCAA official will round out your research.
- **Piggyback on something in the news.** Look for ways to make your story timely. When you pitch your article to an editor, point out that sports pages too often focus on athletes in trouble. Your article offers a refreshing change from these negative headlines.

Transforming a local story into a national story doesn't involve as much work as you might think. In the case of the student athletes, most of the article is going to deal with what's happening at the nearby campus. The difference is that the writer will use the local example to illustrate a national trend. Statistics and quotes from national sources will help create a larger context within which the local story unfolds.

calendars, should help you figure out if your unsolicited material has a chance of earning a place in a future issue. Good market research can greatly reduce the number of rejection letters that a freelancer receives.

Get to Know the Readers

Magazine staffs know a lot about their readers. They know the gender breakdown. They know how many subscribers live in each of the 50 states. They know their readers' average age, marital status, income and education levels. They know if their readers are predominantly conservative or liberal in their politics. They know what kinds of products their readers buy, where they are likely to travel on vacation and if they prefer to drive or fly to those destinations.

This demographic information is essential when a publication's advertising representatives call on potential advertisers. Companies make advertising decisions based on circulation figures, magazine content and demographic data. It's not good enough to know that a magazine has a million readers. Potential advertisers ask, "Of those million readers, how many are likely to purchase our products?" As an example, a magazine read by young families is a good place to schedule ads for station wagons and vans, whereas a magazine read by upscale singles is a likely match for manufacturers of sports cars. Companies that sell cosmetics are more apt to buy space in magazines read almost entirely by women than in a magazine with an even split between male and female readers. Companies that produce computers want exposure in business publications; companies that make running shoes earmark a chunk of their annual advertising budget for fitness magazines.

The same demographic information that helps advertisers identify publications with the right audiences for their products helps writers identify publications with the right audiences for their articles. Young couples might like to read an article that offers tips on buying a first home, whereas upscale singles might welcome guidance on shopping for a condo. Writers can tune into the demographics of a publication by studying its cover, reading its letters to the editor and taking note of its advertising pages.

Here's how it works. Say you have an idea for a feature article and you want to pitch it to a magazine that you often read. Even if you feel you know the publication well, sit down with a recent issue, skim through it and take notes on these elements.

Cover: Look at the face and study the cover lines. What kind of reader would find this celebrity and these articles appealing? Ask yourself if your article idea would interest that reader. Would the topic of your proposed article make an appropriate cover line for this publication?

Letters to the editor: People typically don't sit down and dash off notes or pound out e-mails unless they feel strongly about something. Do the letters alert you to topics that anger, offend, please or rally the publication's readers? Ask yourself if your article idea would spark a similar favorable or unfavorable emotion.

Advertising pages: Try to discern and describe the consumer who is the target for the advertisements. Remember that certain ad pages—the back cover for one—cost more than others. Ask yourself if your article idea would appeal to that targeted consumer.

Take Note of Editors' Notes

Somewhere toward the front of a magazine you're likely to find a **standing column** written by the publication's editor. These columns usually occupy a single page or less and have accurate but often unimaginative names such as "Editor's Letter" (*Woman's Touch*), "Editor's Note" (*Home & Away*) or "The Editor's Desk" (*Newsweek*). They are easy to overlook because they're usually wedged between major advertising pages or placed near the more interesting table of contents. But don't be tempted to turn the page and move on. Writers trying to tune into a publication's editorial needs should view these standing columns as required reading. They contain all sorts of clues. They explain new directions the publication is taking, announce staff changes and offer hints about the magazine's point of view and its position on issues.

For instance, *Runner's World* promised its readers in 2003 that its editors were in the process of planning major changes to the magazine. In April 2004 the familiar "Editor's Letter" carried the title "A Brave New Runner's World" and detailed exactly what those changes were.[2] Beginning with that issue, wrote the editor-in-chief, articles would include more tips about training, health, fitness, food and nutrition. Also, the magazine was going to start publishing profiles of non-celebrity runners who were doing interesting things. Smart writers paid attention to the note and scurried to produce articles related to training, fitness and diet. They looked for interesting, non-celebrity runners who would make good subjects for profile articles.

Staff changes mentioned in editor's notes are important for a couple of reasons. First, they give you the names of the editors to whom you should address your query letters and article proposals. Second, they might tip you off to changes ahead for the publication. Often publishers expect their newly appointed editors to shake up the content and bring freshness to the magazine. When the managing editor of *Money* wrote his last editor's note before moving to *Time*, he welcomed his successor and mentioned the career path of the new editor. The smart freelance writer would review articles the newly named editor had written. These articles might offer insights as to the type of material the editor would like to see from contributing writers.

While you're reading the editor's note, pay attention to the tone of the writing. Is it conversational or formal? Breezy? Precise? Any attempts at humor? To what kind of reader does it seem directed? Is your style of writing compatible with the editor's style?

Pick Up on Masthead Clues

You can pick up valuable clues by reading the fine print of a publication's masthead. First, how large is the staff? A small staff might mean that the magazine depends on freelance writers for much of its content. That's a good sign. It also might mean that the editors are very busy and may be slow in responding to your query letters. Bad sign.

Look at the titles of the various editors listed on the masthead. Sometimes a magazine with a large staff is very exact in its areas of responsibility. Rather than assigning all nonfiction material to an articles editor, it might break down this general category and divide submissions according to specialties. Depending on the topic of your manuscript, your submission might find its way to the desk of a lifestyle editor, beauty editor, new products editor, legal affairs editor, special projects editor, etc. Addressing your material to the right person in the first place will cut down on response time and display a degree of professionalism on your part.

Some publications won't consider submissions from writers they don't know. Instead, they rely on a group of regular contributors for their content. As we indicated in Chapter 11, these writers often are listed on the masthead as "contributing editors." By comparing the masthead with the table of contents, you can figure out if the publication welcomes submissions from newcomers. If the bylines on published articles are the same as the names on the masthead, this is not a good market for an unknown writer.

One more item to check before you move on: Usually somewhere on the masthead you will find a sentence or two relating to unsolicited freelance submissions. Typically this information is at the bottom of the masthead and takes the form of a disclaimer. It states that the publication assumes no responsibility for unsolicited articles and photos. That doesn't necessarily mean that the editors aren't willing to look at material from new writers; it merely protects them from financial claims if the material is lost.

Study the Table of Contents

Survey several issues of the magazine to identify recurring features or **departments**. Publications frequently ease new writers into their circle of contributors by first buying short items that fit into standing departments. We talked more about these foot-in-the-door opportunities in Chapter 11.

Most magazines are very predictable in their content. They follow an **editorial formula** that they know their readers like. For example, each issue might contain two personality profiles, one major and one minor travel piece, three diet and fitness stories, a roundup of film and book reviews, a couple of advice columns and several how-to articles. Because this lineup varies little from month to month, you can almost predict what submissions the editors are likely to consider.

Read Sample Articles

As part of your analysis, read and critique several articles from different sections of the magazine. Ten questions to answer as you read each feature are:

1. What is the length of the article?
2. What kind of lead does the author use?
3. Does the story have any accompanying sidebars?
4. Is the topic aimed at readers of a certain age group, gender or background?
5. Which one of these words best describes the writer's tone—conversational, formal, sassy, breezy, condescending, authoritative, preachy?
6. Does the author write in first person (I, me, my, our), second person (you, your) or third person (he, she, they, their)?
7. How many sources are quoted?
8. Are there any anecdotes?
9. Does the article fit into a particular category—how to, calendar-related, profile, roundup or personal essay?
10. Is the vocabulary easy or difficult?

After you've read a variety of articles, look for characteristics that are present in all the stories. These probably reflect the preferences of the editors and the readers. Ask yourself, are the articles about the same length? If not, what is the range? Do the articles contain a lot of quotations from expert sources? Do most of the articles have sidebars? Is there a prevailing tone to the writing?

Much like a person, a well-edited magazine has a distinct personality, a unique voice, an established point of view and a certain style. These traits usually resemble the personality, voice, point of view and style of the publication's readers. Even magazines in the same genre—fashion, health, home décor, travel—differ from each other. The challenge for the freelance writer is to identify the characteristics the magazine and its audience share and offer material that is compatible. We often say successful writers are like chameleons; they have the ability to produce articles that blend perfectly into the magazines that publish their work.

Finally, as you analyze the content of a magazine, notice changes in its appearance. A new design can signal a new direction. As an example, late in 2003, *Prevention* assumed a new look and introduced new features aimed squarely at its fastest growing segment of readers—females under 50. The magazine's circulation has skyrocketed in recent years, a fact that its editor links to Americans' fascination with healthy living. Knowing *Prevention* is making an effort to reach out to women by offering articles about nutrition and fitness trends should help the freelancer who is trying to break into that market.[3]

New Kids on the Block

Sometimes it's impossible to read and evaluate content and design because the magazine's editors haven't released their first issue yet. Each year brings the introduction of many new publications to the marketplace. Not all survive. Because start-up staffs often are small, these new magazines are excellent places to send query letters. Getting in on the ground floor has its benefits. But how can a writer get a handle on content without first seeing and reading an issue or two?

The answer is in the mail. To generate excitement for a new publication, its promotional staff usually initiates a mass mailing to describe the product and offer a reduced rate for "charter subscribers." A detailed letter often outlines exactly what the magazine will contain. Sometimes a sample of the magazine—a "premiere issue"—follows. For example, the editor of *Backyard Living* announced the publication's launch in 2004 with a letter that promised articles about gardening and landscaping, outdoor entertaining and do-it-yourself projects. He also promised "humorous stories from your fellow readers" and more than 100 full-color pictures in each issue. Upon receiving this promotional letter, a freelance writer could easily read between the lines and surmise the editor is likely to consider proposals for how-to articles written in a friendly tone and accompanied by strong photos. This evaluation would be right on target. The premiere issue of *Backyard Living* devoted two pages to an explanation of how readers can submit photos and stories about porch and patio living, barbecue grilling and backyard projects. "You can help us write future issues," invited the headline.

Persistence Pays

Even with all the marketing aids available to them, freelance writers receive many more letters of rejection than letters of assignment. Having the right idea and pitching it to the right publication at the right time requires skill, hard work and a bit of good luck. Too many writers, new to the profession, try their hands at freelancing then give up after one or two rejections. A wiser strategy is to remember that writing is a business, and like all businesses it has its share of setbacks. Each publication—and there are thousands out there—represents an opportunity. For the writer in search of a market, persistence pays. Never give up.

Suggested Activities

1. Find and read the editor's column in a publication. Can you pick up on any insights that might help a writer who would like to become a contributor? Locate the masthead. Does the publication have a large staff? Do you see a listing of either contributing editors or contributing writers? Now go to the table of contents. Is it evident that the people listed on the masthead also are the authors of most of the articles in the issue? Based on this preliminary research, do you think this publication would be a good place to send your article ideas?

2. From the magazine listings in *Writer's Market*, *The Writer's Handbook* or the *Christian Writer's Market Guide*, select a publication that is not familiar to you. Read the information and then find the publication's Web site

to locate its writers' guidelines. Based on what you've learned, come up with an article idea that might appeal to the magazine's editors.

3. Compare the electronic Web sites for *The Writer* (writermag.com), *Writers' Journal* (writersjournal.com) and *Writer's Digest* (writersdigest. com). Explain which one seems to offer the most helpful marketing information.

Shoptalk

Clips: Published samples of articles. Often writers include clips of their previous work when they approach editors with ideas for future articles.

Closing date: The deadline for submission of all materials, including advertisements, scheduled for a particular issue of a magazine.

Demographics: Vital statistics such as age, education level, geographic location, employment, gender, political and religious leanings, number of children, hobbies and interests.

Departments: Sections of a magazine published on a recurring basis and covering the same general types of topics in every issue.

Editorial formula: The combination of types of articles used by a magazine on a regular basis. For example, some magazines may publish three news stories and two feature profiles in every issue along with its standing columns.

Standing column: A regular feature that is present in every issue of a publication. The name of the column doesn't change; it usually appears in the same place and is written by the same writer.

Tear sheet: A page torn from a publication that contains a sample of your writing.

Endnotes

1. *The Christian Communicator* and *Advanced Christian Writer* are available only by subscription from their parent company, Christian Writers' Institute in Nashville, TN.

2. David Willey, "A Brave New Runner's World," *Runner's World*, April 2004, 12.

3. Peter Johnson, "Prevention is healthy," *USA Today* (Dec. 8, 2003), 4D.

Chapter 21
Writing Creative Query Letters

The two tasks of a query letter are to pitch an article idea to an editor and to convince the editor of the writer's ability to create the article. Competition for bylines is fierce; this means the query's appearance and content should be excellent. In this chapter you'll learn:

- Five components of queries
- When and how to pitch an idea to an editor
- Benefits of snail mail and e-mail
- Why editors reject ideas

Entire books are available that explain what a query letter is and what it's supposed to accomplish. In short, a letter of inquiry—which is where the word "query" comes from—asks the editor two questions: How do you like this idea? Do you think I have the ability to pull it off?

The stakes are high. If the letter doesn't capture the editor's interest and calm all doubts about the writer's skills, the result is no assignment, no byline, no article. For that reason, queries fall into two categories—winners and losers. There is no middle ground. A "winner" means that the editor says "yes" and invites the writer to submit the article. A query that is a "loser" results in a rejection letter, most often a form letter straight from the office photocopy machine.

If a publication's editors like the query but aren't familiar with the writer, they may ask the writer to submit the article **on speculation**. Translation: The editors have no obligation to buy the article if it isn't as good as the query letter indicates. Beginning writers should be willing to work "on spec" until they have established their credentials in the marketplace.

If the editors like the query and have worked previously with him, they often will send the writer a contract that specifies a deadline, number of words needed and the amount of money they will pay for the finished article. Unlike working on speculation, the writer is assured of payment. That doesn't mean the writer is assured of publication, however. If the resulting article fails to meet editors' expectations, the writer may need to revise the submission. Occasionally editors decide not to use the article at all and, according to the contract, are obligated to pay the writer a **kill fee**. Translation: The writer earns at least a portion of the amount originally specified in the contract. This ranges from 20 percent to 100 percent of the total agreed-to fee.

High Hopes, Long Odds

Queries cannot be marginal, passable or even pretty good. They have to be flawless in presentation and sensational in content. Most are not, which explains why the majority are rejected. Occasionally editors reject query letters without reading a single word. This happened to a travel writer who proposed an article about Florida beaches and included a small scoop of Florida sand to grab the editor's attention. She succeeded. The editor ended up with a lapful of grit and the writer's reward was a quick, negative response. In another case, an editor rejected a query letter from a medical writer without even opening the envelope. The letter was addressed to Ms. Patricia Johnson. The editor's name: Mr. Patrick Johnson. The editor wasn't unduly sensitive about his name; he rejected the query because he doubted the writer's attention to detail. If the author couldn't get gender right, could the magazine trust him to get the facts of a medical story straight?

Many editors never meet their contributing writers face to face. The only way they judge competency is, first, by the appearance of the writer's correspondence and, second, by the content of the correspondence. Let's take a closer look at each of these key elements.

First impressions are important. Flawless presentation means attractive stationery and single-spaced text that is formatted in flush-left and ragged right paragraphs. Paper and envelopes should match; the type font should be simple and professional; the letterhead should not be cluttered with silly graphics—quill pens, inkpots, computer monitors—or quotations from famous authors. Some writers try to underscore their previous article sales by including lists of publications in small print on the left-hand side of the query letter. Be careful; it's a fine line between looking professional and appearing pretentious.

The computer gives the writer the ability to design appealing packages that are extensions of the sender's personality. It also tempts writers to experiment with fonts that are difficult to read and graphics that distract from the text. There is no excuse for a less-than-perfect looking query. The two sample letters included in this chapter give you an idea of correct format. They are businesslike in appearance and creative in content. Notice that each is addressed to a specific person. Beginning a query with an anonymous "Dear Editor" is bringing the letter to no one's attention. Do whatever is necessary to find out the name of the editor who evaluates query letters. This usually is as easy as checking the magazine's Web site, its masthead or making a telephone call.

What's the big idea? Assuming a query passes the appearance test, the editor begins to evaluate the creativity of the idea and the skills of the writer. Knowing if an idea is right for a magazine is the easy part. Editors understand their readers and can gauge reader interest in any given topic. Editors also know how recently their publication has featured a topic, and they typically won't revisit the subject for about three years. The exception is the occasional "update" when a major change occurs or a new angle surfaces. Also, certain evergreen topics are of sufficient interest to warrant regular exposure in some magazines. These include fitness and diet tips in women's magazines, money management advice in business publications and stories about high-profile personalities in entertainment weeklies.

As an editor evaluates the idea, he's also looking for clues to the writer's ability. A misspelled word raises questions of accuracy. A writer who includes clichés in a query is likely to include more clichés in an article. If run-on sentences, endlessly long paragraphs and difficult vocabulary are problems in a query, they will be even greater problems in an article. The query serves as an indicator of things to come—good and bad.

Essential Components of a Query

Most successful queries contain five components, strategically arranged for maximum impact. Unfortunately, many beginning writers confuse the order, put the least important element first and are disappointed when their letters fail to yield favorable responses. Here are the components that we recommend, listed according to their correct placement within the query:

1. Compelling lead paragraph
2. Summary of the topic
3. Statement of timeliness
4. Nuts and bolts information
5. Writer's credentials

Just as the lead paragraph of an article has to grab a reader's attention, so does the introductory paragraph in a query letter have to spark an editor's interest. For this reason, many successful queries begin with anecdotes that plunge the reader into the stories the writers are proposing. Notice how the two sample queries included in this chapter begin with compelling anecdotes. Notice, too, that the word "I"—referring to the writer—does not appear until the fourth or fifth paragraph. The rule: A query should never begin with a statement about the writer. That information is the least important element of the letter. The writer should place his credentials toward the end, and, if he runs out of space, he should omit the credentials entirely.

Sample Query Letter #1

Sarah Brzowsky
Senior Editor, *Parade*
711 Third Avenue
New York, NY 10017

Dear Ms. Brzowsky:

Shon Bolden of Hillsboro, Ore., is a 23-year-old tire store worker who attends college part time. About four years ago, he tried to change his bank account to another bank, but the new bank refused to do so. When he asked why, the bank said it ran his Social Security number through a credit bureau and found 14 people were using his Social Security number. Later he started receiving bills on items he never purchased. Shon found out that his financial identity had been stolen. Identity thieves had opened accounts in his name at about a dozen retail stores and had run up big bills. His credit rating suffered. Although he has enough money, he was turned down for a car loan. He describes his 1983 Oldsmobile as "on its last legs."

Shon is one of half a million Americans each year who are victims of identity theft—the country's fastest growing crime. He was one of several persons who testified before the House Banking and Financial Services Committee last October. Those hearings resulted in the passage of the Social Security Number Privacy and Identity Theft Prevention Act of 2000. But already there are some who say the bill doesn't go far enough. Just recently Rep. Ron Paul (R-Texas) introduced a bill into the 107th Congress—the Identity Theft Prevention Act of 2001, which would require the Social Security Administration to issue new Social Security numbers to the 280 million people who now hold them. The first federal law on this issue was passed in 1998.

One FTC survey found that about 55 percent of identity theft victims said their Social Security numbers were misused in obtaining credit cards. These cards were used to make purchases, for which the victims were subsequently billed. Eighteen percent of the victims said that checks were written on their bank accounts or money was fraudulently withdrawn in other ways. And another 10 percent of the victims said that loans had been illegally obtained using their names.

I would like to offer a 1,200-word article on identity theft, how it usually happens and 10 steps readers can take to prevent it. I have already been assigned to write an article on this topic for a local magazine, but I will write a new article for a national audience for *Parade*. I plan to interview Shon Bolden; Beth Givens, director of the Privacy Rights Clearinghouse in San Diego; Rep. Ron Paul; and two identity theft victims whom I know. One of these is a student whose identity theft occurred when she was studying in London. I can deliver this article in about a month.

I am a journalism professor and teach courses in magazine and feature writing. I have published hundreds of magazine articles and write an article on American magazines for the Encyclopedia Britannica Yearbook every year. The enclosed clips will give you some idea of my skills from previously published articles.

Sincerely,
David E. Sumner

Sample Query Letter #2

Lara Evans, managing editor
Delicious Living! Magazine
1401 Pearl St. Suite 200
Boulder, CO 80302

Dear Ms. Evans:

Her doctor at Central Indiana Orthopedic diagnosed a persistent, aching cramp in the arch of her foot as a stress fracture. Because it took more than a year to heal, she was referred to Dr. Kathy Beals, Ball State University nutritionist, who recommended she get a bone scan at the campus lab. The test results showed that she had an astounding 17 percent bone loss, the most visible deterioration in her lumbar vertebrae. Her condition was labeled osteopenia, borderline osteoporosis. Shocked by the news, she now feels as though she is walking on the fragile eggshells that are her bones. Her doctor warned her that low bone density makes her prone to new stress fractures and increases susceptibility for the previous one to return, as she will be on her feet for long hours during the golf season. Stacy Lods is 21. A college junior and a student-athlete, she epitomizes the overlooked trend for calcium deficiency that leads to early bone loss in young women. Stacy never thought she was the type of young woman who would have bone loss; she says she is a big-boned girl.

Osteoporosis, a decline of bone mass to a level conducive to fractures, is strongly influenced by the degree of bone mass attained in the first two-to-three decades of life and the rate of loss in subsequent decades. By about age 20, the average woman has acquired 98 percent of her skeletal mass.

Many risk factors for premature bone loss are uncontrollable, but few people realize the delayed positive effects of consuming enough high-quality calcium early in life. The truth is, if a young woman consciously alters her calcium intake while she is in her late teens or early 20s, she can safeguard from early bone loss and minimize the risk of osteoporosis for life.

It is regarded as a disease for the elderly, called the "silent disease" because it frequently occurs without recognizable symptoms. Calcium intake negligence during late-teen and young-adult years contributes to half of women over 50 experiencing an osteoporotic fracture in her lifetime. More than 8 million American women have osteoporosis and millions more have low bone density, says the AMA.

I'd like to write a health article about calcium deficiency in college-age women, highlighting some ways to enhance diets to get the daily recommendations for adequate calcium. I will interview Stacy Lods, a college junior who recently found out she has early bone loss, and Dr. Denise Amschler, Ball State department of physiology and health science professor of women's health who experienced premenopausal bone loss. The article can be up to 1,000 words and is deliverable in two weeks.

Sincerely,
Laura J. Adkins

An anecdote is only one effective way to begin a query. Other methods include a provocative question, a startling statistic or a witty remark from an interviewee. Often a strong opening paragraph of a query letter can do double duty. It may re-emerge as the article's opening paragraph.

If the first paragraph of the query succeeds in hooking the editor's attention, the second paragraph summarizes the article idea. It can resemble the nutgraf or billboard paragraph we described in Chapter 7. As an example, the first paragraph in a query letter that a writer submitted to an editor in 2004 began with this anecdote:

> For five years Sue Smith, a secretary from Little Rock, has set aside $10 a week to pay for her dream vacation in Paris. Now that her stash is sufficient to underwrite the adventure, she's having second thoughts. Miffed by France's refusal to support the United States' effort in Iraq, she's trading in her euros and looking at destinations closer to home.

Because the topic that the writer proposed is much bigger than one woman's scuttled travel plans, the second paragraph needed to place the Sue Smith anecdote in a larger context. It summarized the total article this way:

> Smith isn't alone. This year France expects to lose $500 million in U.S. tourist dollars. The rift in relations between the two countries is so serious that it has prompted one in five Americans to stop buying products manufactured in France. The result is that those travelers who venture to the City of Light in the next few months will find smaller crowds and bigger bargains awaiting them.

The last sentence of the above paragraph provided the third essential element in our list. It established the timeliness of the story. It alerted travelers to what they might encounter on a trip to France. The editor receiving the query knew the topic would be appropriate for a spring issue because many Americans plan European vacations for the summer months.

After creating the necessary paragraphs that build interest, summarize the topic and establish timeliness, the writer next must outline the nuts and bolts of the proposal. This involves answering several pertinent questions: How many words will the article contain? Will there be any sidebars? What kinds of photos are available? When will a draft be ready? Who are the sources of information? Will "experts" be quoted?

The final paragraph of the query letter offers a sentence or two about the author. At this point mention anything that establishes you as the appropriate person to write the story you have described. Be selective. Try to choose something that relates to your topic. For example, if you are pitching the article about France and you are a frequent visitor to Paris, that fact is worth mentioning. Recapping your academic degrees will have little impact. Explaining that you once had a poem published in your high school newspaper will impress no one.

Remember that a query letter is a sales letter. As such, you should feel comfortable including anything that enhances the chances of making a sale. A clipping of a recently published article—not your high school poetry—is a good way to establish credibility. If you are a writer who also takes photographs, you might want to include a sample of your work.

A business card attached to the query may well lead to a future assignment. Editors sometimes reject a query because the idea isn't right for their publication but they like the writer's style. They file the business card with a notation on the back. The next time they need an article from a certain geographic region, they flip through their cache of business cards.

What Not to Include in a Query

Beach sand isn't the only thing that you should omit from a query. Although some writers always state in a pitch letter the kind of rights they are willing to sell (see Chapter 22), we think that discussion is better delayed until after the editor expresses interest in the article. Most publications are willing to negotiate rights at the point when the editor offers a contract to the author. Introducing the topic into the conversation at the query level seems as inappropriate as typing your Social Security number on a submission in anticipation of payment. Save it for later.

Another pet peeve of many editors is a paragraph of gushy praise for the magazine. Avoid sentences such as, "I just love your publication and read it from cover to cover as soon as it arrives each month." The editor will know that you read the magazine "from cover to cover" if your query letter proposes an article that is exactly right for the publication's readers.

On the other hand, few things frustrate editors more than proposals that are so wrong for a magazine that it is obvious the writers never took time to review the publication. For example, a favorite war story of Ohio writer Bob Hostetler dates back to his three years as editor of *The Young Soldier*, a Salvation Army publication geared to youth. "In the Salvation Army, adult members are called 'soldiers,' and children are called 'junior soldiers,'" explains Hostetler, now a freelance author of more than a dozen books. "Anyone familiar with the Salvation Army or with the magazine would know this. Still, every so often I would receive a query letter proposing an article for *The Young Soldier* about how to disassemble and assemble an M-16 rifle or about the newest developments in tank warfare. Obviously those writers had no idea what I did from 8:30 to 4:30 every day."[1]

Whereas freelance writers should never exaggerate their credentials in a query letter, neither should they tell negative tales on themselves. Lines that a writer should not include in a query are: "I don't know anything about this topic but thought it might be fun to learn," or "I'm a student and my journalism professor is making me write and submit this article" or "I just retired from my real job and have decided to become a writer."

When to Query

Some beginning writers go to all the trouble of researching and writing their articles before they submit query letters to see if any editor is interested in the topics. This makes little sense. The writer-editor relationship often involves an exchange of dialogue as an article takes shape. The dialogue begins but doesn't end with the query letter. Frequently an editor will say "yes" to a proposal and then will offer suggestions as to length and angle. The editor may request that the submission take the form of a how-to article or a profile with a sidebar. The writer who has completed the project has to start over.

Most veteran writers submit their query letters at two points in the writing process.

1. They have an idea and have decided on a slant: Query
2. They have an idea, have chosen the slant and have conducted their interviews: Query

The advantage of sending a query at the first point in the process is that you have invested little time and energy. If no editor expresses interest in the idea, you've lost nothing. You file the idea for the future and move on to another project.

The advantage of sending a query at the second point, after you've done your interviews, is that the query will have more substance. You can include a comment from one of your sources. You can create an anecdote based on your research. If your spadework has caused your enthusiasm to surge, that excitement will spill over into the query and may be contagious enough to infect the editor. You'll have a good idea of how long the article should be, and you can pitch any ideas that you have regarding sidebar possibilities. The only disadvantage to querying at this point is that you have invested several hours in research. If no editor asks to see the finished article, that time is lost. However, if the topic isn't time-dated, you may be able to revisit it in the future.

Snail Mail vs. E-Mail Queries

Should you or shouldn't you? Only editors can answer the question of whether a writer should FAX a query, send it by e-mail or let the U.S. Post Office do the honors. As we indicated in Chapter 20, the writers' guidelines of a publication usually state if electronic submissions are acceptable. E-mail queries work well in three instances: if your proposed idea is time-sensitive and you need an immediate reply from an editor, if you and the editor have a long-standing professional relationship or if the magazine has stated that its editors prefer e-mail rather than other types of correspondence.

An e-mail query has the same two "jobs" to perform as a traditional query. It has to propose a great idea and convince the editor that the writer can deliver an equally great manuscript. The length is often shorter, but the author should include enough details to help the editor make the right decision.

Here's a sample of a query that pitches an article to an editor of a national general-interest magazine. Sending it by e-mail is permissible because the writer, Holly Miller, needs to find a buyer for the idea before the topic loses its timeliness. Also, she has written previous articles for the editor, is on a first-name basis with him and doesn't have to convince him of her skills. The major challenge is to ignite his enthusiasm for the topic she is proposing.

Dear Ted:
The city is magnificent in spite of itself. With scaffolds encasing its monuments and clean-up crews scaling its spires, St. Petersburg, Russia, is withstanding another siege—this one, a massive makeover in preparation for the city's 300th anniversary celebration. The party will peak on May 27.

The perception persists that what's left of the old Soviet Union surely must be gloomy if not dangerous. A few assurances: Russia is safe, and Big Brother won't hassle anyone who aims a point-and-shoot camera at a government building. English is widely understood, and most places accept U.S. dollars as readily as rubles. American money goes far here, but shoppers aren't tempted to part with much of it. Antique stores offer icons and other remnants of the monarchy, but the buzz is that buyers have to relinquish all treasures at the border. The safest purchases are the most predictable—fake fur hats, T-shirts and an endless supply of nesting dolls. Among the most bizarre set of dolls are those that depict Russian leaders and include Gorbachev with his signature head splotch, a woozy Yeltsin and a nondescript Putin. A favorite T-shirt reveals a profile of Lenin and the word "McLenin's" superimposed over the familiar Golden Arches of McDonald's. The back of the shirt carries the old communist symbol, the red star, and the message: "The Party Is Over."

But residents of St. Petersburg hope the party is just beginning as they roll out the red carpet for tourists who want to celebrate the upcoming anniversary. What these visitors are likely to see is the subject of an article I'd like to write for the spring issue of your magazine. May I send you a draft on speculation? Great photos accompany the 2,000-word story that I have in mind.

—Holly Miller

Whether or not the editor agrees to consider an article about St. Petersburg won't depend on the writer's ability to deliver a good story. He is familiar with her work and her e-mail confirms her skill. However, that doesn't mean that he will say "yes" to her proposal. Editors reject article proposals for reasons that go beyond the ability of the writer or the value of the idea. Here are the top four reasons for rejection:

1. The magazine has a backlog of articles to publish before its editors buy new material.
2. Another writer is under assignment to produce an article on the same topic.
3. The article isn't quite right for the magazine's readers.
4. The magazine published a similar article a few months ago.

P.S. Try Again

Writers who bypass the query and send their completed articles to publications often are in for a long wait. Unsolicited submissions typically end up in the slush pile where they might spend several months before anyone looks at them. Editors evaluate query letters; they forward the slush to a **first reader** who is likely to open each envelope and, simultaneously, reach for a printed rejection slip. Professional writers submit queries; beginners send manuscripts.

There are exceptions. In a few instances, even the professionals send completed articles. This is the case when a writer is dealing with a newspaper or magazine that states in its guidelines that it prefers manuscripts to queries. Editors of daily publications in particular often don't have time to engage in back-and-forth correspondence with freelance writers. They want to see the finished product. Magazine editors who usually prefer queries to manuscripts will make an exception for articles that are very short—two or three pages—or those that fall into the category of humor. Since it is difficult to describe what is funny, they like to judge for themselves.

Although rejection letters are part of every writer's life, some such letters are easier to take than others. Occasionally an editor will scrawl a postscript on the bottom of the dreaded rejection note. A personal comment—"great idea, but not right for us"—is meant to encourage the writer to keep trying. The unwritten message is: "Don't give up."

Suggested Activities

1. Create a paragraph that could be used as the closing paragraph for all your query letters. In it, explain in honest but positive language your qualifications as a writer. Keep it on file for frequent use.

2. Choose an article that you have already completed. Write a query letter that uses the first paragraph of your article as the opening paragraph of your query. Write subsequent paragraphs that summarize the story and identify your sources. Add the closing paragraph that explains your qualifications.

3. Create a query letter for an article that you have not yet written. Outline your idea and include the research that you plan to conduct. Add the closing paragraph that explains your qualifications.

Shoptalk

First reader: Often an intern or part-time employee, this person opens unsolicited manuscripts and sorts them according to quality. If an article is publishable, the first reader directs it to the attention of an editor.

Kill fee: An amount of money that an editor pays a writer to cancel an assigned article. Typically a kill fee is at least 20 percent of the amount the magazine was going to pay the author for a published article.

On speculation: These words, often included in a query letter, indicate a writer's willingness to submit an article without any guarantee that the editor will accept it for publication.

Endnotes

1. Workshop lecture, May 21, 2004.

Chapter 22
Copyrights and Wrongs

Although copyright law gets complex, it has three simple applications that you need to understand: How it applies to selling your work to publications; how it applies to protecting your work against infringement; and how to avoid infringing on other writers' rights. This chapter covers these basics and addresses copyright law's applications to the Internet. You'll learn:

- How to market your intellectual property
- Advantages of copyright registration
- How to avoid plagiarism and understand "fair use"

USA Today published a story on Jan. 14, 2004, that began:

> A comparison of a July 9, 1998, *Washington Post* story from Darra Adam Khel, Pakistan, and one published by *USA Today* from the same town on Sept. 2, 1998, showed striking similarities, the newspaper learned Tuesday. *USA Today*'s story carried the byline of Jack Kelley, a foreign correspondent who resigned last week after editors determined that he misled them during an internal investigation of some of his stories.[1]

A subsequent investigation into Kelley's stories between 1993 and 2003 found that Kelley had plagiarized at least two dozen quotes or other materials from competing publications. The uproar at the newspaper led to the resignation of *USA Today* editor Karen Jurgensen three months later.[2]

Jayson Blair's widely reported plagiarism at *The New York Times* in 2003 led to his dismissal and the resignations of two of his editors. These and other recent incidents serve to warn writers that plagiarism can ruin their careers, violate federal laws and increase the public's mistrust of anything they write.

As a writer, you need to understand that the applications of copyright ownership allow you to sell some rights to publishers while retaining other ownership rights. You also need to know how to protect **intellectual property** against unauthorized use by others. Finally, so that you don't commit plagiarism, you need to know what's legal to use and not use when you do research.

The U.S. Copyright Act has specific criteria covering all three areas. Its purpose is to protect "original works of authorship." Congress purposely chose the broad term "works of authorship" to avoid having to rewrite the Copyright Act every time a new "medium" was developed. That means the Copyright Act (Title 17, U.S. Code) protects Internet pages and articles, computer software and multimedia CDs even though these items didn't exist at the time the law was passed in 1978.

The Internet hasn't changed the copyright laws. It has simply made plagiarism easier and more tempting. If you publish an article on the Internet, whether for a personal or commercial Web site, copyright law protects it as soon as it's published regardless of whether the copyright symbol appears or whether the copyright is registered. If someone else copies and publishes your Internet article elsewhere, you can sue for copyright infringement using the same 1978 Copyright Law.

Creative works by writers, musicians, artists, sculptors or computer programmers are their intellectual property. The law says that they alone hold the rights to reproduction, distribution, public performance or public display of their work. That includes the right to sell part or all of their ownership. Theft is theft whether it occurs in the intellectual or material domains of life.

Marketing Your Intellectual Property

What do you have to do to copyright your written work? Nothing. Some writers mistakenly believe they have to register their work with the U.S. Copyright Office to protect it. The law recognizes that you own the copyright to your original work as soon as you write it. Because of the 1978 revision of the Copyright Law, works of authorship are automatically protected from the moment of their creation for the author's life plus an ad-

Five Common Copyright Questions

1. What is copyright?
Copyright is a form of protection grounded in the U.S. Constitution and granted by law for original works of authorship. Publication is not necessary for copyright protection, but the material must be original and preserved in a "fixed, tangible form," that may include paper or computer disk.

2. How does copyright differ from patents or trademarks?
Copyright protects original works of authorship, whereas a patent protects inventions or discoveries. A trademark protects phrases, symbols or designs identifying the source of the goods or services of a party and distinguishing them from others.

3. What is a "poor man's copyright"?
The practice of sending a copy of your own work to yourself is sometimes called a "poor man's copyright." However, there is no provision in the copyright law for such protection, and it doesn't substitute for registering a copyright.

4. Can I copyright the name of a band?
No. Names and titles are not protected by copyright law. They may be protected under trademark law, which requires a different registration process. Contact the U.S. Patent and Trademark Office for more information.

5. Can I register the copyright for something written by someone else?
No. You can register a copyright only if you own the rights to a work by will, contract or legal inheritance. Ownership of the physical work itself doesn't convey copyright privileges.

---

ditional 70 years after the author's death. Prior to that revision, registration was necessary for authors to protect their works. There are still some advantages to registering a copyright, and we'll get to that later.

The only two requirements that the law makes are, (1) that the article or other intellectual property be "original" and (2) that it's in a "fixed and tangible form." That means it doesn't even have to be printed on paper because as soon as it's on the computer screen, it's copyrighted. Courts have ruled that a copy stored in the random access memory of a computer is a copy for copyright purposes, even though it disappears when you shut off the computer.

The copyright symbol on a document, however, serves as a reminder that federal laws protect its author against unauthorized copying or distribution. It may help to include the copyright symbol on copies of articles or handouts given to others. That tells users that it's your original creation, and you don't intend for them to photocopy or give it to others.

If you decide to use a copyright notice, place it in the upper right corner of the first page and include the following three elements:

- The symbol (c) (the letter C in a circle) or the word "copyright." On many computer programs, you can put a "c" between two parentheses, which automatically converts to a copyright symbol after the next space.
- The year of the first publication of a work
- The name of the copyright owner

Example: © 2005 David E. Sumner

How To Sell Your Rights

The U.S. Copyright Law gives copyright owners the rights to reproduction, distribution and public performance or public display of their work. Copyright lawyers call these the "copyright bundle of rights." Selling an article to a publisher means relinquishing partial rights in exchange for payment. Generally speaking, the more you are paid, the more rights you give up.

So it's a tradeoff. In business dealings, the relationship between a writer and a publisher resembles that of a merchant and a customer. The merchant wants to relinquish as little merchandise as possible for the highest possible price. The customer wants as much merchandise as possible for the lowest possible price. In this case, you're the merchant. Most writers don't enjoy the business side of publishing. That's why professional writers hire agents to do their negotiating. Agents, however, usually charge a 15 percent commission and generally work only for authors of books and screenplays.

Most magazines are registered with the U.S. Copyright Office as single collective entities. The individual articles that appear in the magazine are not copyrighted individually in the authors' names. Magazines typically purchase partial rights to each article from freelance writers. The distinction between different kinds of rights gets complicated as writers progress to books, screenplays and international publications.

Beginning writers, however, need to understand only three kinds of rights: **First rights**, **all rights** and **reprint rights**. When you submit a manuscript, you should indicate whether you're offering "first rights" or "reprint rights" in the upper-right corner of the first page. If a publisher wants to purchase "all rights" or any other form of rights, then he will let you know.

First Rights

Publications most typically purchase "first rights" or "first serial rights" from freelance writers. Serial is a librarian's term for any periodical published on a regular timetable, such as daily, weekly or monthly. By selling **first serial rights**, you give the magazine the first opportunity to publish the article. After the article is published, you retain the right to sell reprint rights to other publishers as many times as you wish. Sometimes magazines purchase "First North American serial rights," which means they become the first North American publication to publish it. The writer can still sell "first rights" outside of North America at any subsequent time.

Reprint Rights

While the formal term is "second serial rights," it's usually called **reprint rights** and means exactly what it says. Most print and online publications purchase reprint rights if the original publication's readership doesn't overlap with their own. Only the highest-circulation periodicals insist on buying editorial material that's never appeared elsewhere. Usually payment for reprint rights varies from 10 to 50 percent of the magazine's payment schedule for first rights. One writer, however, sold an article for $250 to a regional magazine published in several large cities and later sold reprint rights for $500 to a magazine with an international circulation. The two publications' overlapping readership was small. There is no limit to the number of times you can sell reprint rights to the same article.

All Rights

If you sell all rights, you give the publisher full copyright ownership for reproduction and distribution. You should avoid selling all rights unless the publisher insists and payment is sufficiently high. All rights means the publisher can publish the article in its magazine, put it on its Web site or publish portions in another magazine it owns or in a subsequent book or CD-ROM with a collection of articles. Unfortunately for writers, an increasing number of large publishers want to purchase all rights because it gives them the freedom to use the material in a variety of print and electronic formats.

While first rights, reprint rights and all rights are the most frequent rights that beginning writers encounter, there are a few other terms that you need to learn about as you become a more accomplished writer.

Work Made For Hire

This legal term, which appears in the federal copyright code, refers to the creative work done by a writer (or any kind of artist) for an employer. Articles written by full-time newspaper, magazine or public relations writers usually come under the provisions of "work made for hire." The employer owns all of the rights to the work unless the employer gives specific permission to the writer to sell elsewhere. So if you become a full-time writer for an online or print publication, make sure you get permission from your employer before trying to sell reprint rights to anyone else.

Some publications ask freelance writers to sign a "work made for hire" agreement. That's the same as the writer agreeing to sell all rights. *Encyclopedia Britannica,* for example, asks all of its freelance writers to sign "work made for hire" agreements. That gives the book publisher the rights to use their material on its Web site, CD-ROM editions and in its annual yearbooks.

Simultaneous Rights

Also known as **one-time rights**, simultaneous rights allow you to sell the same article at the same time to several publishers. Syndicated newspaper columns are the best example of one-time or simultaneous rights. A column by a writer who has sold simultaneous rights may appear in several hundred newspapers during the same week. Simultaneous rights are also useful when you have an article with timely material that will quickly become out of date if not published. Since the process of selling an article may require one week to several months of review time, simultaneous rights let you sell it to the publishers who are willing to accept it most quickly. Although they are not sold, press releases sent from companies or nonprofit organizations fall under the "simultaneous rights" designation.

Electronic Rights

These rights cover a broad range of electronic media from online magazines to CD-ROM anthologies. If you sell material to a Web publisher, make sure the agreement clearly states whether the rights include the Web site only or whether the publisher could use it in subsequent print media.

Subsidiary Rights

Subsidiary rights refer to book publishing. The primary right included in book publishing contracts is the right to publish the material in a print edition. Subsidiary rights include all others such as movie or television rights, foreign editions, book club rights, audio book editions or electronic rights. The book contract should specify who controls the rights (author or publisher) and what percentage of sales from these other rights goes to the author.

Will an Editor Steal Your Work?

Beginning writers worry more about protecting their literary creations than they need to. Theft or misuse of freelance articles by magazine editors rarely occurs. Editors know the copyright laws better than most writers and will not risk theirs or their publication's reputation for the sake of a single article. Why would a magazine editor risk a lawsuit and damaged reputation for the sake of an article worth a few hundred dollars? Though it may help to put the copyright symbol on your article, freelance writers almost never register a copyright with the U.S. Copyright Office. Books, screenplays and movie scripts—yes. Articles—no.

Advantages of Copyright Registration

If your work has potential for substantial financial returns, registering it with the U.S. Copyright Office protects it in these ways:

- Registration establishes a public record of the copyright claim.
- Registration is necessary before you can file an infringement suit.
- Copyright registration within three months of publication permits the plaintiff to win up to $30,000 in statutory damages plus attorney's fees in court actions. Otherwise, the court can only award actual damages to the infringed copyright owner.
- Registration allows the copyright owner to record the registration with the U.S. Customs Service and prohibit the importation of infringing copies.

You can find the necessary information and required forms at www.copyright.gov. Print and complete Form TX (used for a "nondramatic literary work") and return it to the U.S. Copyright Office in Washington, D.C., with a $30 registration fee. If you're going to spend $30, however, save it for your book, play, computer program or hit song.

What Copyright Doesn't Protect

We know of one writer who sent a query to a newspaper's feature editor proposing an article about how people celebrate Christmas with a job that requires them to work on the holiday—medical and law enforcement personnel, pilots and flight attendants and so forth. The writer never received a reply, but on Christmas day the newspaper published a feature on that identical topic. Of course, the writer was angered, but there's nothing he could do. He later learned this isn't an original idea since many newspapers and magazines publish articles on this topic every Christmas. Even if it was original, he had no grounds for copyright infringement. That's because ideas can't be copyrighted. At least six types of material are generally not protected by copyright. These include:

- Unpublished works that have not been fixed in a "tangible form of expression." That included speeches, conversations or performances never written or recorded.
- Titles, names, short phrases and slogans; variations of typographic ornamentation; and lists of ingredients or contents. That means you can't copyright titles of songs or articles.
- Works from the **public domain** with no original authorship, such as calendars, telephone directories and lists taken from public documents. After a copyright expires for copyrighted material (currently 70 years after the death of the author), that material falls into the public domain.
- Press releases. Companies and organizations that send out press releases want their information to be published. They put it in the public domain and allow writers to use anything they want—facts, quotes or anecdotes.
- Published works of the U.S. government or government employees.
- Ideas, procedures, methods, processes and concepts.

The last item is particularly important for writers. As we previously noted, you cannot copyright the idea for an article; you can only copyright the particular way in which the idea is expressed and written. That's good news and bad news for writers.

The Good News and Bad News

The good news is that you're free to browse through newspapers, magazines and Web sites to look for ideas you can use. Ideas and concepts can't be copyrighted. Take any idea you find, interview your own sources and write your own article. That's legal.

Another "good news" consequence of the dichotomy between ideas and their expression is that copyright offers no protection for basic facts or **common knowledge**. For example, *Newsweek*, *The Washington Post* and CNN can all write stories about the latest episode in the Middle East without intruding upon each other's copyright. Copyright does not protect the ideas and facts of any particular news event, but only the arrangement of words and phrases in a particular story.

The bad news is that it's conceivable that you could send your query letter to an editor who steals your idea and assigns it to a staff writer. It's legal, but rarely occurs, at least among reputable magazines.

Avoiding Plagiarism and Understanding "Fair Use"

Three prominent historians who have written dozens of books and often appeared on television talk shows were all charged with plagiarism between 2001 and 2004. All of them admitted to inadvertently quoting other authors' material in their books and failing to give proper credit and attribution. While none was taken to court, one of them made an out-of-court settlement with the author she had inadvertently quoted.

While plagiarism can occur unintentionally, it still violates copyright law and its consequences can be just as serious as intentional plagiarism. All three of these historians damaged their reputations and received fewer invitations to the television talk shows.

What You Can't Do

"Lifting quotes" is one of the most common forms of unintentional plagiarism. We know of one writer who interviewed a well-known celebrity and published a profile about him in a national magazine. Another writer lifted one of those quotes and used it in his article without giving proper attribution to the first writer. The original writer protested and forced the second magazine to publish a clarification and proper credit in the next issue.

Since journalistic writers don't use footnotes, you have to give proper credit within the context of the article. If you choose to re-quote a source from another magazine, you should attribute it this way:

According to a *Newsweek* article, the secretary of state was quoted as
saying . . . .

"We're losing our ratings," the TV program's producer told *The New York
Times*.

The latest edition of the *MLA Handbook for Writers of Research
Papers*, published by the Modern Language Association, has an entire section devoted to unintentional plagiarism: "Plagiarism," it says, "sometimes happens because researchers do not keep precise records of their
reading, and by the time they return to their notes, they have forgotten
whether their summaries and paraphrases contain quoted material that is
poorly marked or unmarked."[3]
The *MLA Handbook* goes on to distinguish between three types of plagiarism:

- Repeating or paraphrasing a few words without giving credit
- Reproducing a particularly apt phrase
- Paraphrasing an argument or line of thinking[4]

In each case, the plagiarist misrepresents to readers the intellectual
property of others as if it were his or her own.

What You Can Do

Section 107 of the U.S. Copyright Law covers "fair use." In general, "fair
use" means you can use brief quotes from other sources as long as you
give proper credit. The law gives permission to build upon the work of
others for "purposes such as criticism, comment, news reporting, teaching
(including multiple copies for classroom use), scholarship or research."
"The primary objective of copyright is not to reward the labor of authors," wrote Justice Sandra Day O'Connor in a 1991 Supreme Court decision, "but to 'promote the progress of science and useful arts.' To this
end, copyright assures authors the right to their original expression, but
encourages others to build freely upon the ideas and information conveyed
by a work."[5]
The fair use provision doesn't say how many words or how much information you can borrow without permission from the author. Writers
generally agree you should not exceed 250 words in any circumstance and
sometimes even less. The law uses four general guidelines to determine
whether fair use applies to the use of someone else's intellectual property:

1. The purpose and character of the use, including whether such use is of a commercial nature or is for nonprofit educational purposes
2. The nature of the copyrighted work
3. The amount and substantiality of the portion used in relation to the copyrighted work as a whole
4. The effect of the use upon the potential market for or value of the copyrighted work

Plaintiffs file many lawsuits each year over the meaning of "fair use." In general, the courts have ruled that the first criteria (a profit motive for its use) and the fourth (its damage to market sales) are the most important. But the courts also have ruled that educational use of copyrighted material doesn't automatically make it "fair use." For example, a state court ruled against a New York school system that made copies and distributed videotapes to avoid purchasing them from the publisher.

If you copy someone else's intellectual property (electronically or manually) without giving credit or paying for it, then you are violating fair use. Copying a CD and giving it to a friend so he doesn't have to buy it is a copyright infringement. Prosecutions can and do occur. Think of how you would feel if someone made a copy of your intellectual work to avoid paying for it.

Plagiarism can quickly damage a career, even an outstanding one. Jack Kelley was *USA Today's* Employee of the Year in 2002 and a Pulitzer Prize finalist in international reporting in 2001. His editors at one time gave him free rein and an around-the-world reporting trip in the company's jet. As a result of his fabrication and plagiarism, however, it only took days for his high-profile career at *USA Today* to end.

Plagiarism is not only wrong, but bad for your career. To avoid Kelley's fate, be sure you know your copyrights and wrongs.

For More Information

U.S. Copyright Office (www.copyright.gov): Library of Congress, Copyright Office, 101 Independence Ave., S.E., Washington, DC 20559-6000. (202) 707-3000.

The Authors Guild (www.authorsguild.org): 31 E. 28th Street, 10th floor, New York, NY 10016-7923. (212) 563-5904. E-mail: staff@authorsguild.org

The National Writers Union (www.nwu.org): 113 University Place, 6th floor, New York, NY 10003. (212) 254-0279. E-mail: nwu@wu.org

Suggested Activities

1. Discuss why it is or isn't legal to make a copy of a CD from your favorite band and give it to a friend.

2. Save and print a copy of an e-mail message that you have sent to a friend. Read the copyright rules and print a copy of form TX from the U.S. Copyright Office (www.copyright.gov). Discuss whether they allow you to register a copyright for that e-mail.

3. Discuss the various ways you can properly attribute a quote that you have borrowed from another printed source.

Shoptalk

All rights: All rights mean the publisher can publish the article in its magazine, put it on its Web site or publish portions in another magazine it owns or in a subsequent book or CD-ROM with a collection of articles. The writer gives up any opportunity to sell or re-use the material.

Common knowledge: Information that's available from several published sources and, therefore, not protected by copyright. Common knowledge issues arise in many fields such as art, geography, science, history, music, medicine and technology.

Electronic rights: Rights that cover a broad range of electronic media from online magazines to CD-ROM anthologies.

First serial rights (first rights): Rights sold to a publisher giving it the first opportunity to publish the article. After the article is published, writers retain the right to sell unlimited reprint rights to other publishers.

Intellectual property: Any work by a writer, musician, artist, sculptor or computer programmer capable of commercial use or distribution. Original creators hold legal rights to reproduction, distribution, public performance or public display of their work. They also have the right to sell part or all of their ownership.

One-time rights: See simultaneous rights.

Public domain: Any intellectual property not protected by copyright law that anyone may use. Published material more than 70 years old and anything published by the U.S. government is generally in the public domain.

Reprint rights or **"second serial rights"**: Rights that give a publication the opportunity to reprint previously published material. Most publications purchase reprint rights if the original publication's readership doesn't overlap with their own.

Simultaneous rights or **one-time rights**: Simultaneous rights allow the writer to sell the same article at the same time to several publishers. Syndicated newspaper columns are the best example of the use of simultaneous rights.

Subsidiary rights: Used in book publishing, subsidiary rights include all other rights such as movie or television, foreign edition, book club, audio book edition or electronic rights.

Work made for hire: The creative work done by a writer or artist in which the employer retains full copyright ownership to the work. Articles written by full-time newspaper and magazine employees usually fall under "work made for hire" provisions.

Endnotes

1. Peter Johnson, "Similar wording is found in 'Post,' *USA Today* stories," USA TODAY (Jan. 14, 2004), accessed at USAToday.com, July 5, 2004.

2. Associated Press story, "USA Today editor retires amid plagiarism scandal involving former reporter," *Boston Herald* (April 21, 2004), Accessed at www.bostonherald.com, July 5, 2004.

3. Joseph Gibaldi, *MLA Handbook for Writers of Research Papers*, 6th ed. (New York: Modern Language Association, 2003), 68.

4. Ibid.

5. Justice Sandra Day O'Connor (Feist Publications, Inc. vs. Rural Telephone Service Co., 499 U.S. Code 340, 349), 1991.

Appendix
Back to Basics

This section covers some of the mechanics of writing. While some readers could benefit, others might not need it. That's why we've included it as an appendix. It covers a few main points about these topics:

- Most common writing mistakes
- Stylebooks and proper usage
- Improving parallel structure

Dozens of editors say they automatically reject a query letter (and even a cover letter with a job application) if it contains any grammar, punctuation or typographical errors. They reason that if the writer is too careless to proofread the letter, then that writer is likely to display as much carelessness in researching and writing articles. The purpose of this chapter is to help you avoid these pitfalls that damage your writing career.

Most Common Mechanical Mistakes Among Writers

"Grammar is not just a pain in the ass; it's the pole you grab to get your thoughts up on their feet and walking," writes Stephen King.[1] Most students cringe at the idea of learning grammar in a writing course. Grammar isn't typically a serious problem among students in our feature and magazine writing classes. Yet, we find some mistakes that seem to occur over and over.

Run-on Sentences

Run-on sentences are the most common grammar mistakes among beginning writers. For example: "Students who don't know grammar write run-on sentences, they usually get a failing grade." The preceding type of run-on sentence is sometimes called a "comma splice" because a comma is used to "splice" two sentences. Here are three acceptable revisions:

- Writers who don't know grammar write run-on sentences, and they usually get failing grades. (Add the conjunction "and.")
- Writers who don't know grammar write run-on sentences; they usually get failing grades. (Separate the sentences with a semi-colon.)
- Writers who don't know grammar write run-on sentences. They usually get failing grades. (Re-write as two separate sentences.)

Sentence Fragments

Every sentence requires a noun and a verb. The most frequent sentence fragments begin with subordinating conjunctions such as "although," "because" or "which." They're called "subordinating" because they create a clause that is subordinate to the main clause. Therefore, the subordinate clause isn't complete and can't stand by itself. For example:

Incorrect: Although most people didn't think he needed to. (fragment)

Correct: The mayor apologized although most people didn't think he needed to. (complete sentence)

Pronoun Agreement

If you use a singular noun, use a singular pronoun when you refer to it later. If you use plural nouns, use plural pronouns when you refer to them later. That's what **pronoun agreement** means. The most frequent problem comes from "collective nouns"—singular nouns that describe a group of people. For example, use "it" and not "they" when you refer to a committee, company or university. Use "it" and not "they" when you refer to the name of a store, a magazine or an organization.

For example, "The popular magazine announced that it (not "they") will no longer accept cigarette ads," or "The downtown store is having its (not "their") annual sale.

Possessive Nouns and Pronouns

The most common misuse of possessive nouns and pronouns comes with confusing plural and possessive forms of many nouns and pronouns. For example:

The committees (two committees) are meeting now.

The committee's (singular possessive) assignment is difficult.

The committees' (plural possessive) tasks are varied.

Another common mistake results from confusing "its" (the possessive form of the pronoun) with "it's" (a contraction for "it is"). Normally you do form the possessive word by adding an "s" with an apostrophe, but with the word "it," the apostrophe forms the contraction for "it is."

Unnecessary Capitalization

Beginning writers are more likely to capitalize a word that shouldn't be capitalized than fail to capitalize one that should be. The most common mistake occurs when referring to a collective noun that doesn't occur as part of a proper noun. For example, most writers know to write "University of Massachusetts" or "Jones Manufacturing Company." But when you refer to them later, you should say "the university" or "the company" and not "the University" or "the Company." Both the Associated Press and Chicago style manuals follow this rule.

Proper Use of Colons and Semi-Colons

Colons introduce. Use a colon to introduce a list of items, names of people or a long quotation. Examples:

He made big promises: no new taxes, more services and less government.

Smith had this to say about the changes: "I am in favor of progress, but these proposals will cost too much, take too long . . . ."

Semi-colons separate. They divide two or more complete sentences that are related to each other in theme or content. A semi-colon can always be replaced by a period, but never by a comma. For example: The day is long; the students are tired; it's time to go home.

Misusing Commas—A Special Problem

Commas are the most frequently misused punctuation marks. In most cases, students use more commas than necessary. The reasons for the misuse are, first, that style manuals vary in designating how and when to use the comma. Second, in a few situations, not even English and journalism scholars agree on proper comma usage. Remember that commas have one purpose: slow down. Just as road signs tell drivers to slow down to avoid danger, commas tell readers to slow down to avoid confusion. Here are the most common rules about comma usage:

Do Use a Comma

To separate items in a series:

> **Example:** The new dean enjoys sailing, cooking, stamp collecting and gardening.

> (The *AP Stylebook* specifies no comma before the final item, while the Chicago, Turabian and other style manuals do.)

After years or names of states or countries when they fall in the middle of a sentence:

> **Example:** He left school on May 13, 2005, to go to Evansville, Ind., to take a summer job.

Between complete sentences (two subjects with two verbs) separated by a conjunction:

> **Example:** The fire alarm went off for the third time, so the motel clerk called the fire department.

To set off introductory clauses and phrases from the rest of the sentence:

> **Example:** When the fire alarm went off for the third time, the motel clerk called the fire department.

To set off **non-restrictive clauses**, phrases and modifiers from the rest of the sentence. Non-restrictive clauses begin with "who" or "which." They add interesting information to the sentence, but aren't essential to its meaning.

> **Example:** My two sisters, who are older than I, live in Alaska.

> **Example:** The motel fire, which started around midnight, did not cause serious damage.

To set off appositive phrases—phrases that follow and explain a noun:

> **Example:** John Smith, vice president for finance, said the company expects a shortfall.

To set off quotes preceding or following the attribution verb "said":

> **Example:** John Smith, vice president for finance, said, "The company expects a shortfall."

Do Not Use a Comma

To set off **restrictive clauses**, phrases and modifiers from the rest of the sentence. Restrictive clauses begin with "that" or "who" and restrict the meaning of the nouns they modify to a particular person or thing. Omitting a restrictive clause can confuse the sentence's meaning.

> **Example:** Two sisters who sought refuge in a church suffered injuries when the tornado struck the building.

> **Example:** The tornado also damaged two storage buildings that are owned by the Smith farm.

To set off subordinate clauses and phrases that come at the end of the sentence:

> **Example:** The motel clerk called the fire department when the fire alarm went off for the third time.

Between compound verbs in a sentence with only one subject:

> **Example:** The motel clerk called the fire department and started notifying guests about the fire.

To set off a month and a year when there is no specific day:

> **Example:** He graduated from Michigan State in May 1986 before entering the U.S. Army.

Here is the most simplified version of common usage: If the reader won't be confused without the comma, then leave it out. If the reader might get confused, then use it. If in doubt, then omit it. After all, who wants to see a 40 mph speed limit sign on the wide-open highway?

Style Manuals and Proper Usage

"Rules of style" are matters of preference and somewhat flexible. You may have used the *AP Stylebook* or *Chicago Manual of Style*. Newspapers are primary users of the *AP Stylebook*, whereas magazines and book publishers often use the *Chicago Manual of Style*. Some publications develop their own **style manuals** for their writers and editors.

Do you write "29" or "twenty-nine"? Do you add or omit the last comma in a series—such as "coffee, sugar and cream"? The *AP Stylebook* says "29" and "no comma," whereas the *Chicago Manual* answers, "twenty-nine" and "use the comma." The Modern Language Association and American Psychological Association publish two other style manuals, which are used mostly for scholarly writing. So what's a poor writer to do with all this conflicting advice?

The answer is easy. Follow the style manual required by your teacher or editor. We have written this textbook following the *AP Stylebook* because it's most commonly used in journalism schools, writing classes and newspapers. That's why that last sentence didn't have a comma before "and newspapers."

Parallel Structure

Parallel structure means writing with a consistent verb, noun, adjective and clause structure. It aligns related ideas and offers them to the reader through similar patterns of grammar. If you use compound elements in a sentence, make sure both are nouns, both are verbs, or both are adjectives. Make sure verbs are in the same tense and voice. Make sure clauses or compound sentences have a similar noun/verb/direct object structure.

Parallel structure gives your writing greater clarity, unity, rhythm and balance. It makes your writing sound better to the ear and look better to the eye. Lack of parallel structure in writing means sentences are longer, more convoluted, confusing or difficult to read.

> **Poor:** Both mayoral candidates said they would make sure property taxes go down, but that street improvements would be increased and new industries would be attracted.

> **Improved:** Both candidates promised to decrease property taxes, increase street improvements and attract new industries.

Parallel structure may be used to introduce complementary, contrasting or sequential ideas. For example:

- **Complementary relationship:** both . . . and; not only . . . but also
  Both the class lectures and the homework assignments will be on the final exam.
- **Contrasting relationship:** either . . . or; neither . . . nor
  Either the university creates more parking spaces, or the students revolt, the editorial warned.
- **Sequential Relationship** First . . . second . . . third
  First, turn down your thermostat; second, insulate your water heater; third, weather strip your windows.

Inappropriate Uses of Parallel Structure

Mixing parts of speech in a series:

Poor: He enjoys books, movies and driving his Corvette.

Improved: He enjoys reading books, watching movies and driving his Corvette.

Inconsistent verb tense or verb structure:

Poor: I enjoy touring the country and then to meet new people.

Improved: I enjoy touring the country and meeting new people.

Changing voice:

Poor: The Senate passed the trade bill, but the budget bill was returned to committee.

Improved: The Senate passed the trade bill, but returned the budget bill to committee.

Unnecessarily changing subjects (second person to third person, etc.):

Poor: You should study hard for finals; students should know that by now.

Improved: Students should study hard for finals; they should know that by now.

Using clauses inappropriately:

> **Poor:** She explained magazine markets, payment rates that are growing and that editors especially look for celebrity profiles.

> **Improved:** She explained writing style, growing payment rates and editors' demand for celebrity profiles.

Most writers are better at following the rules of writing than at articulating them. Sometimes they know that a comma belongs in a particular place, but, if asked, they can't explain why. We hope this section has helped you in both articulating and applying "the basics" of writing.

In conclusion, if you want to become a great writer, then don't settle for a career choice that merely offers a paycheck. We urge you to read and write every day. Fill your mind with great ideas while you follow your dream. Before success arrived, authors of many great books from *Gone With the Wind* to *Chicken Soup for the Soul* have had their manuscripts rejected by dozens of publishers. The oldest, simplest advice is still the best: Never give up.

Shoptalk

Non-restrictive clause: A phrase beginning with "who" or "which" that adds interesting information to the sentence, but isn't essential to its meaning. Non-restrictive clauses are often called "non-essential clauses."

Parallel structure: Writing with a consistent verb, noun, adjective and clause structure. Parallel structure aligns related ideas through similar patterns of grammar.

Restrictive clause: A clause beginning with "that" or "who" that restricts the meaning of the noun it modifies to a particular person or thing. Omitting restrictive clauses can confuse the meaning of the sentence, and they are, therefore, sometimes called "essential clauses."

Run-on sentences: Two complete sentences (both containing a subject and verb) separated by a comma. Complete sentences must be separated by a conjunction with a comma, a period or a semi-colon.

Style manuals: Guides for writers concerning proper word usage. Style manuals may differ in some forms of punctuation and capitalization, which is why it's important to follow the style manual developed or designated by the publication.

Endnotes

1. Stephen King, *On Writing: A Memoir of the Craft* (New York: Simon and Schuster, 2000), 121.

Index